CONGRESS
TWO DECADES
OF ANALYSIS

Harper's American Political Behavior Series
Under the Editorship of DAVID J. DANELSKI

HARPER & ROW, PUBLISHERS
New York, Evanston, and London

CONGRESS
TWO DECADES
OF ANALYSIS

RALPH K. HUITT

Assistant Secretary for Legislation
Department of Health, Education, and Welfare
(On leave, The University of Wisconsin)

ROBERT L. PEABODY

The Johns Hopkins University

CONGRESS: TWO DECADES OF ANALYSIS

Copyright © 1969 by Ralph K. Huitt and Robert L. Peabody

Library of Congress Catalog Card Number: 69-11945

CONTENTS

3.75

Midwest

11/20/73

v

PREFACE

TWO questions might reasonably be asked of my contribution to this book. Why were these essays written in the first place? And more to the point, why should they be reprinted now?

Generations are so short nowadays that it's hard to recapture the climate of twenty years ago. Hard—but helpful in this case.

Literature on the legislature then was less profuse than now, generally of good quality, but concerned for the most part with formal aspects and the prospects for reform. Legislative scholars were confident that they knew what a really good legislature would be like and they thought it useful to measure the real article against the models they constructed.

Then came Stephen K. Bailey's case study of the enactment of the Employment Act of 1946, *Congress Makes a Law*. His concern was what went on in the two houses where an intellectual's dream of a national commitment to full employment was converted into a bill that could pass. The idea of paying attention to what legislators do was revolutionary, and legislative scholarship was never quite the same after that.

The revolution, however, was not complete. Bailey's frame of theory was not the legislature itself but something called "a responsible two-party system" which seemed important at the time. But why should not Congress be studied as a legislature, and the behavior of its members analyzed against the institutional demands of the legislative process?

My own attempt to do this had a long and tortuous beginning. Again, it is hard now to remember when professors wore elbow patches, taught ten hours a week, talked to alumni clubs, and got one summer of research support every three years. But those conditions did obtain, and they explain my concern in the case study of a congressional committee with inventing a way to study the U.S. Congress from a library in Madison, Wisconsin. It looked as if I might never get away from there.

Many people helped me then, but one especially must be mentioned—Burton R. Fisher, a patient and generous teacher of professors who has saved more than one scholarly job from the inadequacies of its authors. And most of all, my wife and Frank and Cindy, participant-observers in a case study of what the word "tenure" really means.

The Ford Foundation changed that. Through its Fund for the Advancement of Education it financed some young professors in the year each really wanted to have. This was my ticket to Congress. My friend and graduate professor, Emmette S. Redford, happened also to be a lifelong friend of Lyndon B. Johnson (then beginning his remarkable eight years as Democratic Leader in the Senate) and so was able to get me a place in the Johnson office. There I studied legislative process from a master of the intricate skills of putting a majority together. Since that time I have not ceased to learn from him. I was helped immensely to understand what I saw by George E. Reedy, mentor and friend, who has combined action and thought in his own life as effectively as anyone I know.

Three other practitioners have taught me a lot. Jack Brooks, congressman from my old Texas district, who has thrived as a liberal in a hard climate. William Proxmire, who as a freshman senator expanded my understanding of the range of creative senatorial roles. Gaylord Nelson, who in a thousand frank conversations about the ends and means of politics has sharpened and deepened what I know.

And the preeminent legislative scholar of his generation, the late George B. Galloway. A true and gentle man, he opened the vast store of his knowledge of Congress to me and every other student who came, without regard to rank.

My professional life, it should be clear by now, has embraced action and reflection, deed and question. Whether this is the best life for a scholar or a family man will get some argument. Whether it is a rich and full life for a certain kind of man I have answered to my own complete satisfaction.

There remains the question why these pieces should be reprinted now.

The answer is suggested in another question, which Alfred E. Prettyman of Harper & Row put to me with classic simplicity: "Other people have got royalties from reprinting your articles. Why not you?"

Why not indeed?

RALPH K. HUITT

ACKNOWLEDGEMENTS

A S ROBERT K. MERTON, among others, has pointed out, "we all are dwarfs standing on the shoulders of giants." Our knowledge of how an institution like Congress works is dependent on insights and understandings gained not just from Woodrow Wilson and his successors, but also on the contributions of such seminal thinkers as Freud and Lewin, Marx and Weber. More immediately, I should like to express my deep indebtedness to three political scientists who have shaped my thinking about the legislative process and ways of researching it: Heinz Eulau, Ralph K. Huitt, and the late V. O. Key, Jr. I am also appreciative of the cogent criticisms and comments of three colleagues and friends on an earlier version of the essay: Milton C. Cummings, Jr., Richard F. Fenno, Jr., and John F. Manley. Jean Torcom has been of invaluable assistance in the editing of my essay and the compilation of the bibliography. My secretary, Mrs. Evelyn Scheulen, has been of great help all along the way and not just in typing and proofreading. Ralph Huitt and I both are grateful to Jere Grant of Harper & Row, whose warm interest and help have gone beyond her highly competent professional help.

Finally, I wish to thank my wife, Judy, and my daughters, Susan, Lynn, and Jennifer, for providing the kind of love, support, and laughter which makes working at home a delight as much as a challenge.

The judgments in the essay about the merits of individual books and articles are, of course, mostly my own. But I owe a great deal to many students and colleagues for helping me come to these evaluations. The errors that have crept in, substantive or factual, are the work of the devil.

ROBERT L. PEABODY.

PART I
RESEARCH ON CONGRESS:
A COMING OF AGE

ROBERT L. PEABODY

RESEARCH ON CONGRESS: A COMING OF AGE

R ESEARCH on Congress has reached an important middle stage in its development. Over the last two decades and especially since 1960 a proliferation of empirical studies have yielded much new data, richer insights, and a better understanding of the internal workings of Congress, executive-legislative relations, and the representative process. Despite these significant advances, political scientists have not yet produced a conceptually clear and comprehensive theory of congressional behavior. Toward this end, it would seem useful to examine the state of congressional research as of the mid-1940s, to survey the principal findings that have emerged from the more recent qualitative and quantitative studies, to examine the directions of current work, and to speculate about the most appropriate research strategies for the future.

How have political scientists approached the study of Congress? At least two mainstreams can be identified. The first is traditional, legalistic, and reformist in orientation. It is at least as old as Woodrow Wilson's classic analysis of Congress in the 1880s, an era of legislative supremacy.[1] It was the dominant approach during the development of political science as a discipline from 1900 through the 1940s. Prior to World War II the emphasis was placed upon constitutional doctrine, statutory au-

[1] *Congressional Government* (1885). For a more complete citation for this and subsequent works reviewed in this essay, see the bibliography at the end of the present book.

3

thority, and formal institutions. Few attempts were made to discover and describe the complexities of ongoing political activity. The focus was not on government as it is, but government as it was supposed to be. Congress was seen as one legal institution among several operating within the framework of a constitutional democracy. These studies were mainly reformist for several reasons: the sharing of powers among institutions was misunderstood; it was assumed that legal prescriptions would work; and, finally, a formal, unmodified democratic theory was supposed to be relevant.

Beginning about 1950 a second mainstream began to predominate —an approach that was behavioral and empirical. It was behavioral because the legislator and his interactions with other participants in the policy-formation process became the primary units of analysis. Implicitly or explicitly it was understood that the legislator, his perceptions, and actions must be examined in the light of the various social and political systems within which he operates: his committees, congressional party, and house. In the first phase of this behavioral-empirical approach, research was exploratory and essentially qualitative. Firsthand observation and focused interviews were the principal means of data collection. Somewhat paradoxically, this qualitative phase of the behavioral approach also had its forerunner in Wilson's *Congressional Government* (1885). According to his biographers, the young Ph.D. candidate never bothered to travel the forty miles from the Johns Hopkins University campus to Capitol Hill to watch congressmen in action, let alone talk to them.[2] But in his classic essay he was attempting to break away from formal and literary treatments of the Constitution to a description of how the federal government actually worked.

As the relevant political and social variables became identified, a shift from qualitative to quantitative methods, characterized by increasing attempts to systematize the data, took place. Although this second phase of the behavioral-empirical approach can be traced back to A. Lawrence Lowell's turn-of-the-century attempts at roll call analysis (1901) and the pioneering methodological contributions of Stuart Rice in the 1920s, this phase did not fully develop until the late 1950s. While a strong reformist orientation continues to preoccupy

[2] Ray Stannard Baker, *Woodrow Wilson: Life and Letters, Youth, 1856–1890*, Vol. I (Garden City, N.Y.: Doubleday, 1927), pp. 217–218; Arthur S. Link, *Wilson: The Road to the White House* (Princeton, N.J.: Princeton University Press, 1947), pp. 12–19.

a segment of the discipline, research in the 1960s has been characterized by increasing efforts at integrating the most positive aspects of qualitative and quantitative methods.

Space will not permit a comprehensive review of all relevant research on Congress, even if limited to the most important contributions over the past two decades.[3] What I propose to do is first to sample the traditional and reformist literature of the 1940s and then trace the qualitative, quantitative, and integrative phases of the behavioral-empirical approach through the 1950s and mid-1960s. This analysis of two decades of congressional research will emphasize underlying assumptions and methodological innovations rather than substantive findings.

Before beginning this review, my own biases, if they have not already been revealed, had best be made explicit. An approach or theoretical framework dictates the problems that are seen as relevant for research. Early students of Congress were confronted not so much by unanswered questions as by problems as yet unformulated. Their approach to a large extent inhibited this very formulation. A good problem is one with a high probability that its solution will contribute to theory or a way of understanding how component parts relate to the whole. The problem, in turn, dictates the method or methods to be used. No one should approach a research problem "qualitatively" or "quantitatively." Instead, one selects whatever tools will help resolve the problem. As George C. Homans has observed, "methodology . . . is a matter of strategy, not of morals. There are neither good nor bad methods, but only methods that are more or less effective under particular circumstances in reaching objectives on the way to a distant goal."[4] The extent to which a problem is resolved, the appropriateness of research strategies, and the inherent or potential contributions to theory can be sensed intuitively by the researcher. But his success, near success, or failure is judged, first by his contemporary professional peers and ultimately, by his contributions to

[3] This review concentrates on research on Congress from the mid-1940s to 1967. For overviews of legislative research at the state as well as national level, see Meller (1960, 1965), Wahlke (1962), and Eulau and Hinckley (1966). See also an annotated bibliography on *The Role of Political Parties in Congress*, by Jones and Ripley (1966); also extensive commentaries in two recent first-rate texts that treat of both Congress and the state legislatures: Keefe and Ogul (1968), and Jewell and Patterson (1966).

[4] George C. Homans, *Sentiments and Activities* (New York: Macmillan, 1962), p. 257.

the growth of a body of knowledge and a discipline. Congressional research may have passed through its adolescence, but as the concluding sections of this essay argue, we will have a ways to go before attaining maturity. There still remains the primary need for theory that describes, explains, and predicts not only how the principal components—congressmen, staff, committees, state delegations, congressional parties, House and Senate—relate to one another, but also how Congress functions in relation to the broader political system.

I. TRADITIONAL AND REFORMIST VIEWS OF CONGRESS

How did students of government view Congress just before and after World War II? Most of the books and articles of the 1940s reflect two common characteristics. First, there is an increasing preoccupation with the functions of Congress and whether or not they are being adequately discharged. For the most part, scholars of this period are unhappy with what they see. A strong normative and critical viewpoint dominates a number of the leading texts, especially George B. Galloway's *Congress at the Crossroads* (1946) and James MacGregor Burns's *Congress on Trial* (1949). Several reports issued by committees of the American Political Science Association, *The Reorganization of Congress* (1954) and *Toward a More Responsible Two-Party System* (1950), are strongly reformist in orientation. During this period, a major congressional reform bill was passed, the Legislative Reorganization Act of 1946 (Cooper, forthcoming).

A second common characteristic of works of the 1940s is a continuing institutional, historical, and low-level descriptive orientation. Empirical studies are rare. Most scholars rely upon historical analysis and a rather uncritical acceptance of the public record. With the exception of the increased emphasis on reform, there is little that distinguishes books and articles of this period from earlier traditional studies of Congress such as De Alva Stanwood Alexander's *History and Procedure of the House of Representatives* (1916), George Rothwell Brown's *The Leadership of Congress* (1922), and W. F. Willoughby's *Principles of Legislative Organization and Administration* (1934).

Floyd M. Riddick's *The United States Congress: Organization and Procedure* (1949) is one of the more useful contributions. "There is no attempt here to give a history of the development of legislative procedure, nor are any suggestions for a better system proposed. The study is merely a description of the House and Senate legislative machines, and of their political and parliamentary procedures in action" (p. iii). Chapter II is typical: a listing of ten functions of Congress with a page or more devoted to each. The author makes extensive use of the *Congressional Record* and the parliamentary precedents of the House and Senate for illustrative purposes. Riddick, an employee of the Senate since 1947, became its parliamentarian in 1965.

One of the more informative of representative articles from this period is Clarence A. Berdahl's "Some Notes on Party Membership in Congress" (1949). His problem is to find "who are the Republicans or the Democrats [in Congress], and in case of doubt, what are the respective criteria of Republicanism and of Democracy" (p. 311). Relying extensively on newspaper accounts and the *Congressional Record*, Berdahl traces the history of party bolters and what happens to them in the House and Senate caucuses, from the middle of the nineteenth century up to 1948. During this period the Republicans had numerous membership controversies. In contrast, "the Democrats have had relatively little difficulty, whether because of a more harmonious party, a higher sense of party loyalty, a stricter party discipline, a more tolerant attitude toward party rebels, or for whatever reason" (p. 721). Berdahl's reluctance to generalize is typical of the congressional research of this period.

Galloway's *Congress at the Crossroads* (1946) represents a blend of the descriptive and the normative. His objectives are

. . . to analyze the evolution of the essential functions of Congress since 1789, to describe how Congress works under modern conditions, to diagnose its defects, and to prescribe a comprehensive program for its reconstruction as an effective instrument of representative government adequate to meet its responsibilities in the postwar world. [p. vi]

The author's strong reformist orientation reflects his prior experience. From 1941 to 1945 Galloway served as chairman of the American Political Science Association's Committee on Congress. In 1945 this group published its suggestions for *The Reorganization of Congress*. During 1945 and 1946 Galloway served as staff director of the Joint Committee on the Organization of Congress—chaired by the late Senator Robert M. LaFollette, Jr., and Representative (now Senator) Mike Monroney—which drafted the Legislative Reorganization Act of 1946. A number of the recommendations proposed by the APSA Committee on Congress, including an increase in committee staffing and a consolidation of committee jurisdictions, were incorporated into the reorganization. Galloway's revised text, *The Legislative Process in Congress* (1953), somewhat moderates its reformist spirit. However, the author believes that "Congress is still at a 'moral crossroads.'" He has designed his book "both as an objective study of our national legislature in action for the use of teachers and students and as a revelation of the limitations of the legislative process that will induce the American people to support its reform" (p. v). From 1946 to 1967 Galloway served as a Senior Specialist in American Government on the staff of the Legislative Reference Service of the Library of Congress.

Burns puts *Congress on Trial* (1949) and finds it wanting. With the exception of the opening chapter—a composite portrait of the career and beliefs of a "typical" congressman—and three short case studies of legislation, almost the entire book is given over to pointing up the shortcomings of Congress and some rather naive notions about what can be done to improve our national legislature. Several of the chapter titles—"The Impotence of Party," "House of Misrepresentatives," "Can Congress Reform Itself?"—indicate the general tone of the argument. Congress is slow to act and ineffective because the parties are undisciplined and decentralized. For Burns, "the best hope for the future of American politics and government lies in a fruitful union between presidential power and party government" (p. 195). His book concludes with proposals for shifting power from state and local party organizations to the national level.

The case for more centralized and better-disciplined parties is given its most definitive statement in the 1950 publication of the American Political Science Association's Committee on Political Parties, *Toward a More Responsible Two-Party System*. The purpose of the 70-page report was "to bring about fuller public appreciation of a basic weakness in the American two-party system."

Historical and other factors have caused the American two-party system to operate as two loose associations of state and local organizations, with very little national machinery and very little national cohesion. As a result, either major party, when in power, is ill-equipped to organize its members in the legislative and the executive branches into a government held together and guided by the party program. [p. v.]

The reformers call for a realignment of the Democratic and Republican parties into two distinct ideological groupings, one liberal and one conservative, each highly disciplined and modeled after the British political parties. Party organization in Congress is to be "tightened up." "In both the Senate and the House, the various separate leadership groups should be consolidated into one truly effective and responsible leadership committee for each party" (p. 59). More specific reforms deal with the selection of committee chairmen, committee assignments, minority staffing, the House Rules Committee, and Senate cloture procedures.

The report aroused considerable controversy among political scientists,[5] but the nation's political leaders largely ignored it. Plans to disseminate the committee's recommendations among a broader public were further frustrated by the outbreak of the Korean War.

Interest in the reform of Congress has never been abandoned. Typically, clamor for reform mounts whenever the program of the President is having difficulty in Congress. Some representative works of the 1960s would include James MacGregor Burns's The Deadlock of Democracy (1963), a restatement of the responsible parties argument; Senator Joseph S. Clark's Congress: The Sapless Branch (1964), a critique of congressional practices by one of the Senate's strongest advocates of reform; and the proposals put forth by the House Republican Task Force on Congressional Reform and Minority Staffing, We Propose: A Modern Congress, edited by Mary McInnis (1966).

Taking a contrary stance to the usual reform arguments, Alfred de Grazia has coordinated a series of essays with the common objective of organizing changes in Congress according to a model of a strong national legislature, Congress: The First Branch of Government (1965). Three Dartmouth College scholars, Roger H. Davidson, David M. Kovenock, and Michael K. O'Leary, have brought a fresh perspective in a study of Congress in Crisis: Politics and Congressional Reform (1966). Their evaluation is based on structured interviews with over 100 House members of the 88th Congress (1963–1964). Since reform of Congress must be approved by the congressional leadership and/or an overwhelming majority of the members, the treatment of reform

[5] See, for example, Austin Ranney, "Toward a More Responsible Two-party System: A Commentary," American Political Science Review, XLV (1951), 488–499; and Ranney, The Doctrine of Responsible Party Government (Urbana, Ill.: University of Illinois Press, 1954); Murray S. Stedman, Jr., and Herbert Sonthoff, "Party Responsibility—A Critical Inquiry," Western Political Quarterly, IV (1951), 454–468; and Julius Turner, "Responsible Parties: A Dissent from the Floor," American Political Science Review, XLV (1951), 143–152.

by the Dartmouth group usually makes more sense than a number of the proposals advocated in the de Grazia-edited volume.

The most thorough collection of materials on congressional reorganization has been the product of the Joint Committee on the Organization of Congress in the 89th and 90th Congresses. Created by concurrent resolution on March 11, 1965, this committee has published some sixteen volumes of hearings and reports. On March 7, 1967, the Senate passed S. 355, a rather pallid reorganization bill, but as of the end of 1967, it and several House versions were still hung up in the House Committee on Rules. Senator A. S. Mike Monroney (D., Oklahoma) and Representative Ray J. Madden (D., Indiana) served as cochairmen of the Joint Committee in both Congresses.

II. THE QUALITATIVE PHASE OF BEHAVIORAL-EMPIRICAL STUDIES

Earlier works on Congress with but a few exceptions concentrated on formal organization, the mechanics of rules and procedures, and the legal technicalities of bill drafting and amending. Although these facets of the legislature cannot be ignored, they are, of course, only a part of the process. To understand legislative policy-making it is necessary to move beyond formal and legal descriptions to the attitudes and behavior of the people who make up the legislature as well as those who try to influence policy-making. Although a number of the principal studies of Congress during the early 1950s still contained strong overtones of the "responsible parties doctrine," it was apparent that a renaissance in congressional research was under way. In large measure these developments can be traced to the impact of the behavioral sciences—anthropology, sociology, and psychology—on traditional ways of viewing politics.

One of the first books to take advantage of field observation and extensive interviews is Stephen K. Bailey's *Congress Makes a Law* (1950). This book is a landmark study for two further reasons. First, it remains a classic analysis of the passage of an important piece of legislation, the Employment Act of 1946. Second, it can be viewed as a bridge between the traditional-reformist viewpoint and the newer qualitative phase of a behavioral-empirical approach to the study of Congress.

The body of the book is empirical and descriptive. It is "an attempt to present a reasonably objective analysis of the formulation of a public policy in the Congress . . ." (p. ix). Bailey's major intellectual debt is to Pendleton Herring, whose earlier works had described the policy-making process as the interaction of individuals, interests, ideas, and institutions.[6]

In the narrowest sense this book is an attempt to describe how these four I's interacted in a particular historical context in relation to a particular economic issue. In a much broader and more fundamental sense, however, this is a study of the types of forces which impinge upon, or work through, the American Congress as it attempts to formulate major public policies in the middle of the twentieth century. [p. x]

His narrative is based on over 400 interviews, including a number held in the home districts or states of the twelve members of the Senate-House Conference Committee which put the final language of the Act together.

Bailey, however, was unable to divorce himself from the moral overtones of traditional political science. The conceptual baggage of the responsible parties school is present in the preface and conclusions. His analysis is

. . . conditioned by certain underlying assumptions which I hold concerning desirable standards of performance in our national legislature. These standards may be reduced to three general propositions: first, that Congress should act responsibly—that is, that it should act in such a way that the voting public may be able to hold individual members and the separate parties reasonably accountable for their actions; second, that Congress should act democratically, that is, that it should formulate policy through a process of majority rule while allowing for the free expression of minority opinions rather than vice versa; and third, that it should act in the public interest rather than in the interest solely of local or narrowly vested group pressures. [p. ix]

How are these standards to be met? Bailey fails to see how a responsible political system can be obtained "except by strengthening the only two instruments in our political life which have an inherent responsibility to the nation as nation: the President and the national political parties" (p. 239). He would not go so far as "to suggest a sudden adoption of the British system, a change which is out of the question," but clearly the two parties must be made more cohesive and centralized.

[6] Pendleton Herring, The Politics of Democracy (New York: Norton, 1940; new edition, 1965), p. 26.

Bailey, in cooperation with Howard D. Samuel, extends the case study approach to cover other aspects of congressional activity in their text *Congress at Work* (1952). The reader gains a measure of insight into the 1950 elections of three congressmen—Senator Herbert H. Lehman (D., New York), Representative William H. Ayres (R., Ohio), and Representative Frank E. Smith (D., Mississippi)—and how each organizes his office and allocates his time during a typical legislative day. Other chapters provide case studies of a range of legislation from a private bill and pork barrel projects to major legislation such as the Taft-Hartley Act of 1947.[7]

Another study of congressional policy-making, Robert A. Dahl's *Congress and Foreign Policy* (1950), also illustrates the responsible party bias of the immediate postwar period. The author posits three useful criteria for evaluating the method by which decisions are made about public policy. To what extent does the decision-making process (1) provide for responsible leadership, (2) facilitate agreement among citizens of the community, and (3) lead to national policies?

In the American democracy, as indeed in any other, much of the burden for securing responsible leadership, for maximizing agreement, and for developing a more rational understanding among the electorate ought to fall upon the legislative body. Yet the plain and ominous fact is that Congress faces tremendous difficulties in discharging this burden. [p. 5]

Why is this the case? "The great gaping hole in the structure of responsibility," concludes Dahl, "is the empty place left by the American party system. Without responsible parties, Congress cannot be responsible; and unless Congress is responsible, it has slight claim to enforce responsibility on the President" (p. 182). For Dahl, the preferred solution for a democracy is certainly not a modern dictatorship based on techniques of mass persuasion nor even presidential supremacy in the foreign policy area. His concluding chapters make the case for a third alternative, "a high degree of collaboration between executive and Congress in the formulation and conduct of foreign policy" (p. 264).

---

[7] The usefulness of a collection-of-case-studies approach was demonstrated, again, by two young political scientists, John Bibby and Roger Davidson, in their paperback text, *On Capitol Hill* (1967). The authors describe "typical" days of Representative Albert Quie of Minnesota and Senator Mike Monroney of Oklahoma, which they observed at first hand; they also include descriptions of campaigns and elections, the organization of a Congress and the selection of a minority party leader, and several short case studies of the passage of legislation.

Dahl acknowledges insights gained from discussions with three Senators, eight members of the House of Representatives, and several top staff personnel. His book is one of the first to make some use of roll call data and public opinion surveys. The main thrust of the book, however, is qualitative and theoretical with some strong moralistic overtones.

Another extremely influential work of this period was David B. Truman's theoretical analysis of interest group behavior, *The Governmental Process* (1951). In his attempt to provide a systematic statement of the role of groups in the political process, Truman builds upon Arthur F. Bentley's pioneering work, *The Process of Government* (1908). Bentley's principal thesis was that the raw material of politics is group activity. For the most part the suggestions of Bentley lay dormant even after a spate of studies of pressure group activity in the late 1920s and 1930s.[8] Not only does Truman revive Bentley, but utilizing the theory and findings of social psychology and anthropology, he attempts and to a considerable degree succeeds in integrating the findings of these disparate case studies. Two chapters are devoted to the relationships between interest groups and legislators. Chapter XI outlines how formal structure brings about advantages in access for some groups, disadvantages for others. It also suggests how the legislators' multiple and overlapping group affiliations condition legislative decision-making. Chapter XII discusses techniques of interest group activity, including suggestive insights on the formation of alliances and the practice of logrolling. Truman's call for further research on these important problems was, with several important exceptions, ignored until the early 1960s.

However, this view of a legislature as an arena for the adjustment and compromising of group interests was given an even more explicit statement in a leading congressional text of the period, Bertram M. Gross's *The Legislative Struggle* (1953). Relying heavily on Truman's group theory, Gross also brought to his work an awareness gained from more than a decade of staff work on Capitol Hill, including a key role in the passage of the Employment Act of 1946.

---

[8] Among the most important of these studies were Peter H. Odegard, *Pressure Politics: The Story of the Anti-Saloon League* (New York: Columbia University Press, 1928); Pendleton Herring, *Group Representation Before Congress* (Baltimore: Johns Hopkins Press, 1929); E. E. Schattschneider, *Politics, Pressures and the Tariff* (Englewood Cliffs, N.J.: Prentice-Hall, 1935); and Oliver Garceau, *The Political Life of the American Medical Association* (Cambridge, Mass.: Harvard University Press, 1941).

The contributions of Huitt and Dexter

No observer of the congressional scene has had more impact in shaping the directions of research over the past fifteen years than Ralph K. Huitt. Chief among his contributions have been four landmark articles published in *The American Political Science Review*, one in 1954, one in 1957, and two in 1961. These four articles form the core of the present book.

In the first of his four articles, "The Congressional Committee: A Case Study," Huitt generates a series of hypotheses from the Bentley-Truman-Gross group approach to analyze and explain the roles of congressional committee members. He examines hearings held before the Senate Committee on Banking and Currency during the spring of 1946 on the question of the extension of price control programs as a means of exploring a number of generalizations about committee behavior. Among the principal roles identified were those of national party leader, defender of the administration, representatives of sectional and specific constituency interests, and the "errand-boy." Huitt concludes:

. . . [t]he congressional role probably is most usefully conceived not as a single role but as a multiplicity of roles, defined for the congressmen by the varying expectations of the groups which he represents or with which he identifies. These roles may be and frequently are conflicting, requiring the individual congressman temporarily to abdicate one or another of his roles, or to find some way to conciliate them, or perhaps to withdraw from the conflict which he cannot resolve. [p. 84]

First published in 1954, this article is notable for its imaginative use of public records. Within a decade a number of political scientists, building upon Huitt's analysis, would begin to combine review of the public record with the intensive interviewing of committee members in order to develop generalizations about committee structure and the legislative process.

Huitt's second article, "The Morse Committee Assignment Controversy: A Study in Senate Norms," is also dependent upon analysis of the public record, with one further refinement. After he completed his study, "persons were interviewed in Washington who had first-hand participant knowledge of the [Morse] controversy." As Huitt notes, "some refinements were made, but the conclusions . . . did not have to be altered as a result of the interviews" (p. 116). The core of the article deals with the treatment of Senator Wayne Morse of Oregon and his appointments to standing committees after he bolted the Republican party during the 1952 presidential election. This controversy is set forth within the larger context of party bolters in the Senate and variations in party discipline since the 1920s.

Huitt's third article, "Democratic Party Leadership in the Senate," is a modern classic. It begins by discussing the reasons why those who seek to reform Congress along responsible party lines have failed. The two most insuperable obstacles to central party leadership are the congressmen's direct ties to constituency and the system of specialized standing committees. The major portion of the article treats of how the principal elective officer of the Democratic party in the Senate, the floor leader, works within these constraints. Particular attention is given to the strategies, tactics, and persuasive powers of Senator Lyndon B. Johnson of Texas, Democratic floor leader from 1953 to 1960. Although operating as a majority leader without the additional leverage that would have been furnished by a President of his own party, Johnson made extremely effective use of what limited powers he possessed. As Huitt concluded, "the successful senatorial leader is one who (1) can and does help individual senators to maximize their effectiveness in playing their personal roles in the Senate, and (2) structures roles and alternatives so that a maximum number of senators can join in support of the proffered solution of an issue" (p. 158).

Huitt's fourth article, "The Outsider in the Senate: An Alternative Role," is a participant-observer analysis of Wisconsin Democrat William Proxmire's first year in the Senate. Huitt served as legislative assistant to Proxmire during that year, 1957–1958. In the introductory section he draws upon two books, William S. White's *Citadel: The Story of the U.S. Senate* (1957) and Donald R. Matthews' *U.S. Senators and Their World* (1960), to establish a system of Senate norms or folkways about which there appears to be a high degree of consensus. What happens to a senator who does not conform? For roughly half of his first session, Huitt reports, Proxmire worked hard at being a model freshman senator. Then, increasingly dissatisfied with that role, he decided to change: ". . . he would 'be a senator like Wayne [Morse] and Paul [Douglas]'; he would talk when he pleased on whatever he chose and would not worry about his influence in the Senate" (p. 166). While this choice of the Outsider role may have made Proxmire less effective as a legislator, the Senate seemed to tolerate his behavior without recourse to sanctions. Huitt concludes that the Outsider is not a deviant but an alternative role. "The behavior associated with the Outsider may be functional for protest groups seeking a spokesman, dysfunctional for groups needing leverage inside the legislative body. It may even be functional for the leadership, to the degree that it makes more persuasive the middle position usually taken by the leaders" (p. 178).

Although these articles treat of four different aspects of Senate behavior—committee roles, the punishment of party bolters, floor leadership, and nonconformity to Senate norms—they have several characteristics in common. In the first place, Huitt is consistently interested in the interplay between *status* and *role,* concepts adopted from anthropological and sociological research. Again and again he explores the range of permissible behavior, the alternatives that seem to work. Secondly, although he makes extensive use of case studies, in each article he is explicitly seeking higher order generalizations. All of the articles, but especially the last two, convey a rich intuitive feeling for the activities of the Senate.

Lewis Anthony Dexter is another scholar whose approach to Congress and interviewing techniques have had a strong impact on congressional research during the 1960s.[9] One of the first of his articles deals with how congressmen respond to the mails, especially communications from businessmen (1956–1957). A second article, "The Representative and His District," is a landmark contribution. First published in an applied anthropology journal, *Human Organization,* in 1957, it has subsequently been revised and reprinted in several anthologies.[10] The author draws on a rich variety of interview sources in his examination of "the ways congressmen view representation and on the ways in which their pictures of the world determine what they hear, how they interpret it, whom they represent, how they influence representations by others, and how they view other representatives" (p. 28). Dexter largely discounts simple-minded explanations in terms

[9] "Role Relationships and Conceptions of Neutrality in Interviewing," *American Journal of Sociology,* LXII (1956), 153–157; "The Good Will of Important People: More on the Jeopardy of the Interview," *Public Opinion Quarterly,* 28 (1964), 556–563.

[10] The quotations which follow are excerpted from a revised version reprinted in Peabody and Polsby (1963), pp. 3–29.

of "pressure politics." As he notes, "what you call pressure, or what you feel to be pressure, depends on how thick your skin is. . . . Until a congressman definitely makes up his mind, it isn't pressure—it's communication or instruction" (pp. 26–27). Dexter was one of the first congressional scholars to base his work on extensive interviewing of congressmen and staff. From 1953 to 1957 he conducted over 400 interviews, more than 100 with congressmen, about influences imping-ing upon the formulation of policy. From this data comes what is per-haps the most penetrating analysis yet written of how congressmen make or fail to make military policy (Dexter, 1963). These materials also form the core of a comprehensive analysis of postwar reciprocal trade policy by Raymond Bauer, Ithiel de Sola Pool, and Dexter. The resulting book, *American Business and Public Policy* (1963), is evalu-ated below (Section V).

The late 1950s and early 1960s witnessed an extraordinary awaken-ing of congressional research, especially studies of (1) the standing committees, (2) other formal and informal groups such as policy com-mittees and state delegations, (3) party leadership, and (4) executive-legislative relations. Rather than review all of this research, I shall concentrate on studies of congressional committees to illustrate com-mon research trends. Only brief mention will be made of some of the most significant work carried out in the other three areas.

The study of congressional committees

I know not how better to describe our form of government in a single phrase than by calling it a government by the chairman of the Standing Committees of Congress. This disintegrate ministry, as it figures on the floor of the House of Representatives, has many peculiarities. In the first place, it is made up of the elders of the assembly; or, by custom, seniority in congressional service determines the bestowal of the principal chairman-ships; in the second place, it is constituted of selfish and warring elements; for chairman fights against chairman for the use of the time in the assembly though the most part of them are inferior to the chairman of Ways and Means and all are subordinate to the chairman of the Committee on Ap-propriations; in the third place, instead of being composed of the associ-ated leaders of Congress, it consists of the disassociated heads of forty-eight "little legislatures" (to borrow Senator Hoar's apt name for the committee); and, in the fourth place, it is instituted by appointment from Mr. Speaker, who is, by intention, the chief judicial, rather than the chief political officer of the House. [Wilson, *Congressional Government*, pp. 82–83]

Congress in session is Congress on public exhibition, while Congress in its committee rooms is Congress at work. [*Ibid.*, p. 69]

If these and other sweeping generalizations about the importance of the standing committees of Congress are true, one wonders why Woodrow Wilson's observations did not stimulate a great deal of research on congressional committees. That they did not, but instead, became widely quoted "truths," is an interesting commentary on the state of political science as a discipline from 1885 up through 1950. Richard F. Fenno, Jr., offers a convincing explanation of why these strong statements did not generate an avalanche of empirical work:

One reason . . . may lie in the fact that Wilson deeply deplored what he described. His study, had, therefore, a normative-reformist component as well as a descriptive one. And Wilson's disciples, too, have deplored. They read Wilson's book as a call for congressional reform, and not as a call for empirical research. It is as if the very eloquence of his description plus the abstract logic of his plea for change rendered further empirical research superfluous. In any case, *Congressional Government* has nourished a long train of plans to bring about the reform of Congress through the reform of its committees. Still, the empirical side of Wilson survives. And, in recent years less reform-minded students of Congress have begun utilizing his insights for more descriptive purposes. [1966, p. xvii]

A few committee studies were published at the beginning of World War II, most notably Albert C. F. Westphal's study of *The House Committee on Foreign Affairs* (1942), Eleanor E. Dennison's examination of *The Senate Foreign Relations Committee* (1942), and Arthur W. Macmahon's classic articles on congressional oversight of administration through the appropriations process (1943). But the bulk of the committee studies were not launched until the late 1950s and early 1960s.

One of the most thorough of these studies is Holbert N. Carroll's examination of *The House of Representatives and Foreign Affairs* (1958). By constitutional mandate and tradition the President and the Senate have dominated the making of foreign policy. But as the United States assumed the leadership of the free world following World War II, the House became increasingly involved.

Complex policies requiring legislative action and sustained public support, the fact that the life of each constituent is touched by these policies, and the need for immense sums of money to support the nation's global business—all of these factors have combined to enhance the influence of the House, the body closest to the people and the traditional guardian of the nation's purse. [p. xi]

The core of Carroll's analysis deals with the two House committees most centrally involved with foreign policy, the Committee on Foreign

Affairs, and the Committee on Appropriations. Other chapters treat briefly of the ways in which other standing committees impinge upon the foreign policy process, the relationship of the House to the Senate and to the executive branch of government. In the main, Carroll's approach is traditional and historical. He follows some fifty bills and resolutions through the legislative process and relies extensively on several hundred policy documents published by the executive and legislative branches during the decade immediately following World War II. In addition, he discussed the process with some 25 individuals —congressmen, committee staff, and executive branch officials.

Some additional insights into the policy-making process in Congress are provided by Charles O. Jones's article on representative processes in the House Committee on Agriculture (1961). As would be anticipated, all but one of the 34 committee members come from districts with significant interests in farm policy. Furthermore, there is a high correlation between the dominant crops in a member's district and the commodity subcommittees to which he was assigned. At the subcommittee level members are most apt to follow the dictates of their "policy constituency," that is, to vote in favor of their district's dominant crop interest. As the measure moves to the full committee and floor, other considerations, particularly party allegiance, come to the fore. Jones concludes that "if a representative has a multiplicity of conflicting demands upon him in any series of actions on policy, he can satisfy many of them, over a period of time, because of the multiplicity of action points at successive stages in the legislative process" (p. 367). His study is based on standard documentary sources, plus focused interviews with 30 of the 34 Agriculture Committee members in the 85th Congress.

The most influential committee study of this period, particularly in its application of systems and role theory and its contribution to our understanding of how congressional committees work, is Richard F. Fenno's analysis of *integration* in the House Committee on Appropriations (1962). A committee is highly integrated when there is mutual support among its subgroups, a fairly consistent set of norms, and a minimum amount of conflict among its roles. Fenno suggests five important characteristics that help to explain the Appropriations Committee's high degree of integration. First, there is a well-articulated and deeply rooted consensus on the Committee's principal goal—the safeguarding of the federal treasury. Second, the Committee's integration is facilitated by the nature of its subject matter—annual appropriations.

A money decision—however vitally it affects national policy—is, or at least seems to be, less directly a policy decision. Since they deal immediately with dollars and cents, it is easy for the members to hold to the idea that they are not dealing with programmatic questions, that theirs is a "business" rather than a "policy" committee. [p. 312]

Third, recruitment patterns favor the selection of "responsible legislators," those who will work within the norms of the Committee and the House of Representatives. Fourth, not only is the Appropriations Committee initially attractive, but once on the Committee, members are likely to stay. "Of the 106 members in the 1947–1961 period, only two members left the Committee voluntarily; and neither of them initiated the move" (p. 313). Finally, the membership of the House Appropriations Committee is exceedingly stable. "The 50 members on the Committee in 1961 had served an average of 13.1 years in the House" (p. 314).

Fenno next turns to the activities and roles of the key subgroups on the Committee—subcommittees and majority or minority party groups. Each subcommittee—there were 14 in the 87th Congress— operates with relative independence from the others and guards its autonomy with zeal. Partisanship tends to be muted by the key subcommittee norms of specialization, reciprocity, and unity. Except for the Chairman, ranking minority members, and a few of their senior confidants, each member is expected to concentrate on the work of one, or at most two, subcommittees. Conflict between subcommittees is minimized by a mutual acquiescence to each other's expertise. Widespread support of a proposed bill or resolution is sought within each subcommittee before it goes to the full Committee, and eventually, the floor of the House.

What are the consequences of high committee integration for the broader legislative process? First, high internal integration of the Appropriations Committee seems to explain a great deal of the extraordinary stability of appropriations procedures since 1920. Second, integration has clearly reduced the influence of party groups on the appropriation process. Finally, it would appear that the greater the degree of Committee integration the greater the probability that its recommendations will be accepted by the House and in conference committes with the Senate. All of these hypotheses received extended analysis in Fenno's large study, *The Power of the Purse* (1966), a book reviewed in detail in a later section (V).

In sharp contrast to the House Appropriations Committee, the House Committee on Education and Labor appears to operate with a rather poorly integrated internal structure. Fenno's study of House action on proposed federal aid to education legislation from 1945 to 1962 suggests many of the reasons (1963).

Most of the Committee's internal problems are consequences of the fact that within its jurisdiction fall a high proportion of the most controversial, the most partisan, and the most publicized issues of American domestic politics. The Committee, activated in 1947, cut its legislative teeth on the Taft-Hartley Bill and has been a domestic political battleground ever since. [p. 198]

Sharp ideological conflicts on labor policy between Democrats and Republicans have carried over into the field of education. Members on both sides tend to be "strongly issue-oriented, personally contentious, and vigorously committed" (p. 202). Committee procedures and the style of decision-making promote a legislative free-for-all rather than a search for accommodation and compromise. Seniority tends to be overlooked. Little deference is paid to the work of subcommittees or the views of subject-matter experts. Finally, Fenno suggests, the House Education and Labor Committee suffered from a notable lack of positive, constructive leadership. The main tactics of one of its strongest chairmen, Democrat Graham Barden of North Carolina, were "to delay, divide, and conquer" (p. 209). His successor, Adam Clayton Powell of New York, became notorious for first providing support for his subcommittee chairmen, then withdrawing it at crucial moments, or absenting himself altogether.

The balance of Fenno's article consists of a summary analysis of the House record with regard to federal aid to education legislation from 1945 to 1962. Proponents of this legislation had to wait until the advent of overwhelming Democratic majorities to the 89th Congress (1965–1966) before federal aid to elementary and secondary schools became the law of the land.

John F. Manley makes a still further contribution to the comparative analysis of congressional committees with his insightful analysis of the House Ways and Means Committee (1965). He builds on the analytical framework set forth by Fenno, viewing the committee as a political subsystem of the House, and focusing upon committee norms, roles, and the socialization process. Like Education and Labor, this powerful social welfare and tax-writing committee often splits along partisan lines, but its members operate under norms more comparable to those of the House Appropriations Committee. "Friendly and cooperative relations between the chairman and the ranking minority member, plus well established norms of deference governing the degree and kind of participation by senior and junior members, constitute a system of decision-making which is marked by restrained partisanship" (pp. 938–939). In addition, Manley examines the leadership style of one of the most successful committee chairmen in the history of the House, Wilbur D. Mills of Arkansas. Since Mills became chairman in 1958, he has only been beaten on the floor three times on bills of any consequence. Manley's analysis is based on interviews conducted in 1964 with 20 of the 25 members of the committee, plus additional discussions with staff, lobbyists, and executive-branch personnel.

What happens to bills after they have been considered and reported out by the standing committees of the House such as Education and Labor or the Committee on Ways and Means? James A. Robinson's careful and detailed analysis of the operations of the House Committee on Rules provides many of the answers (1963). Noncontroversial bills, which amount to almost nine-tenths of the work load of the House in any given session, are brought to the floor through a variety of scheduling devices such as unanimous consent requests, suspension of the rules, and various calendar and special legislative days. Controversial legislation, the kind that arouses interest group activity and promotes newspaper headlines, almost always comes to the floor through the granting of a special order or "rule" from the Committee on Rules. The Committee's wide-ranging powers come from "its opportunities to give or withhold hearings for rules, to give or withhold rules, to trade a change in the bill for a rule, to permit or forbid amendments and set the length of debate, to take advantage of time constraints near the end of a session, to arbitrate differences between legislative committees, and to initiate action in the absence of legislative committee decisions" (p. 21). Based on interviews with the members and meticulous examinations of Committee records and floor debates, Robinson sets forth the extent to which the Committee on Rules has used or abused these wide-ranging powers from 1937 to 1962. Other chapters consider historical developments and changes in the Rules

Committee's role since 1910 and relate the previous congressional experiences and constituency characteristics of members to committee decision-making.

Milton C. Cummings, Jr., and Robert L. Peabody (1963) shed further light on the complex relationships between the Committee on Rules, the leadership of the two parties, and the House at large in their case study of one of the most crucial legislative fights in recent Congresses, the 1961 vote to enlarge the Rules Committee from twelve to fifteen members. With the aid of 22 Republican votes, Speaker Rayburn and the Democratic majority won by a 5-vote margin. Peabody (1963) provides a follow-up study assessing the role of the enlarged Committee on Rules from the point of view of its ten Democratic and five Republican members. Based on interviews with all fifteen members, this study examines their perceptions of committee functions and some of the consequences of the shift in control from a conservative bipartisan committee bloc to a more liberal Democratic majority leadership.

The early 1960s saw a number of committee studies published. Among the most important of these were two books on the Senate Committee on Foreign Relations and foreign policy by David N. Farnsworth (1961) and Malcolm E. Jewell (1962), James A. Robinson's examination of *Congress and Foreign Policy-making* (1962), and Harold Green and Alan Rosenthal's study of the Joint Atomic Energy Committee (1963). The latter study seeks comparative generalizations along the theoretical dimensions set forth by Fenno.

A major constraint on the activities of committee members, at least since the late nineteenth century, is the institutionalization of the seniority system. Perhaps no set of norms of Congress comes in for more continuing criticism than the practice of giving great, if not absolute, weight to length of service in the choice of committee chairmen, the awarding of office space, and the assignment of members to committees. In addition to summarizing the arguments, pro and con, George Goodwin, Jr., examines the operation, historical development, and principal effects of seniority in the House and Senate (1959). His data covering the 80th to 85th Congresses (1947–1958) do not lead to as devastating a case against seniority as some of the critics of the system seem to claim.

Chairmen are older on the average than their colleagues, and yet with luck a number of younger men are singled out for chairmanships. The districts which produce chairmen are not as stagnant as is often suggested, and the degree of party unity and presidential support among chairmen is not as low as many believe. [p. 430]

Goodwin concludes his article with an overview of practices that have ameliorated the most stringent effects of the system and a summary of the principal alternatives that have been proposed from time to time.

More than any other legislature in the world the work of Congress is specialized by committees. Some committees, such as the Senate Committees on Appropriations, Finance, and Foreign Relations, or the House Committees on Appropriations, Rules, and Ways and Means, are more prestigious than others. On some committees such as Public Works or Agriculture, a member can do more for his constituents and thus enhance his chances of re-election. For these and other reasons the assignment of members to committees is among the most vital decisions affecting a congressman's legislative career. Nicholas A. Masters examines the operations of the groups charged with making these committee assignments—the party committees-on-committees in the House of Representatives (1961). Utilizing data derived from interviews with members of these committees, deans of state delegations, and other congressmen and staff, his survey covers the 80th through the 86th Congresses, with special attention to the 1959–1960 period. "Although a number of factors enter into committee assignments—geography, group support, professional background, and so forth—the most important single consideration," according to Masters, "is to provide each member with an assignment that will help to insure his re-election" (p. 357). The evidence supporting this generalization is less than conclusive.

What do party leaders and the members of the committees-on-committees look for in selecting members for the major committees? Both House parties look for members from relatively safe districts, the kind of district that will enable them "to make controversial decisions on major policy questions without constant fear of reprisals at the polls" (p. 353). Both parties tend to follow the practice of selecting members from the same state as the member who vacated the seat in order to maintain geographical balance. Above all, party leaders look for congressmen who are "responsible," that is, members who have a respect for party leaders, fellow members, and the rules, procedures, and customs of the legislative process. "On specific issues, no matter how firm his convictions and no matter how great the pressures upon him," the responsible legislator, "demonstrates a willingness to compromise" (p. 352).

Other areas of research

A number of scholars have examined other working components and subgroups in Congress beyond the standing committees. In 1958 Hugh A. Bone published one of the first descriptions of the Senate and House policy and campaign committees. Charles O. Jones provides an in-depth analysis of the House Republican Policy Committee from 1959 to 1964 (1964). Mark Ferber (1964) and Kenneth Kofmehl (1964) have examined the formation and operations of the Democratic Study Group in the House of Representatives. However, no comparable studies exist of the organization and strategies of southern conservative Democrats or the House Republican social clubs. A number of state delegations in the House have come under close examination —New York Democrats by Alan Fiellin (1962), the Washington State delegation by John H. Kessel (1964), and Chicago Democrats and Republicans by Leo M. Snowiss (1966). All of these studies are useful complements to David B. Truman's more quantitative explorations of the effects of state delegation membership on voting in the House of Representatives, Chapter VII of *The Congressional Party* (1959).

Some of the most exciting research in recent years has focused upon party leadership in the two houses. Studies by Huitt (1961) and Matthews (1960) remain the definitive treatments of Senate leadership practices. A number of younger scholars have focused upon leadership in the House of Representatives, especially Nelson W. Polsby, Robert L. Peabody, Randall B. Ripley, Lewis A. Froman, Jr., and Charles O. Jones.

In his study of the Albert-Bolling contest for House Majority Leader in 1962, Polsby (1963) sets forth two basic strategies of influence, inside and outside:

The inside strategy is likely to define situations as "family matters," and to feature face-to-face interaction among members. The outside strategy is likely to evoke a more ideological, issue-oriented definition of the situation. Interaction among members is more likely to take place through third parties, lobbyists, and the press. [p. 268]

Bolling's attempt to win from the outside failed for several reasons, chief among them Albert's popularity and the fact that the final vote, if it came, would be by secret ballot. This voting procedure, which allows members to vote relatively free from outside influences, also figured heavily in Ford's upset of Halleck in the contest for the House Minority Leader in 1965 (Peabody, 1966).

Both of these contests were among nineteen cases of leadership change or attempted change taking place in the House of Representatives during the 84th–89th Congresses (1955–1966). Peabody (1967) makes use of these cases to illustrate a typology of leadership change and to suggest conditions that promote contested or relatively peaceful modes of choosing House leaders. During this twelve-year period the Republican minority resorted to contests in seven out of ten cases. In contrast, the Democratic majority was able to resolve its problems of leadership selection through uncontested means in eight out of nine cases. Even the one exception, the Albert-Bolling contest, did not go to a final vote. The personality of the leaders, majority-minority status, and the aggregate outcomes of national elections—all have an influence on the timing and type of leadership change.

Randall B. Ripley has contributed a number of articles and books on party leadership in Congress. A six months' internship in the Office of the House Democratic Whip led to a 1964 article that chronicles the development of party whips in the twentieth-century House of Representatives, discusses the activities of the Democratic whip organization over two sessions of Congress (1962 and 1963), and suggests the broader importance of the whips in the House. Lewis A. Froman, Jr., another political scientist with intern experience in the Office of the House Democratic Whip, and Ripley explore some of the institutional restraints under which House party leaders operate, relying on firsthand observation, whip polls, and roll call votes for their generalizations (1965). Ripley's Brookings Institution study, *Party Leaders in the House of Representatives* (1967), contains a judicious blending of historical materials and insightful analysis of the activities of contemporary House leaders. His book covers the development of party offices, caucuses, and committees, from 1861 to 1967. He relies on four years of close observation and over sixty formal interviews with members of the 88th Congress to describe the roles of recent party leaders, the communication process in the House, and attitudes of party loyalty among both majority and minority members. Ripley also makes extensive use of historical analysis in his forthcoming study of majority party leadership. This book—the second in the American Political Science Association–Carnegie Corporation Study of Congress series—concentrates on twentieth-century majority party leadership practices in both the House and Senate. A great deal of attention is also paid to the relationships between Presidents and congressional leaders.

Jones is in the process of completing a comparable volume on minority leadership practices for the Study of Congress series. Some of the preliminary results of this study are published in an article titled "The Minority Party and Policy-making in the House of Representatives" (1968). Four Congresses—the 63rd (1913–1914), the 73rd (1933–1934), the 85th (1957–1958), and the 87th (1961–1962)—are utilized to illustrate various political conditions that set the range of strategies for the congressional minority.

Jones and Ripley are, of course, not the first or only congressional scholars to place increasing reliance on historical analysis. George Galloway sets forth some broad general outlines in his comprehensive *History of the House of Representatives* (1962). Joseph Cooper has explored the historical development of the standing committees in great depth (1960). David J. Rothman contributes new insights into institutional change in his examination of Senate party machinery from 1869 to 1901 (1966). James S. Young's brilliant analysis of the Washington political community from 1800 to 1828 contains the most thorough study yet made of Congress in the pre-Civil War period (1966). Polsby makes imaginative use of statistical time series in his study of "The Institutionalization of the U.S. House of Representatives" (1968).

Political scientists have only begun to explore the politics of executive-legislative relationships. Richard E. Neustadt contributed two important articles in the mid-1950s: one on the development of the Bureau of the Budget as an agency for central clearance of legislation (1954), the other on planning the President's legislative program (1955). Roger Hilsman has speculated about congressional-executive relations in the development of foreign policy (1958). More recently, Seymour Scher (1960, 1963), Joseph P. Harris (1964), John F. Bibby (1966), and others have added to our knowledge about congressional oversight of administration.

What distinguishes this qualitative phase of behavioral research undertaken since about 1950 from the more traditional studies prior to that time? First, and most obvious, is an abandonment of normative and reformist orientations in favor of descriptions as objective as possible. Almost without exception these political scientists are attempting to describe "what is" rather than attacking or defending the status quo. Only after the evidence has been gathered are they prepared to suggest alternative objectives or methods of operation and the probable consequences of their use. Second, the search is for a higher level of generalization and not just a recitation of facts and figures. The theories may be incomplete and the data limited and uneven, but the efforts to be more scientific have yielded an increasingly comprehensive understanding of the internal workings of Congress. Third, strictly institutional research has given way to an approach which encompasses the attitudes and behavior of legislators operating with institutional constraints. In direct and in more subtle ways the concepts and findings of related behavioral sciences have enriched ways of viewing congressional activity. Finally, much greater use has been made of firsthand observation and focused interviews. Since interviews have played such an important part in our enhanced understanding of Congress, it will be useful to interpose a brief discussion of varying interview styles before reviewing more quantitative methods and studies.

III. ON INTERVIEWING CONGRESSMEN

Three main types of interviews have been used in the study of Congress: (1) the fully structured, or survey research, type; (2) the semistructured, or focused, type; and (3) the unstructured, or journalistic, type. Most students of Congress have not made use of structured interviews of the type associated with survey research. They have preferred an unstructured, or at most, semistructured type of interview.

A structured interview is characterized by a carefully designed interview schedule, a set number of questions that are always asked in a particular order, and often, a high proportion of questions that have a fixed or closed response. A fixed-response question can be answered by a "Yes" or a "No," "Agree" or "Disagree," or some predetermined set of alternatives. For example, the Michigan Survey Research Center's 1958 Study of Representation asked a series of questions in order to obtain a summary of the congressman's views on certain issues. Question 12 was typical:

First, on the foreign economic aid program, would you generally favor expanding the program, reducing it, or maintaining it about the way it is?

A researcher utilizing a semistructured, or focused, interview would resort to fewer questions, most of which are open-ended. For example, in my 1963 study of the House Committee on Rules, Question 3 was worded as follows:

What would you say are the two or three most important functions performed by the Committee on Rules?
a. Which one do you think is the most important?
b. Why?

A semistructured interview allows more opportunity for probing and gives the respondent considerable freedom to expand on a given question.

The unstructured interview is much like the journalist's approach to interviewing. The answers to factual questions are sought.

What happened at the executive session of the committee?
What are the chances of this bill coming to the floor next week?

The researcher may enter the discussion with three or four areas he wants to explore, but he composes most of his questions as he goes. It is not uncommon for the interview to take on the characteristics of a dialogue with a give-and-take on both sides. Rapport may be easier to develop with this kind of interview, but the yield of systematic and comparable data is generally quite limited unless the interviewer is especially skilled and experienced.

By far the most thorough use of survey research techniques as applied to Congress has been undertaken by Warren E. Miller and Donald E. Stokes of the University of Michigan's Survey Research Center (1963). Immediately after the 1958 congressional elections, professional interviewers from the MSRC interviewed the incumbent congressman, his nonincumbent opponent (if any), and a sample of constituents in each of 116 congressional districts.[11] Some of their

---

[11] Since this study of representation was a rider midway on a four-year panel study of the electorate, the authors were forced to generalize from a rather scanty number of constituents per district. Overall, a sample of less than 2,000 respondents was unevenly divided among the 116 districts (an average of 17 constituents per district). Ideally, one would want several hundred interviews per district, at the prohibitive cost, as the authors point out, of several small nuclear reactors. The more statistically sophisticated student may wish to consult the authors' defense of their sampling procedure and statistical manipulations (p. 46, n. 3).

These same voter panels form the basis of the MSRC's superb contributions to our understanding of American presidential election behavior. See Angus Campbell, Philip E. Converse, Warren E. Miller, and Donald E. Stokes, *The American Voter* (New York: Wiley, 1960) and *Elections and the Political Order* (New York: Wiley, 1966).

substantive findings will be reported in Section IV, below. Here I wish to make several comments about the quality of these survey interviews as compared with less-structured interviewing common to most of the committee and leadership studies previously discussed.[12]

Miller and Stokes employed a carefully designed and comprehensive set of interview schedules, numbering about 70 questions with the wording varying slightly, depending upon whether the congressional candidate was an incumbent or not, and whether he won or lost the election. Over a third of the questions had more than one part. Among the major topics covered were the election campaign, attitudes on the issues of foreign aid, domestic welfare policies, and civil rights, the impact of the administration and congressional leadership on roll call voting, representational processes, the characteristics of the district, the politician's perceptions of constituency attitudes on the same three issues, and his career prospects and alternatives.

Miller and Stokes' 70-question interview schedule is clearly too long for most incumbent congressmen. Some congressmen start off promising a half hour and end up allowing as much as an hour and a half, and for the best quality interviews, two to three hours. The average interview runs a little more than an hour, and in most cases the congressman merely answers "Yes" or "No" or responds with short phrases. (Some interviewers went so far as to tell the respondents that the interview was lengthy, so he had best make his responses brief!). Interviews taken in the home district after the election are uniformly longer and better in quality than all but a few interviews conducted on Capitol Hill.

Overall, the quality of the MSRC interviews was better than I had anticipated. Most of the interviews were completed. At a minimum, most of the precodeable items, such as fixed-choice responses on issues, were obtained. However, large numbers of structured interviews are achieved at a cost. In my judgment, only the top 10 percent or so would match the average quality of depth, content, and sophistication that a close student of Congress can obtain using

[12] The authors very generously gave me an opportunity to read some 250 interviews with incumbent congressmen and their opponents during a summer I spent in Ann Arbor in 1964. My impressions of quality are offered with a constructive purpose in mind. It seems to me that we are approaching a state of knowledge where a full-scale attempt to interview a large sample of congressmen over several Congresses should be undertaken, using a combination of structured and semi-structured interviewing techniques.

focused interviewing techniques. Congressmen, by definition, are among the most skilled politicians in the land. They look for, and expect, specialized knowledge on the part of the interviewer if maximum rapport and candidness are to be achieved.

As would be expected, the quality of the MSRC interviews varies greatly with the professional skill and experience of the interviewer. The best interviews in terms of comprehensiveness and depth of response were those undertaken by Miller and Stokes. Next in quality were those handled by the MSRC interviewing staff, particularly several of the regional supervisors (middle-aged females). With several exceptions, the worst interviews were obtained by rather inexperienced American Political Science Association Congressional Fellows, who undertook a number of interviews on Capitol Hill during the spring of 1959.

In some cases, the structured interview itself helped to develop better rapport. Some congressmen, particularly the younger and better-educated members, were intrigued by the type of questions. The prestige of the MSRC undoubtedly helped gain access. In some cases, interviews were obtained *only* because the interviewer happened to come from the congressman's home district.

Some of the difficulties encountered in utilizing survey-type interviews with congressmen are summarized by Robinson (1962). His study of *Congress and Foreign Policy-making* combines case studies of legislation with data obtained from survey interviews from a sample of 100 representatives and senators who were re-elected to the 86th Congress. Interviews were solicited by sending a one-page letter outlining the purposes of the research, identifying its sponsor, and requesting a half to three quarters of an hour's time. This letter was followed up by a telephone call requesting a definite appointment. At the end of a month, Robinson, several colleagues, and three graduate students had obtained 75 interviews. Of the 100 interviews they sought, 86 were finally secured. Robinson notes several reasons why scholars may have a more difficult time than do journalists in obtaining access and responses to their questions.

Members of Congress are interviewed frequently by Capitol reporters, but these interviews are considerably different from those of the academician. Accustomed as he is to the pattern set by journalists, a member of Congress may be somewhat disturbed by fixed-response questions, by "objective" interviewers who do not take sides or give their own opinions, and by other canons set by survey interviewers. [p. 228]

Some of these handicaps may be modified by researchers who resort to less-structured types of interviewing. But the journalist has a number of additional advantages:

1. He often knows the member personally and often has been on familiar terms with him over a number of years. Few academics have this kind of access to more than a few members.

2. A reporter can offer immediate and direct benefits; namely he can put the congressman in the headlines. However, congressmen, particularly the younger and newer members, are beginning to realize that scholars can put their names in books. They can also explain the problems confronting Congress to students and interested citizens.

3. Generally, the reporter's questions seek factual answers. The researcher is often governed by more abstract objectives. In Robinson's words:

. . . our study was aimed primarily at the "process," or how decisions are made, rather than the substance of policy decisions. Our impression is that members have little time and few occasions to reflect on the process. [p. 229]

4. Journalists and scholars have different time needs. A reporter can usually obtain his information with three or four questions and a few minutes of time. The scholar, on the other hand, can seldom get by with less than a half hour of time, and with good respondents, interviews may run two hours or more. Bothered as they are by heavy demands on their time and frequent interruptions—an important telephone call, the need to greet a constituent, a committee meeting, or a roll call—it is not surprising that congressmen are sometimes reluctant to allow scholars all the time that they would like to have.

5. Journalists have two further advantages over academicians—use of the press gallery and access to the Speaker's lobby. House and Senate rules prevent note-taking in all but the press galleries. Together with tourists and other interested citizens, the student of Congress shares the public galleries. He cannot record his observations until he leaves the gallery. On momentous occasions it is all but impossible to get in. On the Senate side, he may be rotated out after fifteen minutes of viewing. Unlike the reporter, he cannot benefit from senators who climb upstairs to the press gallery for "back-

grounders," nor can he conveniently buttonhole members in the Speaker's lobby, just off the floor of the House.

Some of these obstacles can be at least partially overcome. A number of congressional scholars have taken advantage of opportunities to work for congressmen or to participate in the American Political Science Association Congressional Fellowship program.

During 1963 and 1964 seven political scientists participated in a series of afternoon or dinner meetings with individual congressmen.[13] The style of these group interviews was relaxed and free-wheeling. The discussions ranged across such topics as the congressman's cognitive map of his political world, career commitments, campaigning, orientation to the job, the formal and informal organization of the House, and the relationships of House members with colleagues, senators, the executive branch, interest groups, and constituents. In addition to the information obtained, each of the participating scholars developed a better understanding of shared research interests and common problems of obtaining access to congressmen.

Another technique for eliciting the views of congressmen about their jobs was used by Charles L. Clapp for his book *The Congressman: His Work as He Sees It* (1963). Two sets of House members, nineteen Democrats and seventeen Republicans, were invited to The Brookings Institution to participate in a series of discussions. Each group met separately for eight dinner meetings during the first six months of 1959. Stenographic records were kept, and these discussions were supplemented by fifty individual interviews with the panel participants, other members of Congress, and staff. The result is a sympathetic portrait of the problems and rewards of service in the House of Representatives.

Probably the single most important factor contributing to a good interview, structured or unstructured, is the congressman's receptivity to the purposes of the interview. Some congressmen could be interviewed by almost any reasonably skilled staff person, Ph.D. candidate, or professional researcher. A few congressmen, particu-

---

[13] The participants were Joseph Cooper, Harvard University (now at Rice University); Milton C. Cummings, Jr., The Brookings Institution (now at Johns Hopkins University); Richard F. Fenno, Jr., University of Rochester; Charles O. Jones, University of Arizona; Robert L. Peabody, Johns Hopkins University; Nelson W. Polsby, Wesleyan University (now at University of California, Berkeley); and H. Douglas Price, Syracuse University (now at Harvard University). This project was supported by a grant from the Social Science Research Council.

larly older members set in their ways, may not be responsive even to the most skilled professional. There is no question that a great deal of valuable information can be obtained through structured interviews. For many sensitive aspects of congressional behavior, however, there is no substitute for the techniques of participant-observation and the use of less-structured interviewing by experienced students of Congress.

IV. THE QUANTITATIVE PHASE OF BEHAVIORAL-EMPIRICAL STUDIES

Political science, in common with other sciences, is confronted with a range of problems, a rich variety of data, and the need to formulate a more or less precise language for stating its theoretical propositions and empirical findings. For a great range of political problems, including much that goes on in legislatures, the data—policy statements, the language of legislation, observations, and interview responses—are essentially "soft." Most judgments are qualitative, a matter of "more or less," and the language that is used can seldom achieve much greater precision than is characteristic of ordinary statements in natural language. With more precise data—election returns, biographical and demographical variables, and roll call votes—techniques of quantitative measurement can be used. Instead of "more or less," it is now possible to answer the question "how much more?" There is a natural tendency to view this movement from qualitative to quantitative approaches as if the discipline has progressed from a lower to a higher stage in its development. Up to a point this is true. However, given the nature of politics, quantitative techniques will never replace qualitative approaches. Instead, it is likely that political scientists will increasingly adapt a range of techniques, both qualitative and quantitative, to the study of legislative institutions. As a complement to earlier reviews of essentially qualitative studies, this section examines the use of quantitative techniques in the study of congressional elections, the measurement of power and influence, and the analysis of roll call votes.

The systematic study of congressional elections

Every two years American voters elect one-third of the Senate and all 435 members of the House of Representatives. Every four years the congressional elections are held concurrently with the choosing of the President of the United States. Most of what we know about voting behavior has come from panel and survey studies of the performance of the American electorate in presidential elections since 1940. Congressional elections as another important source of quantitative data have, with several exceptions, only recently been systematically analyzed.

Two of the first scholars to examine sectional and regional patterns of voting behavior in congressional districts were Arthur N. Holcombe (1924) and Paul D. Hasbrouck (1927). In his pioneering work, *The Political Parties of To-day*, Holcombe develops a number of schemes for classifying congressional districts, including breakdowns by metropolitan, urban, semiurban, and rural districts; sectional and agricultural interests; and the comparative strength of the two parties. Hasbrouck's study of *Party Government in the House of Representatives* reports the extent of "standpatism"—the degree to which there is no change in party control of a given congressional seat—for the seven elections between 1914 and 1926. During this twelve-year period, 62 percent of the districts remained in the hands of the same party. He also

. . . calculated the potential change in congressional races by multiplying the number of districts by one less than the number of elections in the period measured. During the 1914–26 period there were seven elections in 435 constituencies. The potential number of changes (i.e., perfect competition by this measure) was 2.610 (435 × 6). He then counted the actual number of changes and divided by the potential change. There were 308 changes or [11.8] percent fluidity. [Jones, 1964, p. 464]

Still another pioneering attempt at developing generalizations about the choice of our national legislators was Cortez A. M. Ewing's study of *Congressional Elections, 1896–1944* (1947).

In his article "Inter-Party Competition for Congressional Seats" (1964), Charles O. Jones extends the analysis first undertaken by Hasbrouck in 1927. He finds a continued pattern of a rather low degree of competition in congressional districts in each of the three decades since the 1920s. Furthermore, the trend is toward less competition in terms of the numbers of districts which change from one party to the other within a decade. Table 1 shows why the Democratic party has retained control of the House of Representatives since 1930, save for but two Congresses, the 80th (1947–1948) and the 83rd

(1953–1954). There has been a gradual increase in the number of no change districts and the Democrats have dominated the additional ones.

Table 1 Party control of no change districts

Time period	Total NC districts	NC districts dominated by Republicans	NC districts dominated by Democrats
1914–26	270	148 (54.8%)	122 (45.2%)
1932–40	304	74 (24.3%)	230 (75.7%)
1942–50	322	147 (45.7%)	175 (54.3%)
1952–60	340	136 (40.0%)	204 (60.0%)

Source: "Inter-Party Competition for Congressional Seats," Western Political Quarterly, XVII (1964), p. 469. Reprinted by permission of the University of Utah, copyright owners.

While the Republicans have been making modest gains in the South—a trend that has continued into the 1960s—elsewhere their party fortunes have remained stable or have declined. Approaching 1968 Republicans seem to have their best opportunity since 1952 to regain control of the House.

In Congressmen and Their Constituencies (1963) Lewis A. Froman, Jr., is primarily concerned with two types of questions. First, what kinds of people are likely to participate in congressional elections in the United States? Second, what is the relationship between the decisions on public policy made by congressmen and the type of constituency from which they come? Two sources are used extensively: The Congressional District Data Book, Districts of the 87th Congress, published by the Bureau of the Census, and The Congressional Quarterly Almanac for 1961.

What factors are associated with higher voter turnout in congressional elections? Froman's findings conform closely to our knowledge of voting behavior patterns based on studies of presidential elections. Perhaps the most important variation in voter turnout is accounted for by regional factors. Northern congressional districts have the highest turnout, border congressional districts the next highest, and southern congressional districts the lowest turnout. Much of this regional variation can be traced to differences in social, economic, and political factors which characterize the three regions.

In general, Froman finds high voting turnout associated with (1) low percentage of nonwhite population, (2) high percentage of owner-occupied dwelling units, (3) high percentage of urbanization, (4) high population density, (5) greater competitiveness in the district, and (6) incumbent Republican districts. Five of these six relationships

. . . help to explain why northern congressional districts have higher rates of voting than do border districts and why border districts have higher rates than do southern districts. Northern districts have higher proportions of urban, densely populated, competitive, Republican districts, and a lower proportion of non-white (all characteristics leading to higher turnout when all congressional districts are taken together) than do border districts; and border districts, in turn, stand in the same relationship with southern districts. The sections of the country do not differ on percentage owner-occupied dwelling units. [pp. 37–38]

Froman also makes use of these constituency variables to contrast the voting patterns of northern Democrats with northern Republicans. Not unexpectedly, he demonstrates that "Northern Democratic constituencies are more urban, more racially mixed, have a lower percentage of owner-occupied dwelling units, and have more people per square mile than Northern Republican constituencies" (p. 92). Furthermore, independent of political party, these constituency differences are associated with more liberal voting records as measured in terms of high presidential (Kennedy) support scores.

Perhaps the major limitation of Froman's analysis is the relatively short time span from which he draws supporting data. For the most part his generalizations are based on but one census (1960), three elections (1958, 1960, and 1962), and roll calls from but a single session of a Congress, the first session of the 87th Congress (1961).

The advantages of working with longer trend data are demonstrated by Milton C. Cummings' study of *Congressmen and the Electorate* (1966). Using election statistics from *Congressional Quarterly, America Votes,* and the biennial reports of the Clerk of the United States House of Representatives, Cummings explores the relationship between the vote for President and the outcome of House elections in presidential election years from 1920 to 1964. He finds a strong interdependence between the votes for President and the selection of House members. On only two widely separated occasions—1848 and 1956—has the electorate sent a President to Washington without a House majority of the same party. When ticket-splitting takes place, its most frequent consequence has been to strengthen the number of the President's opponents in the House of Representatives.

[I]n most presidential years, it is mainly House candidates of the party that lost the Presidency who survive an opposition presidential tide in their district; and . . . most split results occur in districts where the presidential race is close. [p. 47]

Many incumbent House members do obtain a degree of autonomy from the ebb and flow of presidential election trends. "On the average, more than four of every five candidates for Representative who win are already House members" (p. 57). What factors are likely to limit the electoral advantage enjoyed by incumbent congressmen? Major regional revolts against the heretofore dominant party in a region, economic setbacks, strong third-party candidates, and special local and personal problems such as marital difficulties may at one time or another make more difficult an incumbent's bid for re-election.

Subsequent chapters explore policy and personal differences that may characterize presidential and congressional candidates, the impact of minor-party candidacies, and the effect of institutional factors, such as the form of the ballot and the type of constitutency, on the selection of House members. Over sixty tables and figures help illuminate the analysis and yield working hypotheses for further testing. Two topics, mid-term elections[14] and congressional primaries,[15] are treated only incidentally in this otherwise comprehensive study. As the author notes, both merit detailed study.

Quantitative studies of "power" and "influence"

The concepts of "power" and "influence" are among the most widely used terms in the social sciences. For a time, political science under the stimulus of Charles Merriam and Harold Lasswell, saw power as *the* subject matter of the discipline. More recently, these terms have fallen into some disfavor, both because of the ubiquity of the phenomenon and the difficulty in arriving at conceptual clarity, let alone

[14] The literature on mid-term elections is exceedingly slim, but see McPhee and Glazer (1962)—a rather unsuccessful attempt to utilize state and regional survey data in the study of the 1950 congressional election—and see also Hinckley (1967).

[15] A notable article, Julius Turner's examination of "Primary Elections as an Alternative to Party Competition in 'Safe' Districts" (1953), needs replication and up-dating.

satisfactory measurement.[16] Students of the legislative p
been in the forefront in attempts at isolating the phenc
fining its theoretical dimensions, and developing empiric
for the power of elective leaders, committee chairmen
influential members of Congress.

During the 1950s, one of the most promising approaches seemed to
be the mathematical theory of games. A number of theoretical articles
appeared, one of the most rigorous being the Shapley and Shubik
article (1954), reviewed below. Other students—for example, Luce
and Rogow (1956), Dahl (1957), MacRae and Price (1959), and Riker
and Niemi (1962)—have attempted to provide empirical underpinnings for a power index. Partly because the basic assumptions of
game theory are difficult to meet, and partly because the collection
and organization of empirical data have yet to substantiate the theory,
the game theoretical approach to the analysis of congressional power
has not lived up to its initial promise.

Three additional approaches—the already mentioned Miller and
Stokes study of representatives and constituency influence (1963); the
Wolfinger and Heifetz analysis of safe seats, seniority, and power
(1965); and several working papers of David Kovenock on communication and influence—demonstrate the continued interest of political scientists in these elusive, but nevertheless central, phenomena.

Shapley and Shubik offer a method for the a priori evaluation of
the distribution of power in a committee or the division of power
among the various bodies of a legislature. The power of an individual member is defined as the chance he has of being critical to
the success of a winning coalition. Where all legislators have one
vote, each is credited with 1/nth of the power, given n participants.
Assuming that it takes a majority of both the House and the Senate,
plus the consent of the President, or two-thirds majorities of the two
bodies without the President's signature, Shapley and Shubik cal-
culate their relative power values:

We take all the members of the three bodies and consider them voting for
the bill in every possible order. In each order we observe the relative posi-

---

[16] Robert A. Dahl, "The Concept of Power," *Behavioral Science,* 2 (1957), 201–215,
and Dahl, "Power," *International Encyclopedia of the Social Sciences,* 12 (New York:
Macmillan, 1968), 405–415; James G. March, "The Power of Power," in David Easton,
ed., *Varieties of Political Theory* (Englewood Cliffs, N.J.: Prentice-Hall, 1966), pp.
39–70; and William H. Riker, "Some Ambiguities in the Notion of Power," *American Political Science Review,* LVIII (1964), 341–349.

uons of the straight-majority pivotal men in the House and Senate, the President, and also the 2/3–majority pivotal men in House and Senate. One of these five individuals will be the pivot for the whole vote, depending on the order in which they appear. For example, if the President comes after the two straight-majority pivots, but before one or both of the 2/3–majority pivots, then he gets the credit for the passage of the bill. The frequency of this case, if we consider all possible orders (of the 533 individuals involved),[17] turns out to be very nearly 1/6. This is the President's power index. . . . The values for the House as a whole and for the Senate as a whole are both equal to 5/12, approximately. . . . In brief, then the power indices for the three bodies are in the proportion 5:5:2. The indices for a *single* congressman, a *single* senator, and the President are in the proportion 2:9:350. [p. 789]

As the authors point out, these calculations (which are too complicated to be reproduced in the article) are not intended to be representative of "reality." They are hopeful, however, that "the power index computations may be useful in the setting up of norms or standards, the departure from which will serve as a measure of, for example, political solidarity, or regional or sociological factionalism, in an assembly" (p. 791). They do suggest how a possible empirical power index might be constructed, but note the difficulty of applying such a measure without some means of weighting different legislative issues.[18]

Some of the complexities of quantitative analysis, even within a single session of Congress, are highlighted in an imaginative article by William H. Riker and Donald Niemi (1962). They begin by accepting Truman's central thesis (1959)—that Congress is characterized by several fairly cohesive blocs—with some marginal members who shift from one bloc to another to form winning coalitions. They then attempt to pick out these marginal members through the use of an "empirical power index," a refinement of the *a priori* power

[17] Only 533 individuals, because writing in 1954, Shapley and Shubik were dealing with a 96-member Senate, plus the Vice-President as presiding officer, the 435-member House of Representatives, and the President of the United States.

[18] In 1959 William Riker proposed a technique for weighting roll calls which does seem to distinguish objectively between trivial and nontrivial roll calls. In brief: "the *most significant* roll call possible is one in which (1) all members vote, and (2) the difference between the majority and minority is the minimum possible under the voting rules. Conversely, the *least significant* roll call is one in which (1) a bare quorum votes, and (2) the outcome is unanimous. . . . Such an ordering represents legislators' collective judgment, indexed by behavior rather than talk, of the relative significance of all roll calls" (p. 379).

index posited by Shapley and Shubik (1954). More [
a computation (over a series of roll calls, where th
weighted according to their significance) of the avera
each Representative had to be the pivotal or margini
winning side" (p. 58). Although they were not comple
their study does point out the importance of analysis over time, including shifts in blocs over a single session.

This study used all 87 roll calls during the first session of the 86th
Congress (1959), as well as smaller subsets classified in terms of subject matter, and procedural or political considerations. Riker and
Niemi found that the empirical index on all 87 roll calls for each
member of the House varied from zero to .003283, as compared to
an a priori power index of .002288.[19] The medians for party and
regional groupings accord with intuitive notions of coalition-forma-
tion in the House:

All Democrats	.002582
All Republicans	.001810
Southern Democrats	.002554
Northern Democrats	.002553
Border Democrats	.002746

That is to say, majority Democrats are usually on the winning side,
and border Democrats (Delaware, Maryland, West Virginia, Kentucky,
Missouri, and Oklahoma) frequently provide the swing votes.

However, the coefficient of correlation for the empirical power indices of members on the first chronological half of the 87 roll calls
as compared with the last half was only $r = +.484$. In other words,
it was only possible to predict a member's voting behavior with
accuracy about once in four times. On other subsets of roll call votes,
the predictive power was much higher.

Riker and Niemi summarize their attempt to predict power indices
as follows:

(1) A rather imprecisely defined set of blocs did exist in the first session of
    the Eighty-Sixth Congress.
(2) On two kinds of issues (and for 32 out of 87 roll calls) a fairly high

[19] An index of zero was only obtained by those who never voted, most notably,
Speaker Rayburn. As the authors note, "part of the difficulty with the name of the
index is underscored by this curious result: that the man often considered the most
powerful had an 'empirical power index' of zero" (p. 60, n. 9).

degree of consistency of power indices persisted through the session. For these issues the model was to some degree validated. . . .

(3) On the other sorts of issues, the model was not validated, for it turned out to be impossible to predict members' voting behavior with accuracy. . . .

(4) The exact membership and relative strength and position of blocs changes over time. The crucial features of the change seem to be the content of issues and perhaps the skill and strategy of leaders. [p. 65]

The methods employed by Miller and Stokes in their study of constituency influence on styles of congressional representation[20] have already been described in the section (III, above) on interview techniques. Here some of their findings will be reviewed. This Michigan Survey Research Center study was designed to obtain answers to the following two questions:

Is the saliency of legislative action to the public so different in quality and degree on different issues that the legislator is subject to very different constraints from his constituency? Does the legislator have a single generalized mode of response to his constituency that is rooted in a normative belief about the representative's role or does the same legislator respond to his constituency differently on different issues? [p. 46]

The findings of survey research on the mass electorate consistently demonstrate that most American voters are not well informed about the great majority of legislative issues in Washington. They do, however, hold rather general beliefs about how the country should be run, how far government should go to achieve social and economic welfare objectives, and which party is more likely to maintain prosperity and keep the country out of war. As numerous roll call studies have demonstrated, congressmen respond to many issues in terms of fairly broad evaluative dimensions, bolstered by criteria that are rather complex and specific to particular policy problems.

Miller and Stokes make use of three broad evaluative dimensions to compare the policy preferences of constituents and representatives: (1) the extent of approval of government action in the social welfare field, (2) the degree of support for American involvement in foreign affairs, and (3) the extent of approval of federal action to protect the civil rights of Negroes. Guttman-type cumulative scaling

[20] For what has become a standard distinction between a representative's "style" and his "focus," see Heinz Eulau, John C. Wahlke, William Buchanan, and LeRoy C. Ferguson, "The Role of the Representative: Some Empirical Observations on the Theory of Edmund Burke," *American Political Science Review*, LIII (1959), 742–756.

procedures were used in each policy area to order their samples of congressmen, opposing candidates, and voters. Congressmen were further ranked according to their roll call voting patterns in the House. The three issue domains reveal very different degrees of policy congruence:

On questions of social and economic welfare there is considerable agreement between Representative and district, expressed by a correlation of approximately 0.3. This coefficient is, of course, very much less than the limiting value of 1.0, indicating that a number of Congressmen are, relatively speaking, more or less "liberal" than their districts. However, on the question of foreign involvement there is no discernible agreement between legislator and district whatever. Indeed, as if to emphasize the point, the coefficient expressing this relationship is slightly negative (− 0.09), although not significantly so in a statistical sense. It is in the domain of civil rights that the rankings of Congressmen and constituencies most nearly agree. When we took our measurements in the late 1950's the correlation of congressional roll call behavior with constituency opinion on questions affecting the Negro was nearly 0.6. [p. 49]

These correlations are the starting point for a range of further analyses. In this article, the authors are especially concerned with the extent to which the agreements on social welfare and civil rights questions are due to constituency influence on congressmen and not accounted for by other factors. Three necessary and sufficient conditions are required to establish constituency *control:*

[F]irst, the Representative's votes in the House must agree substantially with his own policy views or his perceptions of the district's views, and not be determined entirely by other influences to which the Congressman is exposed; and *second,* the attitudes or perceptions governing the Representative's acts must correspond, at least imperfectly, to the district's actual opinions . . . [and] *third,* . . . the constituency must in some measure take the policy views of candidates into account in choosing a Representative. If it does not, agreement between district and Congressman may arise for reasons that cannot rationally be brought within the idea of control. [p. 51]

Miller and Stokes present evidence that in large part does substantiate the first two conditions. If the two intervening variables of the representative's own policy views and his perceptions of his constituents' views are used to predict roll call votes, the predictions are quite successful. The multiple correlations increase to 0.7 for social welfare, 0.6 for foreign involvement, and 0.9 for civil rights. The correlations of congressional attitudes and perceptions with constituency opinions are weaker. The third condition is more difficult to satisfy, and would seem to necessitate a series of case studies in a number of constituencies with increased numbers of voters in the samples from each district.

The authors conclude that no one style of representation fully accords with the realities of American congressional politics. "The American system *is* a mixture, to which the Burkean, instructed-delegate, and responsible-party models all can be said to have contributed elements" (p. 56). Moreover, each of the policy areas studied seems to be associated with one of these patterns of representation:

The issue domain in which the relation of the Congressman to constituency most nearly conforms to the instructed-delegate model is that of civil rights. . . . The representative relation conforms most closely to the responsible-party model in the domain of social welfare. . . . [To a degree] the present role of the legislature in foreign affairs bears some resemblance to the role that Burke had in mind for the elitist, highly restricted *electorate* of his own day. [p. 56]

Two theories are examined by Raymond E. Wolfinger and Joan Heifetz (1965) which seem to account for the problems that Democratic Presidents have had with Democratic Congresses over the past several decades. One thesis—called the "textbook theory"—runs as follows: "lack of responsibility in the Democratic party is due to control of Congress by Southerners. Their influence is due to their seniority, which is a result of the lack of party competition in the South" (p. 337). The other interpretation—called the "insiders' theory" because of its prevalence in Washington—introduces additional considerations to explain southern influence in Congress. Northern congressmen from safe seats, so the argument goes, do not make use of their "potential seniority." They frequently leave the House in mid-career for a job in state and local government, particularly judgeships. Southern congressmen are seen as more diligent and able than their northern counterparts.

The two authors mobilize a range and variety of statistical evidence which substantially support the textbook theory, and in the main, refute the insiders' theory. Among their major findings are the following:

(1) Congressmen in southern safe seats do not have more congressional seniority than those in northern safe seats.
(2) The post-congressional career patterns of the two groups do not indi-

cate any greater northern inclination to leave the House for another career. [Northerners are, however, more likely to seek state and local public offices; Southerners are more likely to leave the House for careers in business and law.] [p. 342]

(3) The safe Southerners do not have more committee seniority than safe Northerners.

(4) Safe Southerners have more chairmanships than they are "entitled to" only at the subcommittee level, where considerations other than seniority affect the selection process. [p. 343]

Some fragments of data lend credence to the view that southerners are more able and vigorous congressmen than are a portion of the urban, big-city machine representatives. Northerners include more members who first enter Congress at age 50 or older, and their record of absenteeism is somewhat higher than that of southern congressmen.

Wolfinger and Heifetz conclude that "lack of party competition, aided perhaps by southern favoritism in appointment of subcommittee chairmen . . . seems to be an adequate explanation for the disproportionate number of Southerners in influential positions in the House" (p. 349). These factors were heightened by heavy Democratic election losses in the 1946 election, defeats which were confined almost entirely to the North. "One of the long-term consequences of the Republican landslide then was the creation of a 'seniority generation' dominated by Southerners" (p. 348). Wolfinger and Heifetz also emphasize that the number and share of noncompetitive seats held by the North has undergone a substantial increase over the past decade. They suggest that the effect of these trends is likely to be "a decrease in the power of the deviant wing of the Democratic party and therefore an increase in party cohesion" (p. 349).

One further line of promising research on communications and influence has been undertaken by David Kovenock (1964, 1967). His basic methodological tool is a communications audit technique first developed by Benjamin Walter for the study of the flow of information between bureaucrats.[21] Kovenock applies a modified version of this audit to the movement of communications (or decision premises) between six members of a House subcommittee during three sum-

[21] *Bureaucratic Communication: A Statistical Analysis of Influence* (Chapel Hill, N.C.: Institute for Research in Social Science, University of North Carolina, 1963).

mer months of the second session of the 87th Congress (1962). His findings lend concrete support to the impressions of Dexter and Matthews that "a Congressman hears most often from those who agree with him" (Dexter, 1957, p. 5) and that "the vast majority of all lobbying is directed at [those] who are already convinced" (Matthews, 1960, p. 182).

The analysis of roll call voting

The principal means by which legislatures make and legitimate decisions is by voting. Voting procedures vary from legislature to legislature and even within a single legislature. At least three broad classes can be identified (Anderson, Watts, and Wilcox, 1966, pp. 3–4). Votes may be *closed,* or by secret ballot, as is typically the case in the selection of congressional leaders in party caucuses, or in decisions by committees meeting in executive sessions. They may be *semi-open* or anonymous, for example, decisions made by voice, division, and teller votes in the House of Representatives.[22] Finally, votes may be *open* or public. The most common form is the roll call vote: the names of the members are called alphabetically, to which members respond "yea" or "nay." It is these roll call votes, printed in the *Congressional Record,* that have provided students of Congress with an especially valuable source of data for understanding the workings of the representative process.

The great advantage of roll call votes is that they are "hard" data. As Stuart Rice noted more than forty years ago, votes are "the most tangible and measurable units of political behavior."

They are tangible because simple and precise. They are measurable, for although each is really a *gross measure* of opinion, the value of which may differ widely in different individuals, they are nevertheless assumed to have equal value and are counted and recorded officially. [Rice, 1925, p. 60]

[22] Under a voice vote, the presiding officer calls for the shouting of "yeas" and "nays" and then estimates the winning side. A division vote is more accurate. Members are asked to stand and are counted pro and con, by the chair. Under a teller vote, the members line up and pass one by one up the middle aisle of the House, first those in favor, and then those against. Tellers are appointed by the chair to count those for and against the amendment, and they report their counts back to the chair. The Senate, a much smaller body, frequently makes use of the voice vote, but seldom resorts to division and makes no use of the teller voting procedure.

David B. Truman, who adopted techniques invented by Stuart Rice and refined by Herman Beyle to provide us with the most comprehensive roll call study of one Congress yet undertaken, *The Congressional Party* (1959), specifies the advantages of roll call data even more thoroughly:

Like statistics on elections, they represent discrete acts the fact of whose occurrence is not subject to dispute. They do not depend for their validity as data upon verbal reports of action or upon the impressions of fallible observers. Taken in quantity, therefore, they can be examined statistically with more confidence than can be granted to data whose reliability depends upon the objectivity of visual observation or verbal reporting. In the Congress, moreover, the "yeas and nays" closely approximate a record of the principal actions of the two houses. Not all votes are taken by roll call, of course, but it is rarely the case that a matter of real controversy, or one of importance in other respects, is disposed of in either chamber without at least one vote recording the preferences of the individual senators and representatives. [p. 12]

The basic techniques of roll call analysis have been available for many years. As early as 1901 A. Lawrence Lowell used roll call data to study "The Influence of Party Upon Legislation in England and America." During the 1920s Stuart A. Rice developed several indices for measuring party cohesion and likeness in voting (1928).[23] His technique for identifying different blocs within legislatures was subsequently refined by Herman C. Beyle (1931). The analysis of patterns of legislative votes was further enhanced by the development of Guttman scaling (Guttman, 1950). These techniques largely lay dormant until the late 1940s and 1950s, when several important books and a

---

[23] The Rice index of cohesion has been widely used, partly because it is quite simple to compute and understand. When the party or subgroup is split 50–50, the index is at 0. As the group becomes more and more united, the index rises to 100. To derive the index of cohesion, simply convert the "yeas" and "nays" into percentages of the total number of group members voting. The index of cohesion is the absolute difference between the two percentage figures. Thus, if 60 Democratic Senators split 45 for (75%) and 15 against (25%), the index of cohesion is $75 - 25$, or 50. If 40 Republican Senators split 12 for (30%) and 28 against (70%), the index of cohesion is $70 - 30$, or 40.

The Rice index of likeness is the complement of the difference between the respective percentages voting "yea" in the two groups. Again, the index ranges from 0 to 100, with 0 representing complete dissimilarity and 100 representing complete agreement. Thus, in our example, above, the index of likeness would be $100 - (75 - 30)$, or 55.

spate of articles using roll call data were published.[24] As such they reflect broader research trends within political science, including a greater focus on individual behavior as distinct from institutional analyses, an increasing emphasis on policy outcomes, and a greater reliance on quantitative as distinct from qualitative empirical research. The availability of mechanical and electronic aids, especially the advent of computers, has greatly facilitated quantitative analysis in the social sciences.

In his classic study, *Southern Politics* (1949), V. O. Key, Jr., made use of roll call analysis and the Rice index of cohesion to determine the extent of southern solidarity in Congress. Southern Democrats in the Senate were only slightly more cohesive than Republicans, non-southern Democrats, and all Democrats. A genuine southern solidarity was largely confined to votes on the race question. Southern representatives were considerably more united than their Senate counterparts. On 275 roll calls over four sessions (1933, 1937, 1941, and 1945) southern House members had an average index of cohesion of 70.4 as compared with 55.4 for southern Senators on 598 roll calls over seven sessions (every odd year from 1933 to 1945). "The averages of the indices of cohesion on 275 House roll calls for each of the four groups and the comparable figures for the Senate were as follows:" [p. 370]

	House	Senate
Southern Democrats	70.4	55.4
Republicans	66.0	51.8
Nonsouthern Democrats	61.7	46.9
Democrats	58.5	46.0

Put another way, on the average, 85.2 percent of the southern Democratic House members voted together; southern Democratic Senators voted on the same side of all issues an average of 77.7 percent. Thus, regional cohesion was tighter in the House than in the Senate.

Another pioneering roll call study, Julius Turner's *Party and Con-*

---

[24] The findings of five of the most important books—Key's *Southern Poliltics* (1949), Turner's *Party and Constituency: Pressures on Congress* (1951), MacRae's *Dimensions of Congressional Voting* (1958), Truman's *The Congressional Party* (1959), and Mayhew's *Party Loyalty Among Congressmen* (1966)—are briefly summarized below. Among articles applying roll call analysis and Guttman scaling to the study of Congress, see esp. Brimhall and Otis (1948), Belknap (1958), and Farris (1958), all of which are reprinted in Wahlke and Eulau (1959); Jewell (1959); Patterson (1963); Price (1963); Rieselbach (1964); MacRae (1965); and Marwell (1967).

stituency: Pressures on Congress (1951), was completed as a doctoral dissertation at The Johns Hopkins University under V. O. Key's supervision. Turner focused on two sources of pressure: the congressman's political party, and his constituency. The basic data for his generalizations are roll calls from four sessions of the House of Representatives: the first session of the 67th Congress (1921), the third session of the 71st Congress (1930–1931), the first session of the 75th Congress (1937), and the second session of the 78th Congress (1944). He does not claim that these sessions are representative of congressional sessions in general. Nevertheless, the selected sessions "reflect the American system under widely varying conditions of time, party and group control, and economic and military conditions" (p. 15). Among other quantitative measures, Turner makes use of the Rice indices of cohesion and likeness and Lowell's criteria for a party vote.[25]

A number of Turner's findings have yet to be disproved, despite the rather crude quantitative techniques that he employed. His central finding stresses the importance of party on voting behavior. In his words: ". . . in spite of the small degree of party voting in the modern American Congress compared with other countries and other times, party continues to be more closely associated with congressional voting behavior than any other discernible factor" (p. 34). On what issues do the Republican and Democratic parties differ? For the four sessions analyzed, Turner found the most consistent and sharp cleavages registered on issues of tariff, government versus private action, social and labor questions, and farm policy.

Turner also explored the import of a number of additional "pressures" that seemed to affect congressional voting, including metropolitan-rural cleavages, the extent of foreign born versus native stock in districts, and splits based on sectionalism (for example, North-South). "Of the three kinds of groupings studied, foreign-native Democrats differed most, followed in order by North-South and metropolitan-rural" (p. 132). "Sectional pressures were more effective than metropolitan-rural or foreign-native pressures in the Republican party in three of the four sessions" (p. 154). Only in 1944 did the foreign-native division have a slight edge over sectionalism for Republicans.

---

[25] Lowell (1901) defined a party vote as a roll call on which at least 90 percent of one party votes "yea" and 90 percent or more of the other party votes "nay."

However, all of these pressures are much less important than party as a determinant of voting behavior in the House of Representatives.

The first major attempt to apply cumulative or Guttman scale analysis[26] to roll call votes in the House of Representatives was undertaken by Duncan MacRae, Jr. His *Dimensions of Congressional Voting* (1958), like Truman's *The Congressional Party* (1959), is based upon roll call votes from the 81st Congress (1949–1950). In brief, scaling analysis makes it possible to locate the positions of congressmen along a number of variables or dimensions, thus providing a concise description of their stances on issues. These scale positions can then be related to other variables such as constituency characteristics or leadership and committee roles to test hypotheses about representation and the legislative process.

MacRae found a number of major dimensions into which House Democrats and Republicans of the 81st Congress could be scaled. The most detailed scale, a "Fair Deal" scale, divided House Democrats into eight segments along a dimension of economic conservatism-to-liberalism. The votes of Republican congressmen on the same set of roll calls yielded not one, but two scales: one a welfare state dimension, and the other a labor-relations scale. Other major dimensions that scaled for both Republicans and Democrats were race relations, foreign aid, and agriculture.

As MacRae observes, "the significance of scales based on roll-call votes depends in large measure on the degree of generality of the inferences that can be made from a scale to other political behavior" (pp. 253–254). Chapter III relates scale data to two major occupational characteristics of congressional districts: the proportion of farmers and farm laborers among employed males, and the proportion of professionals and managers. MacRae finds that "the direct relation between interest groups and roll-call votes is strongest in the field of agriculture. Here party lines appear to be weakest, and the support of local commodities differentiates most clearly within each party" (pp. 278–279). The author also examines the relationship of scale data to the representative's election margin and positions of formal leadership, including the attainment of the position of committee chairman and ranking minority member. Republicans in the

[26] Louis Guttman, "The Basis for Scalogram Analysis," in Samuel A. Stouffer, et al., *Measurement and Prediction* (Princeton, N.J.: Princeton University Press, 1950), pp. 60–90.

81st Congress "showed some indication of heightened responsiveness to constituency characteristics when they had narrow election margins, but . . . Democrats did not" (p. 286). MacRae's data support the "middleman" hypothesis with regard to elective leaders, the notion that a successful leader must be a compromise among the ideological extremes of his party (Patterson, 1963). Committee chairmen and ranking minority members, however, tended to come from the more conservative elements of both parties, the Democratic South and the Republican Midwest.

As has already been noted, the most extensive roll call study yet completed is David B. Truman's *The Congressional Party* (1959). The author is interested not just in the internal workings of Congress, but also in how the House and Senate relate to the broader political system of which they are a part. His primary focus is upon the Democratic and Republican congressional parties and their leaders, particularly as their behavior is manifested in roll call votes on the floor of the two chambers during the 81st Congress (1949–1950). The principal technique of voting bloc analysis was first developed by Stuart A. Rice in the 1920s, refined by Herman C. Beyle in 1931, and made applicable to large legislative assemblies by the advent of electronic data processing equipment. In essence, the method consists of counting the number of agreements in each House between each party member and every other party member on a series of selected roll call votes, ordered on the basis of their index of party cohesion. The resulting blocs, or clusters of interrelated pairs, are then examined in terms of the personal characteristics of the members, their constituencies, and the relationship of these blocs to majority and minority status, leadership influence, and state delegation and regional cohesion. The roll call data are supplemented by documentary analysis and interviews (the number unspecified).

Only a few of the many generalizations developed by Truman can be summarized here. Like Turner, he finds party as the single most reliable indicator of congressional voting behavior. In the Senate, the Republican minority was a good deal less unified than the Democrats in both sessions of the 81st Congress. In the House, the Democratic majority was generally less cohesive than the Republican minority. However, "the voting behavior of the Republicans when they were divided resembled the kaleidoscopic stereotype, a moving pattern of shifting individuals or small clusters based on state delegations or even less inclusive aggregations" (pp. 190–191). Several of Truman's most important contributions refer to party leadership roles. He finds that "the minority elective leaders in both chambers, despite the higher Republican party cohesion in the House, were collectively less united than were their majority equivalents" (p. 281). Why is this the case? A most plausible interpretation is that the program of the President and majority status tend to increase a party's general cohesion, stabilize its subparty blocs, and give coherence and meaning to the principal party leadership roles. The mediate functions of the legislative party and the changing nature of issues and political fortunes are keys to the roles of the elective leaders. Their powers

. . . are for the most part informal, personal, interstitial, and—somewhat like those of the President—often less extensive than the range of expectations they must meet. . . . [T]here appear to be differences in this respect between the House and Senate party leaders, but in both chambers the influence of the principal leaders depends heavily upon their recurrently improvising effective combinations among fragments of power of the most varied sorts. [p. 294]

This book has several shortcomings. It is a case study limited to a single Congress. Thus its full value cannot be realized until many of its hypotheses have been tested in other Congresses. Yet, true replicative studies are not likely to be forthcoming, not just because of the complexity of collecting and analyzing an immense amount of data. The machine procedure developed for the Rice-Beyle-Truman bloc analysis "could not efficiently handle simultaneously more than 74 roll calls" (p. 322). Today, more versatile machines exist, and investigators are not likely to want to be bound by the constraints within which Truman was forced to work. Another limitation is that the interviews conducted by Truman are seldom referred to and only indirectly used as the basis for making generalizations.

David R. Mayhew's study of *Party Loyalty Among Congressmen: The Difference Between Democrats and Republicans, 1947–1962* (1966) demonstrates the advantages of roll call analysis over a series of Congresses, the 80th to the 87th. His objective is to analyze the operations of the two congressional parties in the postwar House of Representatives on four kinds of domestic issues: farm, urban, labor, and western (mainly water and public power) issues. The House membership of each party is divided into "interested" and relatively "indifferent" congressmen on each of the four sets of issues. Then, Rice indices of likeness and cohesion are used to develop generalizations about bloc voting in the House.

In voting on each of the four sets of issues . . . Democrats from "interested" districts maintained higher cohesion than Democrats from "indifferent" districts. In the Republican party the reverse was true; members from "indifferent" districts demonstrated greater unity than members from "interested" districts. On all four kinds of issues, "interested" Democrats scored considerably higher in party loyalty than "interested" Republicans. House Democratic leaders persistently championed, and Republican leaders persistently opposed, the programs of their "interested" members. [p. 149]

In other words, the Democratic majority (for all but two of these eight Congresses) was a working coalition of the diverse elements within the party. In contrast, "the Republican leadership responded to the legislative demands of each [Republican "interested"] minority by mobilizing the rest of the party to oppose them" (p. 155).

All of these studies of Congress—Turner, MacRae, Truman, and Mayhew—suffer from the shortcomings of roll call analysis in general. A congressman's performance on roll call votes does not necessarily indicate anything about his behavior off the floor or on less public votes: he may have fought to change the bill in committee to make it more compatible with his own preferences or the desires of a majority of his constituents; he may have previously voted for a crippling amendment, which makes the law unworkable or ineffective. As Truman, himself, has observed:

Reservations properly can and should be registered . . . against an uncritical reliance upon roll calls as indicators of the full range of legislative behavior. They are unmistakably a record of decisions taken, of choices made, but they are evidence of only the most public choices. Ordinarily they indicate nothing about measures that never reach the floor of the House or Senate, and they directly reveal nothing about what has occurred behind the scenes. [p. 12]

Furthermore, techniques of roll call analysis are simply a device for ordering complicated data. They do not explain or account for the patterns that may be discerned in voting. The researcher must turn to other independent variables—party, state delegation, committee, characteristics of the constituency, and so on—to try to account for variations in the dependent variable, in this case, the roll call vote. In the last analysis, even roll call votes, which come as close to "hard" data as any data that social scientists attempt to explain, contain certain inherent ambiguities. Two men may cast a "nay" vote for exactly the opposite reasons: one because he thinks the bill does not go far enough, and the other because the legislation is too far-reaching. To get at motivations behind voting, the researcher must turn to other techniques, such as content analysis of speeches and of newsletters, and the use of interviews. This is just another way of saying that all techniques have built-in limitations. Increasingly, social scientists have utilized a balance of research techniques in their study of complex social and political institutions such as the Congress of the United States.

V. THE INTEGRATION OF QUALITATIVE AND QUANTITATIVE METHODS

By 1960 students of Congress were making increasing use of integrative methods. No longer did they tend to rely almost exclusively on either qualitative or quantitative analyses. Instead, they let their research problems guide them to the most appropriate combination of techniques. Three recent books epitomize the integrative approach: Donald R. Matthews' study of *U.S. Senators and Their World* (1960); Raymond A. Bauer, Ithiel de Sola Pool, and Lewis Anthony Dexter's examination of foreign trade policy-making, *American Business and Public Policy* (1963); and Richard F. Fenno's definitive treatment of the congressional appropriations process, *The Power of the Purse* (1966).

The Senate in perspective

Matthews focuses upon the 180 men and women who served in the United States Senate from 1947 to 1957, "who they are, how they behave, and why they behave the way they do" (p. vii). His findings are based on extensive biographical data, over 100 interviews with senators, staff and other close observers or participants, and a wide and varied use of quantitative data and statistical indices.

Working from *The Biographical Directory of the American Congress, The Congressional Directory,* a number of specialized biographical directories, and newspaper accounts, Matthews has put together the most complete composite portrait of the postwar Senate ever compiled. Of the 180 persons who served in the United States Senate from January, 1947, to January, 1957, only three were women. Only one of these, Margaret Chase Smith of Maine, has had appreciable experience. The widow of a former congressman, she served nine years in the House of Representatives before being elected in 1948 to the first of four six-year terms in the Senate. The other two women, both from Nebraska, served in interim appointments for only a few weeks each.

The age of senators during this period ranged from the constitutional requirement of thirty years to over seventy-five, with the mid-fifties the average age. A majority of the postwar senators were born in rural areas, but small towns of from 2,500 to 5,000 population were the most consistently overrepresented birthplaces. Senators come from relatively high-class origins.

. . . [S]enators were sons, with only a handful of exceptions, of men possessing upper- and middle-class occupations. The children of low-salaried workers, wage earners, servants, and farm laborers, which together comprised 66 per cent of the gainfully employed in 1900, contributed only 7 per cent of the postwar senators. [p. 19]

Furthermore, these senators were among the most educated of all occupational groups in the United States. "Almost 85 per cent of them attended college, a level of education achieved by only 14 per cent of the adult population in 1950" (pp. 25–26). About half of the senators were lawyers.

The two major political parties recruit somewhat different types of men for the Senate.

The Democrats were elected at an earlier age and were born and live in larger towns and cities than the Republicans. Their fathers, as a group, possessed somewhat higher occupational class positions but were also more often immigrants, Catholics, Jews, and members of relatively low prestige Protestant denominations. The Democrats obtained more education than the Republicans, but less often at the well-known schools. They were more often lawyers, but they practiced in smaller towns and as members of smaller law firms than the Republicans. [p. 46]

The Republicans were more often businessmen, especially publishers and manufacturing executives. Democratic businessmen tended to be merchants, contractors, oil and gas producers, and insurance and real estate men.

One dominant theme emerges from this biographical data. The "typical" senator is far from being a "typical" American. With rare exceptions, our senators are selected from near the top of our occupational and educational elite. American voters "seem to prefer candidates who are not like themselves but are what they would like to be" (p. 45).

For his description and explanation of the way senators behave, Matthews relies heavily on 109 focused interviews. Twenty-five of these interviews were with senators, and those remaining, with staff members, lobbyists, and Washington journalists. No attempt was made to interview a representative sample. Instead, the author began with friends and contacts on Capitol Hill staffs and gradually expanded his efforts to obtain a rough cross section of the Senate. No notes were taken during the interview, but these were written up as nearly verbatim as possible as soon as the interview was concluded. Most of the interviews were held between January and September, 1956. Direct quotations are used throughout the book, but their sources are not attributed.

One of the most valuable chapters in the book deals with the "folkways" or normative rules of conduct of the Senate. Matthews identifies six such norms: apprenticeship, legislative work, specialization, courtesy, reciprocity, and institutional patriotism. The main thrust of these norms can only be suggested here. New members are expected to defer to their elders, to listen and learn rather than to participate extensively in floor debate. The way to earn respect and get ahead in the Senate is by hard work and specialization. Conflct is toned down and personal attacks are muted through the practice of senatorial courtesy. A number of the chamber's formal rules and conventions, including the use of impersonal forms of address such as "The distinguished Senator from ——," help minimize antagonisms. Reciprocity, mutual accommodation, and implicit bargaining are a way of life. Institutional patriotism runs high: the Senate is seen as the greatest legislative and deliberative body in the world. (As Huitt's study [pp. 159–178 of the present book] of Senator William Proxmire shows, however, a few members consciously adopt a different or "outsider" style of behavior which challenges or ignores a number of these norms.)[27]

Throughout his book, Matthews makes extensive use of quanti-

[27] For Matthews' response to Huitt's discussion and a rebuttal, see Matthews, "Can the 'Outsider's' Role Be Legitimate?," and Huitt, "On Norms, Roles and Folkways," *American Political Science Review*, LV (1961), 882–883, and LVI (1962), 142.

tative data and statistical indices. Some 62 tables and 31 figures help to present the data in a clearcut and meaningful fashion. Several traditional measures, such as the Rice index of cohesion, are used. Other indices, such as an index of conservatism-liberalism and an index of administration support, are adapted from the *New Republic* and *Congressional Quarterly*. The author develops several additional measures, including an index of specialization and an index of legislative effectiveness. The end product of most of these measures is greater rigor and precision of analysis.

However, as Ralph K. Huitt points out in his review of Matthews' book for the *American Political Science Review,* sometimes his "attempts to impose on the data all the quantification they will bear," lead to questionable results:

Particularly is this true when a categorization of senators based on two variables only—social status and previous political accomplishment—is employed. Of the four categories, one contains only seven and another four percent of all the senators, with the result that cells frequently are too small to have much significance.

Again, as an example, the author attempts to determine whether senators who obey the folkways enjoining talkativeness and prescribing specialization actually are more effective (i.e., get more of their bills passed). Leaving aside the obvious complaints that bill-passing is a collective, not an individual, accomplishment, and is not the only nor perhaps even the most important function of the Senate, the results still provoke wonder. When they lead the author to say, "Some rank and file minority senators are more effective than committee chairmen. . . . Some new and very green members of the District of Columbia Committee were, at least during the Eighty-third and Eighty-Fourth Congresses, more effective than very senior senators of the Appropriations Committee," it is time for the common sense which is displayed on every page to assert itself and question what, if anything, is being measured. [Huitt, 1961c, pp. 401–402]

Huitt concludes his review of *U.S. Senators and Their World* with this statement: ". . . the overall judgment nevertheless certainly must be that this book is a solid scholarly achievement which probably will be the standard work on the Senate for a long time." As the decade of the 1960s comes to a close this judgment continues to hold true.

The politics of foreign trade legislation

American Business and Public Policy, by Bauer, Pool, and Dexter, is an impressive undertaking. Some ten years in the making, it treats of the ways in which American business leaders, lobbyists, and congressmen "learn about the outside world, how they integrate that which they learn with their own immediate concerns, and, finally, what leads them to action" (pp. 489–490), and, it might be added, inaction. One of the central conclusions of this book is that "pressure groups" are not especially well organized or effective.

This wide-ranging study employs more diverse methods than either Matthews' book on the Senate or Fenno's analysis of the congressional appropriations process. Partly, this is because the authors bring together and make use of the multiple skills of a psychologist, a political scientist, and a sociologist. Partly, it is because their study goes far beyond the involvement of congressmen in the foreign trade policy process to include the study of interest group activity, the attitudes of businessmen and their impact on policy, the role played by eight communities in the process, and the history of foreign trade legislation with a particular focus on the period 1953 to 1962.

Bauer, Pool, and Dexter's principal data-collection instruments consist of a systematic sample survey of 903 business leaders carried out by the National Opinion Research Center and more than 500 less-structured interviews with members of Congress, their staff, federal executives, lobbyists and trade association representatives, businessmen, labor union leaders, and journalists.[28] These interviews are complemented by case studies of trade policy activity or lack of activity in eight different eastern communities ranging from several small cities to the Wall Street banking community, Detroit (the auto industry), and the state of Delaware (the DuPont Corporation). The first six chapters of the book provide a historical survey of foreign trade policy, especially its formation during the first three years of the Eisenhower administration.

The two most relevant sections for the present review are Part IV, treating of pressure groups, and Part V, dealing with the congressional process.

The main thrust of Bauer, Pool, and Dexter's findings contradicts the view that well-organized and richly financed lobbies bring pressure to bear on congressmen, who in turn pass legislation sympa-

[28] These latter interviews follow "the journalistic principle of asking each man about those matters on which he has something interesting to say, rather than the survey principle of asking each man the same thing" (p. 403, n. 1).

thetic to these powerful interests. When the authors looked at a typical foreign trade lobby, they found that "its opportunities for maneuver [were] sharply limited, its staff mediocre, and its major problem not the influencing of Congressional votes but the finding of clients and contributors to enable it to survive at all." On the whole, lobbies were "poorly financed, ill managed, out of contact with Congress, and at best only marginally effective in supporting tendencies and measures which already had behind them considerable Congressional impetus from other sources" (p. 324). Rather than acting as agents of direct persuasion, most lobbyists functioned as service bureaus for those congressmen already agreeing with them.

The chapters on Congress, based largely on Dexter's 1959 Columbia University doctoral dissertation, "Congressmen and the People They Listen To," contain some of the richest qualitative materials ever published on the legislative process. Sections dealing with the wide variation in how a congressman may allocate his time, how he is likely to react to outside communications, and the range of role conflict he faces are especially insightful. As Dexter and his coauthors conclude:

Congressmen have a great deal more freedom than is ordinarily attributed to them. The complexities of procedure, the chances of obfuscation, the limited attention constituents pay to any one issue, and the presence of countervailing forces all leave the congressman relatively free on most issues. He may feel unfree because of the great demands on his time, but consciously or unconsciously, by his own decisions as to what he chooses to make of his job he generates the pressures which impinge upon him. He hears from voters about those things in which he himself chooses to become involved. . . .

A congressman needs issues in the public eye. He needs people who want favors from him. His stock in trade is his power to take action on things citizens care about. If there were no clamorous demands giving him the opportunity to show his worth, he would have to create them. And that, indeed, is what he habitually does.

Congress is not a passive body, registering already-existent public views forced on its attention by public pressures. Congress, second only to the President, is, rather the major institution for initiating and creating political issues and projecting them into a national civic debate. Congressmen are often the leaders in that debate. [p. 478]

The politics of congressional appropriations

At the core of the national legislative process is the power to appropriate money for the operations of the federal government.

Fenno's comprehensive study of these decisions, *The Power of the Purse* (1966), will be the definitive treatment of the congressional phase of this critical and complex process for many years to come. It is at the same time the most insightful and important contribution to our understanding of committee behavior since Woodrow Wilson's classic study, *Congressional Government*.

Three principal objectives shape the book's organizational structure, dictate its conceptual framework, and guide its selection of research techniques. Fenno succeeds admirably in all three basic aims: "first, to provide an empirical description of the contemporary appropriations process in Congress; second, to demonstrate the importance of committee-centered analysis for increasing an understanding of Congress; and third, to suggest the usefulness of [system and role] theory for students of Congress and its committees" (p. xiii).

In addition to building upon earlier and more limited studies of the congressional appropriations process, Fenno's study nicely complements the more executive-oriented analysis of budget decision-making by Aaron Wildavsky and his associates.[29] Whereas Wildavsky concentrates on the step-by-step decisions of agency budget officers, Fenno takes the President's budget as given. He focuses on the flow of congressional policy-making from the fifty-member House Committee on Appropriations (Chapters One through Eight), to the House floor (Chapter Nine), the twenty-seven member Senate Committee on Appropriations (Chapters Ten and Eleven), and finally, to the conference committee between the houses (Chapter Twelve). The first eight chapters treat not only of the internal committee structure and process, but also of its relationships with the House of Representatives and some 36 executive bureaus in seven of the ten Cabinet departments. Agency appropriations requests and what happens to them at each stage are charted over a sixteen-year period from 1947 to 1962. A number of the expectations and attitudes that guide the behavior of House Appropriations Committee members were summarized in Section II of this review.

Several of Fenno's most important findings deal with the differ-

[29] Aaron Wildavsky, *The Politics of the Budgetary Process* (Boston: Little, Brown, 1964); and Otto A. Davis, M. A. H. Dempster, and Aaron Wildavsky, "A Theory of the Budgetary Process," *American Political Science Review* LX (1966), 529–547.

ences between the House and Senate Committee operations and the results of conference committee activity.

The Senate Committee's (and the Senate's) consideration of agency requests is less extensive, less thorough, and less time-consuming than is the same range of relationships for the House Committee. The Senate Committee, acting as an appeals court, focuses on a smaller increment of the budget than does the House group. The Committee makes smaller adjustments in the appropriations figures which come to it from the House than the House group does on the figures which come to it from the agencies. In comparison with the previous year's appropriations figures, Senate Committee decisions run in the same direction (toward increasing or decreasing appropriations levels) as that of the House Committee. These differences of style, of task, and of output are powerfully influenced by the intractable appropriations sequence, in which the House acts first and the Senate last. All these differences provide support for the assumption that the House Committee is the more dominant—and hence the most dominant—force in congressional appropriations politics. [pp. 614–615]

What happens when Senate and House Appropriations Committee members meet in conference to resolve differences between the two houses? The conferees are faced with twin prescriptions: they must win for their respective houses, but they are also aware that they must compromise their differences in order to obtain any bill at all. House members see themselves as the really responsible guardians of the federal treasury; they view their Senate counterparts as much more free with the public's money. Senators see the House members as more conservative, and acknowledge their own tendencies to engage in senatorial back-scratching. House members are seen as a rule as more specialized and better informed; senators as more prestigious, and perhaps, a little more adept at bargaining. In general, there is considerable congruence in the images that House members have of themselves and how they are seen by their Senate counterparts, and vice versa.

When conflict is present between the two houses, who usually wins?[30] Analysis of appropriations decisions affecting the 36 bureaus from 1947 to 1962 suggest that the Senate has the edge. "Of the 331 cases in which a conflict was present, the Senate conferees won 187 times, the House conferees won 101 times, and in 43 cases the two

[30] For a case study of the 1962 stalemate between the Senate and House Appropriations Committees, see Pressman (1966).

groups split the difference" (p. 663). It is Fenno's conclusion that "The Senate is stronger in conference because the Senate Committee and its conferees draw more directly and more completely upon the support of their parent chamber than do the House Committee and its conferees" (pp. 668–669). However, these winning tendencies of Senate conferees should not be confused with House Committee dominance of the appropriations process as a whole. "Decisions of the greatest magnitude and impact are made in the House; Senate decisions involve smaller increments of money; in conference committee the range of discretion is smaller still" (p. 662).

Fenno acknowledges his indebtedness to other students of congressional committee behavior, especially Wilson (1885), Huitt (1954) [pp. 77–112 of the present book], and Matthews (1960). But this book moves significantly beyond previous studies, both in the development of theory and the marshaling of supporting data. For Wilson, "Congress in session is Congress on public exhibition, while Congress in its committee rooms is Congress at work." Fenno not only brings us inside the committee to see what expectations guide committee work, he also demonstrates the importance of the interdependency between committee decisions and floor action.

The study distinguishes between the Committee's internal and external relationships. Both sets of relationships are examined—separately and as they affect one another—in an effort to discover and to explicate enduring patterns of interaction. As an aid in the identification, examination and explication of important relationships, the study focuses attention on some basic problems which every political system must solve in order to stabilize its activities or "survive" over time. Externally, there is the problem of *adapting* to the demands of other political entities. Internally, there are structural problems of *decision-making* and *integration*. [p. xviii]

As has already been suggested, the overarching theoretical concepts used in this study are *system* and *role*. Here, Fenno draws heavily upon such system theorists as Parsons and Shils; and Easton; and such group and role theorists as Homans; Merton; Thibaut and Kelley; Wahlke, Eulau, Buchanan, and Ferguson; and Gross, Mason, and McEachern.[31] The basic descriptive concepts are the expectations,

[31] Talcott Parsons and Edward Shils, *Toward a General Theory of Action* (Cambridge, Mass.: Harvard University Press, 1951); David Easton, *The Political System* (New York: Knopf, 1953), and Easton, "An Approach to the Analysis of Political Systems," *World Politics* IX (1957), 383–400; George C. Homans, *The Human Group* (New

perceptions and attitudes, and behavior of the various participants: members of the House and Senate, especially the Appropriations Committee members, committee staff, and executive officialdom.

The principal data for the study are of two main sorts: "hard" data in the form of dollars-and-cents appropriations figures, and "soft" data from some 175 interviews with individuals involved in appropriations decision-making. In all, some 576 appropriations case histories are analyzed: the year-by-year success of 36 different bureaus over a sixteen-year period. Fenno makes use of semistructured interviews. A number of key questions, all open-ended, were asked of all respondents holding similar positions. Over the six-year period he interviewed 58 members of the House Appropriations Committee, 18 Senate Appropriations Committee members, some 25 staff assistants, and over 40 executive branch budget officials. The end result is an integration of both qualitative and quantitative data. Structure and process (gained from observation, interviews, and the reading of the public record) are related to legislative outcomes (the appropriation decisions at each stage of the process). As a result of Fenno's work, our understanding of both committee behavior and the appropriations process has taken a significant leap forward.

VI. FACTORS AFFECTING PROGRESS

What can be said about the state of congressional research as we enter the last third of the twentieth century? What work is ongoing? What remains to be done?

It seems clear from this review of the qualitative, quantitative, and integrative phases of behavioral-empirical studies of Congress over the past two decades that our knowledge of congressional behavior has been substantially advanced. This progress has come about for a variety of reasons. First and foremost, it is the result of increased numbers of political scientists engaged in on-the-scene em-

---

York: Harcourt, Brace & World, 1950); Robert K. Merton, *Social Theory and Social Structure* (New York: Free Press, 1951); John W. Thibaut and Harold H. Kelley, *The Social Psychology of Groups* (New York: Wiley, 1959); John C. Wahlke, Heinz Eulau, William Buchanan, and LeRoy C. Ferguson, *The Legislative System* (New York: Wiley, 1962); and Neal Gross, Ward Mason, and Alexander McEachern, *Explorations in Role Analysis: Studies of the School Superintendency Role* (New York: Wiley, 1958).

pirical research. For the most part, these political scientists have self-consciously avoided a dominant reform orientation. Partly, their work has been a reaction to the responsible parties doctrines of the late 1940s and early 1950s. Partly, it reflects some uneasiness about the increasing strength of the Presidency and the bureaucracy as compared with the legislative branch since World War II. But primarily, these students of Congress have been concerned with describing how the Senate and the House of Representatives work, in fact, rather than prescribing how these institutions *ought* to perform. The result has been a substantial increase and new richness of data and insight. Theoretical advancement, however, has not kept pace. Much more work is needed on how component parts—party leadership, committees, state delegations, informal groups—relate to one another and to the outside environment within which Congress operates.

A second reason for the advancement of knowledge about Congress can be traced to improved techniques of research. Capitalizing on a modification of survey-research interviewing skills and the experiences of participant observation, students of Congress have relied heavily on semistructured interviews with members of Congress and other participants in the legislative process. Quantitative techniques, facilitated by the advent of electronic calculators and the high-speed computer, have been further refined and extended during this period. Increasingly, qualitative and quantitative techniques have been combined. Thus, in terms of both substantive knowledge and methodological sophistication, research on Congress has come of age.

Several additional factors have contributed to our knowledge about the people who serve in Congress, how they relate to one another, and to their constituents. At least six may be singled out for brief comment: (1) the establishment of the *Congressional Quarterly* in 1945; (2) the improvement of governmental statistical publications, including the adoption of the congressional district as the unit of analysis; (3) the creation of the American Political Science Association's Congressional Fellowship program in 1953; (4) higher-quality newspaper coverage; (5) contributions from the essays and books of more analytically-oriented congressmen; and (6) improved sources of financial support for the funding of congressional research.

The study of Congress has been greatly facilitated since 1945 by the information services provided by *Congressional Quarterly, Inc.,* a privately owned research institution. Its most valuable service is the weekly publication and annual summary of all congressional roll call votes broken down by party, state, and district.[32] These roll call votes form the core of its *Weekly Report*, which also chronicles congressional and political activity throughout the year. At the end of each year the *CQ Almanac* is published, which distills, reorganizes, and cross-indexes the full year in congressional and national politics. From time to time special reports on such subjects as congressional and presidential elections, campaign financing, lobbying, congressional reorganization, and reapportionment are issued. In 1965 *Congressional Quarterly* brought out *Congress and the Nation, 1945–1964*, a 2,000-page volume summarizing major political and legislative activities in the four postwar administrations of Presidents Truman, Eisenhower, Kennedy, and Johnson. The kinds of materials that used to form the basis of articles in political science journals two decades ago are now standard fare in the publications of *Congressional Quarterly*.

Students of Congress have long had available a number of governmental publications containing valuable biographical and statistical materials. Among the most important of these have been the annual *Congressional Directory; The Biographical Directory of the American Congress, 1774–1961*, which has gone through some ten previous editions; and the Biennial *Reports* of the Clerk of the House of Representatives containing election statistics. Not until 1956 did the U.S. Bureau of the Census begin to publish a few statistics broken down by congressional districts.[33] In 1961 the first of the *Congressional District Data Book* series was published, presenting a great variety of statistical information for districts of the 87th Congress. It also contains maps for each state showing congressional district boundaries, counties, and important urban places.

The American Political Science Association's Congressional Fellowship program has had as its main purpose to equip outstanding

[32] In cooperation with the Inter-university Consortium on Political Research, *Congressional Quarterly* has made available its IBM cards containing roll call data for the most recent Congresses. Under a project launched by Professor Duncan MacRae, Jr., of the University of Chicago, the Consortium hopes to eventually have roll calls for all Congresses available for data processing and subsequent analysis.

[33] U.S. Bureau of the Census, *County and City Data Book, 1956* (Washington: U.S. Government Printing Office, 1956), Appendix G.

young political scientists, journalists, governmental career employees, and law school faculty members with a better understanding of the national legislative process. First launched in 1953 with six Fellows, the 1967–1968 group includes some 40 participants. During the past fifteen years over 330 Fellows have been brought to Washington, D.C., for nine months of full-time work in Senate and House offices.[34] About 30 percent of the participants have been political scientists. A number of them have made substantial contributions to our knowledge of how Congress works, including Charles L. Clapp, H. Douglas Price, James A. Robinson, Stephen Horn, Raymond Wolfinger, John S. Saloma, III, Lewis A. Froman, Jr., John F. Manley, and David R. Mayhew.

Furthermore, through its awards to outstanding young journalists, the APSA Congressional Fellowship program has contributed to an improvement in governmental news coverage. Almost every year two or three of the journalists have stayed in Washington as newspaper reporters or as press aides to congressmen.

Most close observers of the congressional scene agree that newspaper coverage of Congress has improved substantially over the past fifteen to twenty years. Newspapers are alloting more space to congressional activities. Reporters are better trained and there are more of them regularly assigned to Capitol Hill. Only a few of these congressional reporters have the inclination and time to back off from day-to-day coverage in order to present a longer and more general view of congressional operations. However, two of the best overviews of the Senate and the House of Representatives in recent years have been written by journalists—William S. White's The Citadel: The Story of the U.S. Senate (1956), and Neil MacNeil's Forge of Democracy: The House of Representatives (1963). A number of newspaper reporters have also contributed excellent political biographies of leading congressional and national personalities, for example, White's The Taft Story (1954), Robert A. Smith's The Tiger in the Senate: The Biography of Wayne Morse (1962), and Rowland Evans and Robert Novak's Lyndon B. Johnson: The Exercise of Power (1966).

Books written by congressmen have always been a source of valuable information for political scientists. Three that rise above mere

[34] Biographical Directory of Congressional Fellows (Washington, D.C.: American Political Science Association, 1967), Ist ed., p. i.

chronological and anecdotal reporting are Clem Miller's *Member of the House: Letters of a Congressman* (1962), Frank Smith's *Congressman from Mississippi* (1964), and Richard Bolling's *House Out of Order* (1965). Miller goes a long way toward transmitting the flavor of congressional activities as savored by a perceptive freshman representative. Smith, a member from 1950 to 1962, relates his experiences as a southern moderate during a period of increasing civil rights strife. Bolling writes from the seasoned perspective of eight terms in the House, including ten years on the House Committee on Rules as Speaker Rayburn's informal spokesman.

The availability of greater resources to fund social science research has also had its impact on the quantity and quality of congressional research. More political scientists have been able to come to Washington, D.C., and spend a year or more engaged in the study of Congress at first hand. Among the principal foundations and research institutions supporting such studies have been the Carnegie Foundation, the Ford Foundation, the Rockefeller Foundation, the Social Science Research Council, and The Brookings Institution. Universities and graduate schools have also been able to be more generous with financial support for individual scholars in the form of research professorships, sabbaticals, and summer stipends.

In 1964 congressional scholars were provided with a major challenge and opportunity. The American Political Science Association was awarded a $230,000 grant from the Carnegie Corporation to study congressional organization and operations. The decision to seek support for a broad-ranging Study of Congress grew out of a series of small meetings held in 1963 between congressional scholars and congressmen (the latter led by Chet Holifield, D., Calif., and Thomas B. Curtis, R., Mo.) and funded by the Philip Stern Family Fund. A brief description of this ongoing project will set the stage for a discussion of the directions that future inquiries might take.

The APSA study of Congress

Ralph K. Huitt, Professor of Political Science at the University of Wisconsin, was appointed as Director of the American Political Science Association's Study of Congress project in February, 1964. In May, 1964, he invited some twenty-five political scientists already deeply immersed in research on Congress to meet at Airlie House, Virginia, to discuss and criticize the objectives of the project. The broad outlines of the Study of Congress were set forth in Huitt's conference working paper:

Research on Congress with a behavioral bent has come a long way . . . in the last ten or twelve years. Our discipline has produced a generation of scholars sensitive to the influence on the behavior of congressmen of the various roles they assume in the related subsystems of Congress, and to the influence on Congress of the external system with which it interacts. We have sliced into our problem enough ways to give us a notion of what is there and some confidence that we know how to proceed. What we still lack, even with the extensive descriptive and prescriptive work of several generations of predecessors, is any very clear idea, to put it simply, how Congress works—how its principal parts do their jobs and how they are related to each other. That is what the associated studies called the Study of Congress can do: they can provide us with analytical descriptions of Congress, its subsystems, and its relations with its environment; these should (1) fill in the research gaps, suggesting models and relevant variables for future research; and (2) provide some basis for stating the functions Congress performs for the political system, evaluating the performance, and pointing out alternative structural arrangements and modes of action which seem realistically to be open to Congress.

Eight of these political scientists also joined Huitt in the conduct of a seminar on legislative behavior sponsored by the Inter-University Consortium on Political Research and held at Ann Arbor, Michigan, during the summer of 1964. By the end of 1964 some fourteen projects had been commissioned on various aspects of congressional organization and procedure. Several additional projects were added the following year. The eighteen participants, their affiliations and their topics are:

Milton C. Cummings, Jr. Johns Hopkins University	The seniority system
Richard F. Fenno, Jr. University of Rochester	Comparative study of committees
Alan Fiellin City University of New York	Legislative oversight
Lewis A. Froman, Jr. University of California, Irvine	Congressional rules and procedures
Charles O. Jones University of Arizona	Minority party leadership
John F. Manley University of Wisconsin	Ways and Means Committee, taxation, trade and social welfare policy

Roy E. Moor Fidelity Philadelphia Trust Co. (former A.A. to Senator William Proxmire)	Taxation and appropriation policy
Morris S. Ogul University of Pittsburgh	Legislative oversight
David M. Olson University of Georgia (formerly University of Texas)	Congressmen and local party organization
Kenneth G. Olson Governmental consultant (formerly Smith College)	Defense policy
Samuel C. Patterson University of Iowa	Committee staffing
Robert L. Peabody Johns Hopkins University	House-Senate relationships, especially conference committees
Nelson W. Polsby University of California, Berkeley (former Wesleyan University)	Institutionalization of the House; the seniority system
Leroy N. Rieselbach Indiana University	Foreign policy, especially foreign aid
Randall B. Ripley Ohio State University (formerly Brookings Institution)	Majority party leadership
James A. Robinson Ohio State University	Congressional policy-making and urban-rural conflict
John S. Saloma, III Massachusetts Institute of Technology	The evaluation of congressional effectiveness
Raymond E. Wolfinger Stanford University	Centralization of power, presidential and congressional leadership

Little, Brown published in June, 1967, the first book in the Study of Congress series—Lewis A. Froman's *The Congressional Process: Strategies, Rules and Procedures*. The core of the book consists of a careful assessment of the rules and procedures of the House and Senate and their impact on legislative strategy and the substance of legislation. Other initial publications of the Study of Congress include two articles in the *American Political Science Review*: by Charles O. Jones (1968), "The Minority Party and Policy-making in the House of Representatives," and Nelson W. Polsby (1968), "The Institutionalization of the U.S. House of Representatives"; a postscript on the 88th

Congress in Leroy N. Rieselbach's *The Roots of Isolationism* (1966), and a bibliography and research guide, *The Role of Political Parties in Congress* by Charles O. Jones and Randall B. Ripley (1966).

In September, 1965, Huitt took a leave of absence from directorship of the project to become Assistant Secretary for Legislation, the Department of Health, Education, and Welfare. Robert L. Peabody of Johns Hopkins University has served as Associate Director of the Study of Congress since that time.

VII. RESEARCH STRATEGIES FOR THE FUTURE

What lies ahead? What directions should future inquiries take? A great deal of research remains to be done, and this will be true even after the participants in the Study of Congress contribute their articles and books to the growing body of knowledge about the United States Congress. Most of the research trends highlighted in this review—comparisons within and across the two houses, the exploration of historical trends, the use of more sophisticated research techniques, and the integration of qualitative and quantitative methods—can be expected to continue. The payoffs should be rich.

Yet, in order to achieve a major scientific breakthrough, one pressing need must be met and several further developments in research strategy seem imperative.

The critical need is for *theory* at several levels for, quite clearly, in congressional research the generation of data has proceeded much more rapidly than the accumulation of theory. We need more and better theory: First, at the lowest level in the form of propositions that convert isolated facts into working hypotheses and, ultimately, into tested generalizations. Second, we need to move beyond fragmentary or isolated descriptions of the behavior of party leaders, committee chairmen, other influential congressmen, and rank-and-file members to statements about the range of expectations and behaviors open at each level of the organizational hierarchy. How do the activities of the typical freshman member in the House differ from more senior members and their counterparts in the Senate? What rewards and sanctions are available to committee chairmen in the House which are not available in the Senate? How do the elected leaders, such as the Speaker and the Senate Majority Leader, relate to committee chairmen, to rank-and-file members? Answers to questions such as these will increase the need for a higher order of theorizing, the construction of so-called theories of the middle level. For example, a theory of the lawmaking process is needed which will relate and explain the impact of such independent variables as constituency, state delegation, and party upon such dependent variables as frequency of communication between members, the introduction of legislation, and the extent of support and opposition to legislation as expressed through a range of committee action, floor behavior, and final roll call votes.

Third, and at a still higher level of abstraction, the search must intensify for a general, or overarching, theory of congressional behavior. In addition to taking into account the roles and personalities of the incumbents, legislative structure and process, and policy outcomes, this broader congressional theory would have to encompass the other principal actors in the system: the President, other national party leaders, executive officialdom, interest group representatives, the press, and the American electorate. Such a theory would come close to being a theory of the American political process itself. Finally, one may conceive of a theory of legislative behavior which is comparative in the broadest sense, being neither time-bound nor limited to a single nation or culture.

Many of the studies reviewed in this essay have been productive of low-level generalizations, and sometimes even middle-level theory construction. Almost no study, with the possible exception of Fenno's analysis of the appropriations process, has attempted to formulate an overarching, or general, theory of congressional behavior. Systems theory, role theory, and structural-functional analysis have been applied to legislatures with a measure of success.[35] Another promising line of attack would seem to be a theory of political exchange and collective decision-making.[36]

[35] See, for example, Wahlke, Eulau, Buchanan, and Ferguson (1962); Jewell and Patterson (1966); and Fenno (1966).

[36] George C. Homans, "Social Behavior as Exchange," *American Journal of Sociology*, 65 (1960), 545–556; Peter M. Blau, *Exchange and Power in Social Life* (New York: Wiley, 1964); Talcott Parsons, "On the Concept of Influence," and James S. Coleman, "Comment on 'On the Concept of Influence,'" *Public Opinion Quarterly*, 27 (1963), 37–62, 63–82; and Coleman, "Collective Decisions," *Sociological Inquiry*, 34 (1964), 166–181. For more specific applications of exchange theory to legislatures, see Robert L. Peabody, "Organization Theory and Legislative Behavior: Bargaining, Hierarchy and Change in the U.S. House of Representatives" (paper delivered before

The comparative study of legislatures, in the sense of cross-cultural analysis, has barely begun.[37]

How best are these theoretical objectives to be achieved? The answer does not lie in "a moratorium on empirical research, so that theorizing can catch up and find its bearings." As Heinz Eulau and Katherine Hinckley (1966) point out:

This advice . . . would be both futile and foolish. It would be futile because the charm of fresh discovery is too alluring to resist. It would be foolish because theorizing is best advanced in the context of empirical research and not apart from it. [p. 180]

What kind of research will most likely result in major theoretical advances? It seems to me that the discipline of political science has reached a point in its development at which a team of congressional scholars should undertake a comprehensive, long-range, well-organized, and well-financed study of Congress and national public policy-making.[38] Without the advances made by the APSA Study of Congress it would be difficult to conceive of such a research strategy. Yet, this same study also demonstrates the limitations of a series of individual efforts, competent as they may be, formulated without the benefit of a unifying theoretical framework. It would be best if the team of scholars were self-selected.[39] They should meet for several summers to define the principal problems they wish to attack, to develop the theory that seems most promising, and to state the generalizations they wish to explore and test. Preferably, the focus of

---

American Political Science Association, New York City, September 7, 1963); Peabody (1967); James D. Barber, "Leadership Strategies for Legislative Party Cohesion," *Journal of Politics*, 28 (1966), 347–367; John F. Manley, "The House Committee on Ways and Means: 1947–1966" (unpublished Ph.D. dissertation, Syracuse University, 1967).

[37] Lord Campion and D. W. S. Lidderdale, *Parliaments* (London: Cassell, 1962); K. C Wheare, *Legislatures* (New York: Oxford University Press, 1963); and Gabriel A. Almond and James S. Coleman, eds., *The Politics of the Developing Areas* (Princeton, N.J.: Princeton University Press, 1960).

[38] For a parallel suggestion and discussion, see Heinz Eulau's position paper, "Notes on the Study of Congress," prepared for the Behavioral and Social Sciences Survey Committee, National Research Council and Social Science Research Council, April, 1967.

[39] This was not the case in the Wahlke, Eulau, Buchanan, and Ferguson comparative study of state legislatures. For a discussion of some of the problems created by this and other facets of collaborative research, see "The Annals of Research: A Case of Collaboration in Comparative Study of Legislative Behavior," *The American Behavioral Scientist*, IV (1961), 3–9.

this research should be both internal structure and process and the external environment within which policy is formed. An attempt should be made to interview *all* members of both houses, preferably more than once over several Congresses. In addition, extensive interviewing should be conducted with White House staffs, agency officials, interest group representatives, and to the extent that resources permitted it, within a sample of state and local constituencies. A study should concentrate on four or five major policy areas—for example, education, transportation, labor-management, defense and/or foreign policy. Extensive use should be made of demographic, biographical, and roll call data. Such a study should be financed over a long period of time, a minimum of eight to ten years, in order to facilitate comparisons within Congresses by different policy areas, as well as across Congresses. It would be particularly valuable for the study to overlap at least two administrations.

It is, of course, one thing to propose such a grand scheme, something else to raise the several millions of dollars it would cost to finance it, and, perhaps most difficult of all, to bring about the scholarly cooperation necessary to plan and implement such a project. At a minimum it would require three or four experienced students of congressional politics who were willing to bet on themselves and their assistants for at least a decade. As a compromise, such a project might be undertaken in stages by one or more teams—the first stage a thorough study of internal structure and process, with later stages focusing upon the policy areas and congressional representation. Of one thing I am convinced: a continued proliferation of individual studies will not do the job. As individual scholars with limited time and resources, we are like the proverbial blindmen examining the elephant: each of us feels and understands only a part. The relationship of the part to the whole is almost impossible for any one scholar to capture. Single-shot studies make the analysis of change exceedingly difficult. The way out of these research dilemmas is comprehensive, full-scale, team research sustained over time.

PART II
STUDIES OF CONGRESS AND CONGRESSIONAL COMMITTEES

RALPH K. HUITT

ONE
THE CONGRESSIONAL COMMITTEE:
A CASE STUDY

C ONGRESSIONAL government is Committee government" said Woodrow Wilson in 1884,[1] and political scientists since that day have seen no reason to disagree with him. It would be reasonable to suppose then that once committees ceased to meet secretly (as they did when Wilson wrote) and began to keep verbatim public records of their proceedings, the committee process would be subjected to relentless and systematic study. Such has not been the case. The frequency with which Wilson is quoted is as much a reflection of a lack of substantive research by later students as it is a tribute to his intuitive insights.

It would not be hard to make a case for close and continuous study of congressional committees. On every count, they would seem to hold as much interest for the student of politics as administrative bodies or the courts, upon which so much more attention has been lavished. They are decision-making agencies of crucial importance; it is a commonplace that they hold life-or-death power over legislation. Again, they provide a point of focus for the political

The research on which this article is based was made possible by a grant from The Research Committee of the Graduate School, University of Wisconsin.

This article originally appeared in *The American Political Science Review*, XLVIII (June 1954), 340–365.

[1] Woodrow Wilson, *Congressional Government*, preface to 1884 edition.

process; they are "miniature legislatures," "microcosms" of their parent bodies[2]—not in the sense that they epitomize the larger houses, but rather that the committees are subject to the same influences and power drives, which are easier to intercept and analyze here than in the larger and more complex houses themselves.

A third reason for studying the committee is less obvious but no less important. Each house of Congress is a human group, with leadership, a hierarchy of influence, and a set of norms which control, more or less, the behavior of its members. The man who goes to Congress joins a going concern. He accepts and shares a group life.[3] One factor in any decision he makes is the influence on him of his house as an institutionalized group. But the group life of the congressman is exceedingly complex. Like other men he is a member of many groups, with any one of which he might identify in a particular situation; but unlike most other men he is a *representative*, under obligation consciously and deliberately to take into account the wishes of the groups which support him. As we have said, he is part of the status pattern in his legislative house, in which both formal and informal leadership patterns impose obligations and afford access to power. His success as a professional legislator depends to a large extent upon his conforming with the group norms of his colleagues. But congressmen, too, follow the election returns; prestige and influence in the internal system of the legislature are responsive to success in meeting external demands upon the member. In these respects, to be sure, the group life of a legislative body is not different in kind from that of those small groups which have been studied with impressive results.[4] But it certainly is more complex and its members are more sophisticated. Consequently, it presents more formidable problems than do simpler groups.

A study of the group life of Congress might well begin with the standing committee. It *is* a small group, susceptible in most of its operations to close observation. Because its membership is relatively stable, its leaders men of long committee tenure, it has a continuous

---

[2] George B. Galloway, *Congress at the Crossroads* (New York, 1946), p. 53.

[3] See David B. Truman, *The Governmental Process* (New York, 1951), pp. 343–46.

[4] See especially George C. Homans, *The Human Group* (New York, 1950), in which five distinguished studies in social behavior are examined in detail to develop both an organic theory of the human group and a system of analysis for further study of the group.

group life of its own. One factor in that group life, of course, is the pressure from the house whose creature it is, but the committee is worth studying as a human group in its own right. Furthermore, there is the attractive possibility that techniques so developed will be useful in the more difficult undertaking with the larger group of which it is a part. And it is relatively accessible to research: most of its hearings are open to the public and an adequate record is kept. The public hearing is only a part of the activity of a committee, but it is an important and often revealing part.

The standing committee then is a promising group with which to begin a study of the behavior of congressmen in the legislative struggle for at least four reasons. One is the greater *frequency of interaction* of individual congressmen in committees than on the floor of their house. On the floor a congressman may speak seldom, and on a particular issue may confine himself to a single prepared speech. But in a committee in which he is active he talks many times and with less formality. A second reason is that in the committee hearings a group of congressmen are subject to *common stimuli*. They hear the same witnesses and react to the same comments. The third is that the committee is a group of *manageable size* for intensive study. It is possible to observe it closely, and its members are few enough that roles can be kept straight and relationships plotted. A fourth is that it has, within limits, a *continuous life*. Its membership changes, but members are encouraged by the seniority principle to stay on a committee. And the change of membership is never complete and seldom drastic at one time; group norms can easily be transmitted to new members. Thus the committee is a subgroup of its house which is itself a going concern.

I. SOME HYPOTHESES ABOUT THE COMMITTEE

We are not without generalizations about the roles that committees— and inferentially committee members—play in the legislative process. The general literature on legislation and the political process furnishes several which might serve as hypotheses for further testing. One of the most tenacious of the basic concepts has the committee discovering, protecting, and advancing the general interest out of the welter of special interests contending for support. As Professor Chamberlain puts it: "The committee itself must be the guardian of the general public interest, too large and too vague to be organized. What is in the general interest is for the committee to determine, after hearing advocates of the special interests who appear before it."[5] After giving a number of examples of committee actions, he asserts that "the committee played principally the part of a *legislative court,* listening to the evidence of fact and law brought before it by interested parties, considering their suggestions . . . ," then deciding what should be done.[6]

This notion of the committee's function perhaps is accepted implicitly in the recent emphasis on the committee's role as a *fact-finding* agency. Political scientists, and some congressmen, have insisted that committees need professional staff with secure tenure, capable of serving either party with equal competence.[7] To insure the non-partisan and objective character of their service, some have urged a legislative career service, perhaps with staff members to be drawn from a pool, with a professional personnel director in charge of recruitment. The argument is that the professional staff could get objective facts for the committee, thus ending the committee's dependence upon the selected facts of lobbyists and the not disinterested experts borrowed from the bureaus.

A second function, not unlike the first, is that of providing, through its public hearings, an open *public forum*.[8] The special interests still vie with each other, the general interest still must emerge from their

[5] Joseph P. Chamberlain, *Legislative Processes: National and State* (New York, 1936), p. 79.

[6] *Ibid.,* pp. 72–73. Emphasis added.

[7] *The Reorganization of Congress,* A Report of the Committee on Congress of the American Political Science Association (Washington, D.C., 1945), p. 79; Galloway, *Congress at the Crossroads* [cited in note 2], pp. 158–61; Ernest S. Griffith, *Congress: Its Contemporary Role* (New York, 1951), pp. 70–75; Estes Kefauver and Jack Levin, *A Twentieth Century Congress* (New York, 1947), pp. 167–68; *Organization of the Congress,* Report of the Joint Committee on the Organization of Congress, pursuant to H. Con. Res. 18, H. Rep. No. 1675, 79th Cong., 2d sess., pp. 9–11; and Report from the Special Committee on the Organization of Congress, Sen. Rep. No. 1400, 79th Cong., 2d sess., pp. 21–24. See also the frequent recommendations of this nature in *Organization of Congress,* Hearings before the Joint Committee on the Organization of Congress, pursuant to H. Con. Res. 18, 79th Cong., 2d sess.; *Legislative Reorganization Act of 1946,* Hearings before the Committee on Expenditures in the Executive Departments, U.S. Senate, 80th Cong., 2d sess.; *Organization and Operation of Congress,* Hearings before the Committee on Expenditures in the Executive Departments, U.S. Senate, 82d Cong., 1st sess.

[8] Chamberlain, p. 64.

clamor, but the stage is highlighted, and a larger audience participates in the decision.

A somewhat different set of generalizations—or hypotheses—rests upon the conception of the legislative process as simply one phase of the political struggle, in which contending groups seek access to governmental power at a number of points, the legislative committee being one.[9] The committee members are not judges, discovering the general interest; they are themselves participants in the political struggle, as indeed are all other governmental officials. No one knows what the "general interest" is; there is none in which everyone shares. Public policy emerges from the pull and haul of groups, and the whole thing is kept from flying to pieces because overlapping memberships in groups prevent the perfect mobilization of any interest. In this frame of reference Professor Truman sees the committee using its public hearing for three purposes.[10] The first, and probably least important, is that of "transmitting information, both technical and political, from various actual and potential interest groups to the committee." The second use is as "a propaganda channel through which a public may be extended and its segments partially consolidated or reinforced." Thus the public forum is provided but the committee is not neutral; what is presented is not so much a fair debate as a set piece. The third use is to provide a catharsis for frustrations and grievances, "a quasi-ritualistic means of adjusting group conflicts and relieving disturbances through a safety-valve."

This is not, of course, an all-inclusive list of the general propositions about the roles of congressional committees, nor is it suggested that these propositions are mutually exclusive. But they are useful hypotheses for empirical research. The purpose of this study is to see how well these generalizations explain what took place in a series of public hearings before a particular committee on a given issue. The hearings chosen for a case study are those held before the Senate Committee on Banking and Currency in the Spring of 1946 on the question whether the price control and stabilization program of 1942 should be continued, and if so, whether and what changes should be made

[9] See especially Arthur F. Bentley, The Process of Government (Bloomington, Ind., 1949), first published in 1908; Truman, The Governmental Process (cited in note 3); and Bertram M. Gross, The Legislative Struggle (New York, 1953). The latter devotes three chapters (14–16) to a realistic description of the operations of congressional committees.

[10] The Governmental Process, pp. 372–77. Emphasis added.

in it.[11] No claim is made that these are "typical hearings," from which valid generalizations about all committee hearings can be made. No doubt there are numerous "types." But there are several reasons why these hearings are selected for the purposes of this study. (1) The problem is intensely political, i.e., many powerful groups have a stake in the issue and are prepared to make strong efforts to influence the outcome. (2) It is a problem which involves the "general interest"; everybody in the country will be affected in some degree by the outcome. (3) Facts would seem to have some relevance in arriving at the policy decision. There are huge quantities of data available and there are substantial bodies of politico-economic theory to which they can be related. (4) This is not a new problem. It has a history in the three years of administration of public policy in a war economy and nearly a year in a peacetime economy. It is the kind of problem, therefore, which should bring into play all the elements necessary to test the generalizations about committee behavior which we have stated.

The limitations of this kind of study are obvious. It is limited to the public hearings, although much that is important, and perhaps what is decisive, takes place elsewhere. Moreover, it is limited to the printed record of those hearings, where only what is said can be found, and that subject to editing. Inferences therefore must be made from behavior which is recorded incompletely, and perhaps inaccurately. The principal defense of a study thus restricted lies in the fact that it is made with materials which are available in profusion to the kind of people who will make most of the studies of legislative behavior. Few academic persons have data-gathering organizations at their disposal, or freedom for continuous participant-observer research. But the printed record is within the reach of the most modest seminar, making possible endless repetition and refinement. Furthermore, hypotheses which are formulated in crude studies may be used to guide studies which can employ more precise procedures.

II. ROLES OF COMMITTEE MEMBERS

From even a casual reading of the record it would seem that these generalizations may be extended and refined by focusing on the

[11] *1946 Extension of the Emergency Price Control and Stabilization Acts of 1942, As Amended,* Hearings before the Committee on Banking and Currency, U.S. Senate, 79th Cong., 2d sess., on S. 2028. Cited hereafter as *Hearings.*

behavior of individual members of the committee. A multiplicity of roles are played by various members, and sometimes by a single member. The status *committee chairman*, for example, can be described by formal and informal powers attributed to that status. But the human chairman is a man in space and time, interacting with other men. More than that, the human chairman occupies more than one status. He is a committee chairman, but he is also a representative of a district, and a member of a complex of groups which make claims upon him and with which he identifies from time to time. And not even the status *chairman* can be simply defined: at one moment the status is that of the fair presiding officer, under a moral obligation to treat all interested groups fairly; at another moment it may be that of the party leader with a commitment to a program; and again it may be that of a champion of the clientele his committee serves. The role the human chairman will play, his behavior itself, will depend upon many things: upon the constituency, sectional, and party interests in the issue; upon the size of his majority and his hold over it; upon the power and popularity and party of the man in the White House.

The concepts *status* and *role* which we are using here are neither novel nor very complicated. They are used in the sense that Professor Linton uses them in his *The Cultural Background of Personality*.[12] Every culture, no matter how simple, is organized into a number of systems which relate the individual to his culture, among the most important being those of age-sex, family, occupation, and association groups. In a complex society with a high degree of division of labor such as our own, these systems are multifold and overlapping. "The place in a particular system which a certain individual occupies at a particular time" is referred to by Linton as "his *status* with respect to that system." The term *role* he uses "to designate the sum total of the culture patterns associated with a particular status. It thus includes the attitudes, values, and behavior ascribed by the society to any and all persons occupying this status. It can even be extended to include the legitimate expectations of such persons with respect to the behavior toward them of persons in other statuses within the same system. . . . In so far as it represents overt behavior, a role is the dynamic aspect of a status: what the individual has to do in order to validate his occupation of the status." A role thus is defined by

[12] Ralph Linton, *The Cultural Background of Personality* (New York, 1945), pp. 76–77.

what other people expect of the person filling it. Behavior consists of what the person actually does in filling the role. An individual congressman may occupy a number of statuses: he is a middle-aged man, a father, a congressman, a Democrat, a member of the Ways and Means Committee third in seniority, and so on. In each of these statuses he has learned to play certain roles, and to expect other people to play certain roles. He cannot play all these roles simultaneously, of course; "although he occupies statuses and knows roles at all times, he operates sometimes in terms of one status and its role, sometimes in those of another." The congressional role probably is most usefully conceived not as a single role but as a multiplicity of roles, defined for the congressman by the varying expectations of the groups which he represents or with which he identifies. These roles may be and frequently are conflicting, requiring the individual congressman temporarily to abdicate one or another of his roles, or to find some way to conciliate them, or perhaps to withdraw from the conflict which he cannot resolve.

The price control controversy in the Spring of 1946 subjected congressmen to just such conflicting demands, and by the time the issue reached the Senate Committee they were well-defined. The extensive hearings before the House Committee on Banking and Currency, which culminated in a series of proposed amendments to the existing law, made certain of that. It is easy, as a consequence, to identify a representative sample of congressional roles from the behavior of the members of the Senate Committee.[13]

The only person to play clearly the role of a national party leader was Senator Robert A. Taft, and he seemed to play it consistently. To him the price control contest was simply one round in a continuing battle with the Administration. Officials of the Administration he regarded not as individuals but as representatives of a generalized program which he was attacking on all fronts. Taft made this explicit when Chester Bowles protested that Taft was criticizing him for

[13] The Democratic members of the Committee were Robert F. Wagner, New York, Chairman; Carter Glass, Virginia; Alben W. Barkley, Kentucky; John H. Bankhead 2d, Alabama; George L. Radcliffe, Maryland; Sheridan Downey, California; Abe Murdock, Utah; Ernest W. McFarland, Arizona; Glen H. Taylor, Idaho; J. William Fulbright, Arkansas; Hugh B. Mitchell, Washington; and E. P. Carville, Nevada. The Republican members were Charles W. Tobey, New Hampshire; Robert A. Taft, Ohio; Hugh A. Butler, Nebraska; Arthur Capper, Kansas; C. Douglass Buck, Delaware; Eugene D. Millikin, Colorado; Bourke B. Hickenlooper, Iowa; and Homer E. Capehart, Indiana.

opinions which he (Bowles) did not hold: "Mr. Bowles, may I say this: I don't distinguish you from the administration. The administration has one policy; you are the Director of Economic Stabilization. What your particular views are make no difference to me. You are carrying on the policies of the administration. When I say 'You' I should be more explicit. I mean the administration. I am not attacking you personally on it, or anything of the sort. I am criticizing your analysis of the situation which is only affected by administration policy; not by what you personally think. That makes no difference to me."[14] The loan to Britain was a special target of Taft's frequent attacks on aspects of the Administration program not within the Committee's jurisdiction. But in his role of national leader, Taft did not hesitate to tell representatives of specific industries that he did not believe they should be decontrolled.[15] His role apparently was appreciated by the spectators; when he excused himself from the session with Bowles, Senator Millikin noted that Taft's departure cost the Committee half its audience.[16]

There was no Democratic counterpart of Taft. The chief burden for the Administration was carried not by the ageing and ailing chairman, Senator Wagner, but by Hugh Mitchell. It was Mitchell who apparently was forewarned of the nature of impending testimony against OPA, and so was ready to confront a hotel association's witness with the statement of a firm specializing in hotel accounting that "the hotel industry of this country is at its peak"; a meat institute's spokesman with a retail grocers' attack on the institute's market survey; the automobile dealers' representative with a court decision upholding the OPA cost absorption policy complained of; and a retail dry goods association's director with a Small Business Committee report claiming that prevailing prices were not hindering production by established firms.[17] Mitchell's favorite tactics were to call for figures and more figures, and then discredit or interpret the figures if possible. But he was content to undertake no more than his role on the Committee required, leaving a general defense of the Administration to another time and place.

14 *Hearings,* p. 43.

15 *Hearings,* pp. 965, 1265.

16 *Hearings,* p. 29.

17 *Hearings,* pp. 986–87, 1094, 1295–96, 1311.

Another familiar legislative role, that of representative of a sectional interest, was played with almost classic purity in these hearings by Senator Bankhead. His concern was the Southern cotton farmer and the textile industry which buys his product; like a sensitive seismograph picking up vibrations in far corners of the globe, Bankhead reacted to testimony which remotely affected his chief interest. A lumber manufacturer was asked about timber on land owned by farmers, and the price of southern pine compared with western pine. A general discussion of how OPA figured profits was turned into a specific discussion of how it was done on cotton textiles. No suggestion that the industry was doing better than during an OPA base period was acceptable.[18] A general discussion of industry advisory committees led him to point out that the 15-member committee on women's blouses had not a single member from the South, and get a promise of OPA action.[19] Bankhead's interventions were devoted almost exclusively to his one interest, and when witnesses equipped to talk about that were on the stand his usual taciturnity vanished. On one morning the Committee heard seven witnesses, three of whom represented the cotton textile industry.[20] With these three witnesses Bankhead accounted for more than one-third of all the interruptions (questions and comments). Of the other four (representing apartment owners and hotels) he asked no questions at all. Bankhead presided over the hearings on two occasions; on one, the principal witnesses represented the American Farm Bureau Federation, the National Grange, and the National Cooperative Milk Producers Federation; on the other, the witness was the Secretary of Agriculture.[21]

The Committee members seemed most impressive when they were acting as representatives of specific constituency interests in their states.

18 *Hearings,* pp. 704–6, 1730–31.

19 *Hearings,* p. 325. There followed this colloquy:
Senator Tobey: That is not Senator Claghorn speaking. That is Senator Bankhead.
Senator Bankhead: What was that?
Senator Tobey: That was a joke, Senator. I said it was not Senator Claghorn, it was my friend Senator Bankhead speaking about the South.
Senator Bankhead: I am always trying to get justice for them. That is a hard task very often, I will say to my New England Senator friend.

20 *Hearings,* pp. 931–1041.

21 *Hearings,* pp. 637–777, 1043–88.

Here they seemed to speak as experts in their own right. The cliches fell away, the fuzziness and amateurishness disappeared; here the facts were clear and the grasp sure. As a consequence, when the senators talked details of the products and industries of their states with each other they could get together on what they meant, the frustrations of contradictory figures and shifting frames of reference relieved for the moment. Mitchell on the dairy industry in Washington, Murdock and Millikin on dairy cattle in Utah and Colorado, Hickenlooper on land prices in Iowa, Fulbright on strawberries and poultry in Arkansas[22]— these are but a few examples of members speaking easily and with authority on the interests of their states.

This role occupied Senator McFarland to the virtual exclusion of any other. He took very little part in the hearings. His interest was in the subsidies paid to the lead, copper, and zinc industries, which were important in Arizona. Early in 1942 the OPA froze the prices of these metals, and then sought to increase production by awarding subsidies for increments over base-period output on a mine-to-mine and month-to-month basis. McFarland proposed an amendment, supported by the industries, which would shift 60 per cent of the subsidies into the prices of the metals and put the remainder on a noncancelable basis. McFarland came late for Bowles' presentation and made sure the matter had not come up. In the meeting devoted to it, McFarland carefully guided the testimony of the industry representatives and answered many of the senators' questions himself. He displayed no interest in the subsidy question in regard to anything else. He took little part in the remainder of the hearings until the last day, when the OPA administrator of meat prices was called by the Committee in reference to several telegrams from Arizona meat dealers received by McFarland.[23]

There is a difference, of course, in seeking to amend a law, which is the legislative function in its primary form, and interceding with an administrative agency in behalf of a constituent. The latter is the "errand-boy" role, and by the accounts of legislators themselves a large part of their time is spent playing it.[24] There is eloquent testi-

[22] *Hearings*, pp. 176, 687–88, 1046–49, 1721–23.

[23] *Hearings*, pp. 74–75, 436–95, 1733, 1791–93.

[24] See the statements in Galloway, *Congress at the Crossroads* [cited in notes 2 and 7], pp. 57–63.

mony in the hearings to the importance of the role to both legislator and administrator: in the senators' complaints that OPA handled congressional mail slowly, and in Paul Porter's reply that the agency got 1500 congressional letters a week and had a rule, not always carried out, that they must be answered in three days.[25] The errand-boy role was not dropped at the committee room door. Capehart brought up three wires from merchants in Indiana complaining about the trouser problem ("Do you have a trouser expert here, Mr. Porter?"); Taylor the case of a packer in Idaho; Mitchell that of a packing company in Tacoma, Washington; Buck that of a factory in Johnstown, Pennsylvania, about which he had a letter; and Bankhead that of a Mr. Flagg of Florence, Alabama.[26] Names were called and action solicited. Hickenlooper, for example, instructed Porter to "make available to me all of the records of Mr. Slotkin and his meat operations for the last 4 years and whatever investigations you have made and alleged infractions and shortcomings; all the meat quotas and his record of ceiling purchases. . . . I would like to see the file and know why something has not been done about it."[27] Tobey raised the case of a New Hampshire veteran who thought OPA was stopping him from fabricating lumber he had logged himself. The OPA man present could not answer the question, but it was later handled to Tobey's satisfaction, although, curiously enough, not to that of Millikin of Colorado.[28] Senatorial interventions in the administrative process, of which these are samples, were made frankly and the administrators commended for prompt service. Hickenlooper spoke appreciatively of Porter's alacrity in the one case the Senator asked him personally to handle, and Capehart stated: "I personally have been over to OPA on any number of occasions, and I must say that I think my batting average has been about 99 percent in the matter of getting adjustments."[29]

Still another role is involved when an industry brings its problems before the Committee and, in effect, gets a review of the policy and

[25] *Hearings*, pp. 1725–26. Tobey suggested that a review board be established to handle congressional cases faster.

[26] *Hearings*, pp. 175–76, 181, 182, 130–32, 110.

[27] *Hearings*, p. 1743.

[28] *Hearings*, pp. 1667, 1693.

[29] *Hearings*, pp. 132, 111.

rulings of the administrative agency. This happened several times during the hearings. Typically, the industry in question was not one in which any individual senator was particularly interested; it simply was one which was not satisfied with the results it had gotten in its dealings with OPA. The senators allowed themselves to become entangled in the technical details of the industry's problems, frequently accepted the industry's version, and then called on OPA for action. A good example occurred early in the hearings, when representatives of the underwear industry appeared and complained in detail of OPA procedures and policies. It soon became obvious that their problems had a long history and that the Committee was not competent to legislate in detail for the underwear industry. An OPA man was sent for, and there followed a confrontation scene between him and the underwear maker he allegedly was driving out of business.[30]

The usual effect of the Committee's interest in a particular industry or business was that the OPA then tackled the complainant's applications with speed, giving him real service. The Committee thus constituted itself a kind of superadministrative agency, intervening capriciously and depending upon business to initiate the process. Capehart got an assurance that a price increase would be granted the cheese industry, and Taft a promise of immediate action on evaporated milk.[31] In some cases the outcome was ambiguous, as with Capehart's efforts in regard to the price of butter and oil, and Millikin's attempt to "get an airtight promise out of OPA to decontrol poultry."[32] In one instance a glovemaker under suit for alleged violation of the law brought his case to the Committee, and strong pressures were placed on the OPA enforcement chief by Committee members, apparently in an effort to persuade him to drop the case.[33]

One way to intercept the shifting roles of the Committee members is to observe the variations in their behavior when different witnesses appear before them—representatives of the Administration, of interest groups, businesses, etc. The Administration point of view, in support of extension of price control "without crippling amendments," was well represented on the Committee. Wagner, Mitchell, Barkley,

[30] *Hearings*, pp. 229–73.
[31] *Hearings*, pp. 845–46, 1725.
[32] *Hearings*, pp. 853–58, 1087, 1724.
[33] *Hearings*, pp. 1516–38.

Taylor, Radcliffe, Murdock, Fulbright, and Tobey (a Republican), were usually dependable, and sometimes aggressive, supporters of OPA. But it would have been hard to tell it during the testimony of Bowles or Porter, the first two witnesses before the Committee. Despite Bowles' hopeful introductory comment that he would like to read his statement through and then answer questions on it, Taft, Capehart, and Millikin promptly took charge. In his first appearance there is no page of uninterrupted testimony, in his second only three.[34] So intensive was the barrage that at one point the roles were reversed, with Bowles cross-examining Taft on the Senator's statements.[35] In all of Bowles' testimony, there are no more than four interventions by Administration senators to ask leading questions in support of the witness. In the two early appearances of Porter, who on the whole was treated more gently than Bowles, there are only three.[36] It is hard to escape the conclusion that the senators were content to let the bureaucrats take care of themselves as best they could. The role of the legislator versus the bureaucrat is an old one, rooted in an institutional jealousy never hard to arouse. Anti-OPA witnesses were well aware of it: statements that "Congress treated us fairly but OPA interpretation stripped away relief" and charges of "OPA usurpation" were staples of their testimony. And the target was well-chosen; even the gentle Barkley, staunch friend of OPA, remarked once ". . . I won in the Senate, but I lost in OPA."[37] Administration witnesses were not all treated the same, needless to say; Fred Vinson was the only important witness who was allowed to read his statement through without interruption.[38] Among his many services to his country, the Secretary of the Treasury could count six terms in the House of Representatives.[39]

The lethargy of the Administration senators, which hung on through the appearances of several spokesmen of particular industries, disappeared instantly with the appearance of Robert R. Wason, president of the National Association of Manufacturers.[40] Before Wason had

[34] *Hearings*, pp. 6–75.

[35] *Hearings*, pp. 25–26.

[36] *Hearings*, pp. 77–208.

[37] *Hearings*, p. 956.

[38] *Hearings*, pp. 1551–78.

[39] In the 68th to 75th Congresses, except for the 71st.

[40] *Hearings*, pp. 392–428.

read two hundred words of his statement, his right to speak for the public, for industry, or even for the NAM, had been challenged. From that point on the fight seems pretty even, as it was later when James B. Carey, secretary-treasurer of the Congress of Industrial Organizations, appeared.[41] NAM and CIO were the principal ideological protagonists in the fight over the extension of price control, and this was clearly reflected in the interest group split on the Committee when their representatives appeared.[42] Neither man was allowed a page of uninterrupted testimony. The role here was that of legislator pro-or-con interest groups. The senators clearly were identifying with private interest groups in a struggle which cut across the separate branches of the government.

Other group identifications can be perceived in the hearings. For instance, the special position of farm groups in American politics was underlined. In the welter of name-calling and exaggerated charges, there is not one criticism of farmers. Everyone agreed they deserved well of the republic. On one occasion Taylor came dangerously close to a critical remark; in defending the government's paying a premium price for grain, he said: "The farmers knew that they [starving people] had to have it, but unfortunately they have held on to the wheat and corn. I don't think it is to the credit of the American farmers themselves. . . ." But Capehart forthwith restated the official congressional position: ". . . I don't agree with the Senator that the American farmer is unpatriotic. I think they are among the most patriotic people this Nation has and I want the record to so state. I don't agree with that statement at all."[43] Ed O'Neal, president of the American Farm Bureau Federation, reflected the magnificent immunity of the farmers when he blamed the inflation, with fine impartiality and without challenge, on the Congress, both parties, the Treasury, the Federal Reserve, and

[41] *Hearings,* pp. 573–603.

[42] Consider this fine exchange:
Mr. Carey: There are no such things as "natural economic laws."
Senator Millikin: Who repealed those?
Mr. Carey: They never existed.
Senator Millikin: My God! That is astounding information.
Mr. Carey: In the first place, economic laws are a prostitution of the *aims of nature, whose first purpose* is to fill the needs of man . . . (*Hearings,* p. 576. Emphasis added).

[43] *Hearings,* p. 800.

the whole Administration, as well as OPA.[44] Again, it was reflected in the lack of any interrogation of James G. Patton, president of the National Farmers Union, whose record as a political actionist might have been expected to invite cross-examination.[45]

One identification any congressman is likely to make is that with his former, or other, occupation. This is borne out in the lawyer-like conduct of the legislative hearing itself, with its cross-examinations and its concern for "the record." As Ernest Griffith has remarked, "The majority of congressmen were (and still are) lawyers, and, to a lawyer, truth emerges from a battle of protagonists."[46] But other occupations also are represented, and the label "lawyer" frequently covers a variety of activities. It is a virtue of the legislature that it is made up of "general" men, and it is natural that legislators should test what they hear against the commonsense of their own experience. The senators on this committee did so; Murdock, for example, talked to a livestock man about his own grass-fed steers, and Millikin remarked: "I am speaking somewhat categorically on this because I have had considerable experience in the oil business."[47] But this is not the same thing, quite, as identifying with an occupational group and perceiving facts in their frame of reference. That is what Capehart seemed to do. A farmer and manufacturer, Capehart had been in the Senate less than two years. He made reference to both of his other occupations, but it was clear that Capehart saw price control in his role as businessman. Over a quarter of a century of experience had conditioned him to trust a businessman's judgment and resent the bureaucrat's interference in the economy. As he put it himself (objecting to questions asked of a businessman): "My observation is that anyone that comes in here from an industry knows his business. They are the people who are trying to make things and do business under all the difficulties that confront them, and trying to be honest and sincere and conscientious, and in the hope that they will be permitted to remain in business. I think that to question their integrity and

[44] *Hearings,* pp. 668–69.

[45] *Hearings,* pp. 691–99.

[46] *Congress: Its Contemporary Role* (cited in note 7), p. 63.

[47] *Hearings,* pp. 1205, 1718. Millikin is an example of the lawyer in Congress: his biography in the *Congressional Directory* includes law, the army, and politics, but not the oil business.

honesty . . ." To which Barkley replied, in part: "We had a witness here yesterday who questioned the sincerity and honesty and integrity of everybody in the Government and you didn't complain about that."[48] But Barkley, who first went to Congress in 1913, had complained the day before, as he did on every occasion when government officials were attacked indiscriminately.

That Senator Capehart continued to regard price control as a businessman would, so long as he remained a minority member of the Committee, is suggested by his writing in 1951 what President Truman called "the terrible Capehart amendment," which Truman said made price control impossible. But in 1953 Capehart assumed the new status of Chairman of the Banking and Currency Committee, and with it a new role requiring him to accept primary responsibility for the legislation reported by the Committee. In his new role he advocated stand-by controls for prices, wages, and rent. He found it hard to understand the intransigence of groups which were "unalterably opposed" to any concession to the principle of controls, and understandably shocked to hear himself accused by a business lobbyist of espousing a philosophy of the "left." It would be hard to find a more striking example of the effect of a change of status.[49]

Senator Tobey appeared briefly from time to time in his peculiarly personal role of moral prophet. He was inclined to indict the whole people for lacking the moral fiber to resist the tainted opportunities afforded by the black market. In the tones of Jeremiah, later to become familiar to the television audience of Kefauver's crime investigation, he called upon the people "to rise up and say 'Unclean, unclean'."[50]

Some of the roles which might have been anticipated were not played by anybody. That of the dictatorial chairman, sure of his power, was one. That of the subject-matter expert, whose prestige in a given field is widely accepted (e.g., O'Mahoney on economic questions[51]), was another. The hectoring-inquisitor role was not played consistently by anybody.

[48] Hearings, p. 1316.

[49] See Robert Bendiner in "The Apostasy of Homer Capehart," The Reporter, May 12, 1953, pp. 30–32, for an interesting description of the Senator's discomfiting experience.

[50] Hearings, p. 1673.

[51] See Earl Latham, The Group Basis of Politics (Ithaca, N. Y., 1952).

The limitations upon what can be done in a study of behavior from the printed record alone have already been acknowledged. The pattern of interactions among the members can be studied fully only from first-hand observation. What does it mean in the climate of the hearing for a particular member to be present? Or absent? It can be seen from the record that questions, and sometimes tempers, tended to get shorter when Senator Taft was on hand. That is tantalizingly suggestive, but not enough. Who supports, who opposes, whom? Who retreats into silence from whom? Such questions can be answered only by the observer. The item in the record which might reveal significant interactions may be the very one which is subsequently edited from it.

It is hard to evaluate the role of leadership with any method, and especially so when reliance must be placed on the printed record. On the surface, it would appear that Senator Wagner had little control over his Committee in the price control controversy. The power of the committee chairman is justly celebrated in political journalism, but it may be that like so many other concentrations of power in the Congress, it can be used most effectively against a majority only in a negative way. The chairman can prevent committee consideration, prevent a report, prevent floor consideration, much more easily than he can command a balky majority to do something positive. When Congress passes legislation requiring periodic reenactment, as it does so often now, it must counteract to some extent the power of the few to control the many. Wagner was not able to get his way with this Committee. He refused to sign the report. Barkley signed it only to get it on the floor, making clear his opposition to it. What went on in the executive sessions, where the bill was amended heavily over the opposition of the chairman, obviously is not to be learned from the record, and perhaps not in any other way.

Some elaborate studies based on role theory have been made of complex organizations,[52] and the congressional committee would seem to be an inviting subject for such research. That much, at least, seems clear from the foregoing analysis; no generalizations about the committee are valid which do not take into account the varied and

[52] See Eugene Jacobson, W. W. Charters, Jr., and Seymour Lieberman, "The Use of the Role Concept in the Study of Complex Organizations," *The Journal of Social Issues*, Vol. 7, pp. 18–27 (No. 3, 1951), and the publications of the Survey Research Center, University of Michigan, which are listed there.

complex statuses which congressmen hold, and the shifting roles which they play in filling first one and then another of them. A congressional committee is an agency for the implementation of the purposes of congressmen. Functionally, it gives to bills the detailed consideration which the full house cannot, but in other ways it is simply another point of focus of the political process, as its parent house is also. It is a part of "the legislative struggle," to use Bertram Gross's term, but, as he indicates, the struggle is a confused one in which the participants fight for different and changing purposes and represent many and sometimes opposing causes. National and parochial ends are inextricably entwined in the Congress, and so they are in the committee. Taft, holding no elective party office in the Senate and sharing eighth rank in seniority with three others, nevertheless chooses the role of national leader for himself and effectively shapes the expectations of others to that role. The committee hearing is no more than a shift of scene for him. McFarland, soon to lead the Democrats in the Senate, chooses for reasons of his own to use this time and place to plead narrowly for the industries of his state. Therein lies the value of the committee hearing for the student of political behavior: within a more manageable compass, the congressmen behave like congressmen.

III. THE COMMITTEE AS A FACT-FINDING AGENCY

The Committee's performance as a fact-finding agency is worth special consideration. Quantitatively, at least, an impressive job was done. Nineteen days were consumed in public hearings, during which 12 public officials, 38 spokesmen of business and business groups, 5 representatives of organized labor, 8 farm group leaders, and 9 persons representing other groups—72 witnesses in all—testified before the Committee. The printed record ran to 2212 pages, including 541 exhibits, charts, statements, letters, and telegrams. Thousands of questions were asked and answered. Out of this welter of facts and opinions, what did the Committee learn about the problems of economic stabilization? What kinds of questions did its members ask? What picture of the factual situation emerged from the answers they got? In the light of the Committee's performance, what might be done to make legislative committees generally more effective as fact-finders?

These questions would be easier to answer if the Committee had ever formulated a set of questions to which the hearings should supply answers. That the Committee did not do. Nevertheless there were questions which, because of their pertinence, were raised again and again, by the witnesses and by the senators themselves. For the purposes of this study, several of these recurring questions were traced carefully through the hearings, to see whether any or all of them could be answered, unambiguously, from the record. Careful attention was paid to the leading questions and gratuitous statements of the senators, to see what facts they accepted, and whether their conceptions of the "facts" ever changed. From this procedure there emerged, not one picture of the factual situation, but two. The senators who supported OPA accepted one, those who opposed OPA the other. Some sharpening of details in each picture doubtless occurred, but there was no indication of a change in the general picture for either group. Each group seemed to come into the hearings with a ready-made frame of reference. Facts which were compatible were fitted into it; facts which were not compatible, even when elaborately documented, were discounted, not perceived, or ignored. This is not so hard as it sounds. A disagreeable fact is not an isolated fact, but one of a constellation of facts. Which is the relevant one? And when statistics seem accurate beyond dispute, there is the question of selecting the relevant variable or the proper base period, or perhaps of whether there is not a serious contrary trend which began too late to be reflected in the figures. Thus contradictions need not be resolved, and in these hearings they were not resolved. The hearings could be said not to have progressed. At the end the same questions were being asked as at the beginning, and were receiving the same sets of answers.

There was not necessarily agreement within either group over what should be done about price controls. The *pro forma* claim that "I don't know how I'm going to vote on this matter" was made frequently, and most of the senators would say that price controls ultimately would be extended—with modifications. What divided them was that one group would accept statements of fact which put the OPA in a good light, and receive sympathetically the claims of groups which supported the OPA and the Administration. The other group would not. The first group was made up loosely of the Democrats Wagner, Mitchell, Barkley, Taylor, Fulbright, Murdock, and Radcliffe, and the Republican Tobey. The opposing group was composed of the Republicans Capehart, Millikin, Taft, Hickenlooper, Buck, and Butler, and the Democrat Bankhead. Other members of the Committee did not participate frequently enough to be placed with any confidence. The first group's conception of the facts was shared roughly with Administration spokesmen, labor representatives, the president of the National Farmers Union, and several other group representatives purporting to speak for the "liberal" or the consumer point of view. The second group listened most receptively to business spokesmen and the representatives of the other farm groups. These classifications are rough, of course, and should be taken that way. They are not meant to indicate anything approaching complete uniformity.

Some of these questions, and the ways in which the two groups answered them, may now be considered.

What was the "lesson" of World War I?

The Administration clearly thought that the experience of World War I supported the extension of price controls. Every Administration witness mentioned, it, and charts were brought in to support their story.[53] Starting back in 1914, it ran, prices rose precipitously until some voluntary controls were partially successful in checking the rise in 1917–18. After a brief post-Armistice recession, with controls off, prices rose sharply again in 1919–20, causing a snowballing of demand and a hoarding of inventories, in anticipation of even higher prices. Ultimately a buyers' strike caused collapse; deflation and depression were the result of the unchecked spiral of prices. To these witnesses and their supporters the moral seemed clear: weakening the price control program in 1946 would bring the same disastrous results.

To the other side it was not clear at all. They doubted the relevance of the earlier experience to the problem at hand. Or they were impressed with the shortness of the periods of inflation and deflation in World War I. Taking the post-Armistice figures alone (which they frequently did), neither the climb nor the subsequent drop looked so bad. They pointed out that a "flood of goods" had eventually forced

---

[53] The statements used in this section were all selected because they were made many times. Therefore, no attempt will be made to document them except where a particular quotation is used by way of illustration. For a representative Administration statement of the World War I experience, see the testimony of John D. Small, head of the Civilian Production Administration, at pp. 1449–50.

prices down, forgetting that prices had gone up three times as much as industrial production, and that the "flood of goods" had been released—not produced—by deflationary dumping. Even recollections of the period fell conveniently into place; Glen Taylor remembered it as a dreadful experience, Capehart as not bad at all.[54] Millikin was perhaps the most intransigent. He could see on the government's charts only one fact, that prices had gone down. The buyers' strike had prevented an "explosive inflation"—by which he meant not the 150 per cent increase the World I charts showed, but the kind of runaway inflation the Germans had.[55]

What causes inflation?

This question caused difficulty, because whenever it was discussed seriously it took the Committee quickly outside its jurisdictional field. Farm policy, fiscal policy, the wages of labor, and many other things not the Committee's business were involved in the stabilization program. But the question had to be raised. The Administration group saw the principal inflationary threats in the economic forces OPA sought to control. The pent-up demands from the war period, supported by 225 billions in purchasing power, exceeded the total current supply of goods. Production was at a record high level, despite labor shortages and the problems of reconversion, but it would take time to "fill the pipelines" from producer to consumer and meet the demand. In this interim period, price controls were imperative to prevent a disastrous spiral. These were the bed-rock economic facts, but this group suspected more. They believed that businessmen were hoarding inventories, thus aggravating the shortages, in order to make huge profits if price controls were removed. They also believed that speculation—"betting on inflation"—made the control job harder.

The charge of inventory-hoarding is a good example of the influence of group ideology on the perception of facts. It was made repeatedly by pro-OPA witnesses, and apparently believed implicitly. Yet when the opposing senators demanded proof, it was sometimes promised but never furnished. Paul Porter could report an incident he knew about, and surmise that the situation, whatever it was, would get

[54] *Hearings*, pp. 206–7.

[55] *Hearings*, pp. 1585–86.

worse as the date for the expiration of controls drew near.[56] A member of a CIO local told about finding a back room full of oil at a place where he had been told there was no oil.[57] That was the extent of the proof of inventory-hoarding, but the charge would not down; it was an essential element of the version of the facts held by OPA supporters. Their opponents, curiously enough, accepted inventory-hoarding as a fact sometimes, justifying it on the grounds that the hoarders could not make a profit under OPA, or that they hoped OPA would see "the light" and treat them fairly.

Anti-OPA witnesses and senators found the chief causes of inflation in the policies of OPA itself. OPA kept prices unrealistically low, forcing producers to concentrate on high price lines or inferior substitutes. By refusing to recognize rising costs of production, OPA impeded production. OPA propaganda and "scare talk" created an inflation psychology, leading to panic buying and hoarding. Other Administration policies, including the unbalanced budget and the loan to Britain, compounded the pressures on prices. So did the wage increases which the Administration permitted. To this group, wage increase always started an inflationary spiral, just as a price increase did for the pro-OPA group. Similarly, Taft would not agree with Bowles that repeal of the excess profits tax was inflationary, but he was sure the loan to Britain was.[58]

What has been the overall effect of price controls on the economy?

OPA and its friends were sure that OPA had stabilized the economy and prevented inflation. Their charts showed it; the cost-of-living index had risen only about 30 per cent since 1939.[59] They claimed that the cost-of-living had risen only about 3½ per cent since price controls became effective in 1943, and had gone up only .7 per cent since V-J day. In this time, controls had prevented neither production nor profits. Everyone knew that production had been enormous, and the charts showed that it had risen at its wartime peak nearly 140

[56] *Hearings*, p. 198.
[57] *Hearings*, p. 608.
[58] *Hearings*, p. 39.
[59] *Hearings*, p. 1450.

per cent over the 1939 level. Their opponents would contest it, but OPA was prepared to support the claim that business profits had been high, too. OPA believed that it had preserved economic stability and made planning possible.

Its opponents believed that the overall effect of OPA on the economy had been bad. Some were willing to accept it as a wartime necessity, and to make a grudging admission that it had done an acceptable, even a good job, if only its powers could be terminated soon. But others would not concede that it had done a good job. The kindest view was that it was not OPA's fault: the economy was too complex for controls, and besides, price controls could only treat effects, not causes. Some argued that inflation had been serious in spite of OPA (amounting to 32 per cent over 1941)[60] but generally the figures did not seem to matter much; they did not settle the question, as they might have been expected to do. Millikin said again and again that OPA never had held a line when there was real pressure on it, that the goods simply flowed into the black market and the price line became a "fiction." OPA had made it impossible for farmers, dry goods wholesalers, retail meat dealers (and others, explicitly and by inference) to operate legally. The government's figures actually demonstrated a chief vice of OPA: the agency concentrated on controlling the cost-of-living *index*, rather than encouraging production through incentive prices where needed. The bill of particulars against OPA was a long one; in addition to hampering production, penalizing the efficient producer, and diverting goods to the black market, OPA had used its consumer subsidy program to increase the demand for the limited supply of goods. The overall effect of OPA, they believed, had been to aggravate inflationary pressures.

What is the administrative record of OPA?

The administrative performance of OPA was under continuous attack; the agency and its friends never got off the defensive. OPA was charged with handling appeals slowly, with issuing orders that were hard to understand, with tying up business with red tape. It was not improving, or if it were, it still was not good enough. OPA was inflexible; it handled individual firms with industry-wide orders, and

[60] *Hearings,* p. 866.

refused to modify those orders. These criticisms were to be expected, but there were worse. The agency had "continuously and directly violated the Price Control Act,"[61] Taft said, and Goss, master of the Grange, was even more sweeping when he said: "For four years the OPA has thumbed its nose at Congress, has violated the basic law under which it was created, and has pursued an illegal but politically expedient course which has fed the fires of inflation and then tried to control the fire by stopping up the chimney."[62] Its "vicious propaganda" had created a "scare psychology" among buyers. OPA was accused especially of refusing to grant relief in hardship cases, as provided for by law, and of holding up production by maintaining inadequate ceiling prices which they had the power to raise. This line of criticism fell into a syllogism: every increase requested is necessary to production; any delay in granting it holds up production; therefore, OPA is responsible for critical shortages (e.g., in housing for veterans).[63] Since there was no question of the righteousness of every request for an increase, if OPA held one up a year it was only because of administrative ineptitude; the fact that it was granted ultimately proved it was right all the time, without regard to any change in circumstances which might have occurred.

Under this drum-fire of criticism, OPA was pushed into defending itself by citing the number of adjustments it had made and price increases it had allowed.[64] The agency officers contended they had a "realistic" approach to price control (i.e., one which allowed prices to go up). The ambivalence in their position was resolved by claiming that, while they had held the line against general inflation, they had granted adjustments to get production or relieve hardship. The Administration group was willing to admit mistakes, but insisted that OPA's procedures had been improved and made more than reasonably efficient. A detailed account of procedures employed to reduce delay in handling individual adjustment cases was placed in the record, with statistics demonstrating their effectiveness.[65] Breakdowns in production were traced to shortages in labor and materials, not to ad-

61 *Hearings*, p. 1243.

62 *Hearings*, p. 674.

63 *Hearings*, pp. 301–4.

64 *Hearings*. See, for example, pp. 82, 155–56, 159–62, 783–84, 1580, 1727.

65 *Hearings*, pp. 138–45.

ministrative delay. But the criticisms, needless to say, were not affected in the least.

The influence of group ideology on fact perception was clearly reflected in the image of OPA as a human organization which each group held. The opponents of OPA saw the agency people as theorists, inexperienced in business, telling experienced businessmen what to do. The complaint that "OPA does not understand the underwear industry" (or the construction industry, or any other) was frequently heard, and doubtless it was true. As one OPA official put it, it was impossible to have an expert in every line. To a businessman involved in the unique particulars of his own business, the edicts of an agency which of necessity sought to generalize its rules were bound to seem amateurish and arbitrary. Thus the professor, whom the Congress had tried to legislate out of OPA, proved as a stereotype to be ineradicable. Consequently, the anti-OPA senators were prepared to accept assertions of industry representatives that inexperienced men in those branches of OPA were of no avail.[66] The automobile dealers complained that there were no persons remaining in OPA who had experience in the retail automobile business; Porter listed four in the Automotive Branch, and the dealers carried the debate into the appendix of the record.[67] In answer to the lumbermen's charge, Porter listed 17 employees with a total experience in the lumber business of 400 years.[68] But Taft was sure that no retail lumberman knew anything about pricing for the industry. And so it went. That there was more involved than the legislator's stereotype of the bureaucrat is clear from the persistence with which the Administration senators defended the competence and experience of OPA administrators, whom they believed to be able and patriotic men who frequently were hired away from OPA by business.

What are the motives of OPA?

The contrary images of OPA extended to the motives imputed to the administrators themselves. Their opponents saw them as enemies of capitalism, who hated profits, liked controls for their own sake, and

[66] See the list of OPA personnel connected with pricing of textile industries, *Hearings,* pp. 118–25.

[67] *Hearings,* pp. 1272, 1760, 1874–76.

[68] *Hearings,* p. 1713.

wanted to perpetuate their own jobs. "Last year, this year, next year, the year after" was heard again and again, summing up the anti-OPA belief that OPA would always ask for extension of its regulatory powers. The statements were bitter. Bowles was compared to Hitler and Mussolini, without rebuke from anti-OPA senators. OPA officials belonged to that "school of thought that believes that the wholesaler, jobber, and distributor are excrescences on the body politic." Again, ". . . the fundamental philosophy of OPA is the abolition of profits, the regulation of profits, and the stifling of private enterprise." The kindest construction put on their motives was that they were "a group of very sincere, honest young people that want to reshape the world nearer to their heart's desire . . . but they seem to disregard the effect of these regulations on legitimate established businesses."[69] Given this image of OPA, it was easy to believe in specific acts of duplicity and abuses of power. When a price increase was granted an industry the day before its spokesman appeared before the Committee, Capehart was sure the timing was deliberate. The OPA contention that at least two months were required to clear a price order did not move him (although usually he would accept the argument that OPA could do nothing in a hurry).[70] OPA was charged with allowing a rental 50 per cent above ceilings on some new apartment buildings in New York, just to prevent apartment owners from claiming there was no new building under OPA.[71]

OPA's own statements of its policies and practices obviously would not be acceptable to senators who saw them in this light. Porter stated the decontrol policy of OPA this way: ". . . if we can find that there is a reasonable prospect that there will not be inflationary increases to the extent that would jeopardize the general policy of stabilization, we can take [price control] off." But Millikin was sure that if OPA should take "a long look through the future and if you see some little dislocation ahead that might interfere with prices, you are not going to decontrol."[72] Some of the senators favored writing a rigid decontrol

---

[69] Hearings, pp. 1185–86, 1356, 971, 1356. See p. 971 particularly for the contrast in the images of OPA held by the president of the National Apartment Owners' Association and by Senator Glen Taylor.

[70] Hearings, pp. 1311, 1319.

[71] Hearings, p. 1492.

[72] Hearings, p. 1718.

formula into the law, on the ground that OPA could not be trusted to decontrol otherwise. Perhaps the blackest picture of OPA was painted by Millikin in grilling the OPA deputy administrator for enforcement. Millikin insisted that OPA set quotas for its enforcement officers, smeared innocent business men and set traps for them with sweeping injunctions, and forced federal judges to render judgments they knew to be unjust. Murdock finally was moved to protest that OPA did not write the law, nor confirm the federal judges, and "that if you go to the length that Senator Millikin wants you to, we must assume that we have a fool on the bench as well as a rather vicious fool in the OPA Enforcement Section."[73]

The Administration group could see no justification for impugning the motives of OPA officials. As they saw it, "they are all down here on loan from business enterprises and at a financial sacrifice, most of them, and they are anxious to get back."[74] OPA administrators were selfless, patriotic men, who believed in the profit system and allowed for profits in their pricing, and who were motivated by a desire to save the business system from the evil effects of an inflationary spiral.

How has labor fared in the postwar economy?

If one question were wanted, of all those asked in the hearings, to provide an index to the whole constellation of facts accepted as true and relevant by the person answering, this one probably would serve as well as any other. The result would turn on whether the answer mentioned hourly wage rates, which generally were up, or take-home pay, which generally was down.[75] This is another way of saying that the two groups divided sharply on their attitudes toward organized labor. The pro-OPA group, senators and witnesses (including the consumer groups and the Farmers Union), was sympathetic toward it; the other was not. One brief exchange perhaps will serve to illustrate. Ed O'Neal, president of the American Farm Bureau Federation, presented a series of elaborate tables designed to show, generally, that the earnings of labor had advanced much faster than the cost-of-living, and that conversely the cost of food had advanced relatively

[73] *Hearings,* p. 1691. This remarkable cross-examination is worth a complete reading. See pp. 1663–1705.

[74] *Hearings,* p. 971.

[75] See the colloquy of Taft and Bowles, *Hearings,* p. 58.

very little.[76] Senator Mitchell pointed out that the NAM compilation showed the cost of food and the price of farm products as having gone up more than the AFBF figures did. Replied O'Neal: ". . . We farmers are getting awfully tired of the *workingmen in America* and a lot of *propagandists in the administration* blaming the farmer. We are all pretty mad about it." To which Mitchell countered: "How about the National Association of Manufacturers? Their compilation shows that the farmer is getting more out of the increase, a greater increase, than anybody else." But Mitchell could not make O'Neal criticize the NAM.[77]

Obviously, hourly wages and take-home pay are two aspects of the same thing, and both were relevant to the Committee's problem. Hourly wages are part of the cost of production and affect the price at which a producer can sell. Take-home pay is what the worker relates to the cost-of-living; together they determine whether he makes ends meet. But both groups were reluctant in the extreme to consider both factors. Taft, for instance, wanted the AFL to put in the record "a figure on the increase in *straight-time hourly earnings* since before the war." Green did not have those figures, but "I have a few figures here," he said—all showing declining earnings *since VE-day*. Taft did not want postwar figures; he wanted a simple comparison of the increase of the cost-of-living and of straight-time hourly earnings since January 1, 1940, which he believed would show that labor had done very well. Needless to say, when the figures were submitted he got a great deal more than that, but never precisely that, and the showing did not come out his way at all.[78]

The cleavage on facts related to labor never was closed. Earlier in the year a wage increase had been granted to steel-workers, followed by an increase in the price of steel. These related facts were neatly divided in the testimony; neither side willingly talked about both. To one, the wage increase meant that the government had abandoned wage controls; to the other, the "$250,000,000 bribe to the steel industry" was a hard blow at stabilization. Goss and O'Neal, like the businessmen, stressed the wage increase; Patton and Carolyn Ware

[76] *Hearings*, pp. 654–65. Significantly, the only group chosen for comparative purposes is labor.

[77] *Hearings*, p. 667. Emphasis added. Contrast the attack on NAM by James Patton, president of the Farmers Union, pp. 694–98.

[78] *Hearings*, pp. 787–93. Emphasis added.

(speaking for the consumer) said that their organizations had protested the price increase. One group saw labor's preferred position relative to other groups continuously being improved by a sympathetic Administration which allowed wages to rise unchecked and forced businesses to absorb increased costs without price relief. The other saw disadvantaged labor striving to meet increased costs of living with diminished take-home pay, and forced to bargain with businesses which could recoup strike losses from tax returns.

Other questions

Many other questions showed the same division as to what the facts were; a few, briefly treated, will have to suffice.

One of the cliches accepted by everybody was that production was the only thing that would solve the problem of inflation. What, then, was the level of production at the time of the hearings? The Administration group offered figures many times to show that production was at the highest level in our history, that only the pent-up demand of a population loaded with purchasing power made it insufficient.[79] This made the problem simply one of what to do about prices until the excess of demand could be satisfied. Higher prices, they were sure, would not increase production, when the real bottlenecks were shortages of labor and materials. There was no indication that the figures ever convinced anybody. "How do you get production?" remained the crucial question for the opponents of OPA. Even the everyday experiences of the protagonists seemed to be affected by what they thought to be true. Senator Taylor found the evidences of production in the stores; he had found tools he wanted with no trouble. A representative of the National Retail Associations, on the other hand, could not buy a little hatchet, search as he would.[80]

A related question concerned the profits of business. In an economy of hundreds of thousands of businesses, it may be doubted whether aggregates or averages could mean much; but the profits of business were part of the picture and a try had to be made. Some elaborate statistics were presented, but the Committee never really got beyond the question of how profits should be computed. Profits before, or after, taxes? Figured as a percentage of net worth, or net sales? Bowles'

[79] *Hearings,* pp. 870–71, 1449–51, 1461–62, 1708–9.

[80] *Hearings,* p. 867.

figures were based on net worth; Taft countered with tables showing the percentage of national income paid out to various types of recipients between 1929 and 1945, and corporate profits before and after taxes as a percentage of national income for the same period.[81] Similar difficulty was had with a question of business practice. One of the House amendments would require OPA to set a ceiling price for every product which would allow the cost of the product plus a reasonable profit for both producer and distributor. OPA argued that most industries make a variety of products, some of which make high, others low profits and still others no profit at all. What mattered to the industry was its overall profit. OPA supporters could and did buttress, with personal experience, their contention that no businessman expected to make a profit on every item. But their opponents had had contrary experience in business; they were equally sure no businessman ever willingly lost money on anything.[82]

A question with which the public was concerned in 1946 was what had happened to meat, and what should be done to get more of it. The question was extensively discussed in the hearings, by the persons best qualified to give the answers. The several levels of the meat industry all wanted price ceilings removed. They quoted Department of Agriculture figures to show a great supply of cattle, enough to meet demand, and needing to be reduced. They argued that legitimate packers had trouble getting steers because they had been diverted to small black-market operators, who wasted valuable by-products as well as overcharging the public. They estimated that the removal of controls would send prices up 15–20 per cent (again based on Agriculture figures), which was about what they thought people were currently paying in the black market. With decontrol, the industry people believed, meat would flow into legitimate channels, probably forcing prices down. If meat were not decontrolled now there never would be a better time.

The experts in OPA, and their friends on the Committee, thought

[81] *Hearings*, p. 42. Perhaps the most remarkable piece of statistical gymnastics was performed by James Carey, CIO, who put corporate profits during the war years at 52 billion dollars (before or after taxes?). Although he stated that 25.9 billions had been paid to stockholders, he then said: "For every dollar of these unused reserves [sic] it means one hour of unemployment for some American worker. In other words, $52,000,000,000 means 52,000,000,000 man-hours of unemployment" (p. 585).

[82] For representative examples of these exchanges, see *Hearings*, pp. 47–48, 286, 807, 987, 1589–90, 1623–25.

the black market in meat and the wastage of by-products had been greatly exaggerated. They recognized that there had been diversion of meat into the black market, but they pointed out that a new control order put into effect on May 1 had within a week increased the volume of inspected slaughter cattle by 12 per cent to a figure only one per cent below the volume for the same time in 1945. They believed, therefore, that the problem was being solved. Some of them questioned the Agriculture Department's figures; they did not believe there was enough meat. But Patton and the CIO packinghouse workers both thought the "shortage" was deliberately engineered by the large packers.[83] They were sure that the removal of ceilings would send prices up at least 50 per cent, wreck other food controls, and end stabilization. It would be better to decontrol later, when a larger supply of durables and consumer goods would drain off purchasing power and relieve the pressure on foods.

The disagreement extended even to small and ascertainable facts. What is the most efficient use of grain? Fulbright asserted that "a pound of wheat, used in bread, will produce about 2,400,000 calories, and if it is fed to a beef cow it will produce only a little over 200,000 calories." To which Hickenlooper replied: ". . . I am quite certain that the statistics show in every study that has ever been made of ultimate food values that human beings get more definite, substantial value out of grain fed through meat animals than they do from the grain itself. That is, they get more proteins and more vitamins. . . ."[84] Like the large contradictions, this small one remained unresolved.

Many facts, of course, have handles on both ends. Wason, of NAM, for instance, produced newspaper advertisements to show that grocery prices had gone up more than Bowles claimed. This might seem to prove that Bowles had lied and that OPA had failed to control grocery prices, or it could show that the grocers had no reason to complain of OPA.[85] When a CIO member recited high prices he had to pay, it might demonstrate, as he thought, the laborer's need for continued protection; but perhaps it was unwitting testimony to OPA's ineffec-

---

[83] Resolution of United Packinghouse Workers of America, CIO, *Hearings*, pp. 641–44; testimony of James Patton, pp. 698–99.

[84] *Hearings*, pp. 1209–10.

[85] *Hearings*, pp. 395–402.

tiveness.[86] Or take the question of the level of production of any commodity. If it were conceded to be low, and not equal to demand, it could be said to prove that price control was needed until production could meet the demand, or, contrarily, that control should be abolished in order to get production. If it were conceded to be high, it might prove that production and profits could be gotten under price control, or that control could now be abolished with safety.

IV. INFLUENCE OF GROUP IDEOLOGY ON FACT PERCEPTION

What has been argued in the preceding section is that the Committee and its witnesses were made up of two loose groups of people who disagreed, not so much in their opinions upon what should be done about a known or ascertainable fact situation, as upon what the underlying facts themselves were. As advocates, neither side could afford to accept the other's conception of the facts, for that would be to concede the battle; policy is rooted in the assessment of the situation. But if common experience can be trusted, the people on both sides believed in good faith that they were stating *the* facts, and from this flowed the sincerity and even passion with which they seemed to talk. As Walter Lippmann put it, "a public opinion is a moralized and codified version of the facts."[87] The interest group orientation furnished the pattern of preconceptions through which the facts were screened. It was easy for one side to see an entrenched bureaucracy meddling with a free economy, for the other to see a democratic government protecting the helpless from exploitation. After that it was just a matter of filling in the details.

There is, to be sure, nothing new in this conception. It is at least as old as Plato, who expressed it with moving beauty in his allegory of the cave.[88] But it has a relevance for a theory of the group process in politics that has not been sufficiently appreciated. In the price control controversy (and surely in others like it) the senators were

[86] *Hearings,* pp. 604–9.

[87] *Public Opinion* (New York, 1922), p. 125.

[88] This was the central idea of Lippmann's *Public Opinion.* See especially Karl Mannheim, *Ideology and Utopia* (New York, 1951), and Ralph K. Merton's essay, "The Sociology of Knowledge," in *Twentieth Century Sociology,* eds. G. Gurvitch and W. E. Moore (New York, 1945).

not sitting as arbiters of the group struggle, but as participants; it flowed through them. But it was not perceived so clearly and simply as that by those in the struggle. It is generally accepted that there are many opinions, but not that there are many versions of the facts—or at least, not that there is no single *true* one. This is the crucial problem of communication between social groups, as it is, to a greater degree, of intercultural communication. Given its own version of the facts, and believing it to be the only true one, each side could fight for the general interest and impute bad motives to its opponents in all sincerity. In this sense the Committee *was* concerned with promoting the general interest, but so were most of the spokesmen of special interests who appeared before it. Social conflict over group interests, clearly perceived and rightly identified, should be easy to mediate; a rough appraisal of the balance of power and frank bargaining should be enough. It is the quantum of concern for the general interest in every calculation that makes the trouble.

It should be emphasized that the price control question was highly political, with a long history. The kinds of information committee members would want, the kinds of facts they would be able to perceive, their willingness to accept relatively objective data, surely would vary with the kind of question under consideration. Nevertheless, the conception of the social nature of fact perception should be useful to political science. In regard to policy, it suggests one of the limits to the usefulness of uncommitted social intelligence to the politician. In regard to research, perception of the fact situation surely is one of the crucial variables, both in the group struggle which is the political process, and in the behavior of the individual actors in it.[89] Conversely, the perception of the fact situation by public officials might provide a useful index to their group orientations.

V. CONCLUSION

This study began with two sets of generalizations, one of which suggested that committee members sit as judges representing the general interest presiding over the public debate of the special interests; the other suggested that committee members themselves are participants

---

[89] See the distinction between process and behavior made by David Easton in *The Political System* (New York, 1953), pp. 203–6.

in the struggle of contending groups, one phase of which is the public hearing. The analysis of the hearings conducted in 1946 by the Senate Committee on Banking and Currency on the question of extending price control would seem to support the latter. The members of this Committee did not sit as legislative judges to discover an abstract general interest, nor did they seem concerned with presenting a balanced debate for public consideration. On the contrary, most of them did take sides. The Committee hearings clearly were used as a public platform for opposing groups with which the senators identified. A great deal of information was received from interested groups, which the senators accepted or rejected in accordance with their preconceived notions of the facts. What was made perfectly clear was that the groups opposing price control were more numerous and more militant than the groups supporting it. This was, of course, crucial information. The remark of Kefauver and Levin (in urging professional staff for committees), that "Congress cannot function today without lobbyists,"[90] will always be true, for only the lobbyists can tell what their groups will fight for and how hard they will fight. It is reasonable to suppose that some social catharsis was provided by the institutional conflict, as Professor Truman suggested, but there was no way to tell in this study.

But this is not to be taken to mean that Professor Chamberlain's generalizations are wrong. What is suggested rather is that members of the Committee behaved in a variety of ways, depending upon the roles they chose to play. It seems indeed unlikely that we have exhausted the repertory of committee roles; quite the contrary. In hearings on a different issue, under other circumstances, some or all of the members surely might choose the judicial role, some or all of the time. The number and range of roles permitted by the norms of a given committee, the variations in what is acceptable which may exist between committees, are matters for further research.

Other questions should be asked. Why does a legislator choose a particular role, and not another? What is the effect of the subject matter of the hearing upon role selection? Upon the perception of facts, and the willingness of committee members to accept relatively objective data? The records of hearings of congressional committees, readily accessible in embarrassing abundance, can be used extensively

[90] *A Twentieth Century Congress* (cited in note 7), p. 156.

to formulate hypotheses based on these and other questions, which might then be tested in more intensive research. State legislatures, which seldom keep verbatim records of committee hearings, nevertheless multiply the opportunities for studies involving close observation, interviews, and other techniques in the arsenal of behavior research. It should not be too much to hope that ulitimately some general propositions might be fashioned which would contribute to a viable theory of politics.

TWO
THE MORSE COMMITTEE ASSIGNMENT CONTROVERSY: A STUDY IN SENATE NORMS

T HE Senate of the United States, like other institutionalized groups, operates in accordance with a complex of norms for members' behavior which are understood by few outsiders and perhaps not completely by all senators. Formal written rules governing the behavior of members take into account the division of functions between the two major parties and the operation of the Senate's institutionalized sub-groups, the committees. These are supplemented by unwritten rules that are often more consequential. Members have generally-accepted notions of the way the Senate as a body ought to perform its public business and regulate its internal affairs, and the way members ought to behave toward the Senate and toward each other.[1]

This study was made possible by funds granted by The Fund for the Advancement of Education. That Corporation is not, of course, responsible for any of the statements made or views expressed here.

This article originally appeared in *The American Political Science Review*, LI (June 1957), 313–329.

[1] "A possible objection to the word *norm* itself is that we may easily confuse two different things: norm A, a statement of what people ought to do in a particular situation, and norm B, a statistical, or quasi-statistical, average of what they actually do in that situation. Sometimes the two coincide, but more often they do not." George Homans, *The Human Group* (New York, 1950), p. 124. The term is used here, as Professor Homans uses it, in the first sense, as the behavior expected of members of a group by the members themselves, a departure from which in practice is followed by some punishment, such as a decline in the member's social standing in the group.

Senatorial behavior would be difficult enough to study if this were all, but it is not. For one thing, the norms are by no means undifferentiated for the entire membership. Within the Senate a number of identifiable official and unofficial "statuses" (or "positions") besides that of United States Senator can be distinguished, each carrying with it a "role" in the form of the behavior expected by the Senate and the public of the person occupying that status. The leadership positions in the two parties and the committee chairmanships come immediately to mind as examples of official statuses. The status of "elder statesman" occupied at one time by, say, Senators Walter George and Alben Barkley may be suggested as an example of the unofficial kind. Furthermore, even senators who occupy no specialized statuses must accommodate themselves to the demands of many groups. Some of these are sub-groups of the Senate itself: the senatorial party, with its formal and informal structure; the committees; friendship groups; and groups of sectional, ideological, and interest allies. Many are outside the Senate: the national party, with its need to make a record and capture the presidency; the constituency, sometimes conceived broadly as all the people in a state and sometimes more narrowly as the groups that supported the senator; interest groups broader than a state, perhaps sectional or national in their scope. The demands these groups make on a particular member often conflict, and they must moreover be reconciled with the ambitions, philosophy, and personality of the member himself. The "reference group" for the substance of the specific behavior may then be exclusively the one in which the senator is physically participating, the Senate, or it may be one which is psychologically important to him, even though he may not be a formal member of the group. The Senate itself will be the reference group for the style of the behavior and the form in which he interacts with other senators and the symbols and agencies of the Senate.[2]

These are commonplace observations; the existence and power of norms for behavior are apparent to anyone who reads about the Senate in the daily newspaper. When the "liberal" senators mass forces in a vain effort to change the closure rule it is plain that the written rules, including the one that makes a change so difficult, have

[2] See Eugene L. and Ruth E. Hartley, *Fundamentals of Social Psychology* (New York, 1952), pp. 456–81.

crucial importance, as does the unwritten convention that the Senate is a "continuing" body. There is even some general awareness of the more subtle working of the norms regulating the conduct of members toward each other; this is implied in the fairly common reference to the Senate as an "exclusive club." The generally more subterranean operation of norms of this kind comes to the surface when a sanction is applied—when virtual ostracism was imposed on Huey Long, or when a public rebuff is administered to an overly aggressive junior member. The sanction may be covert, as in the Senate's displeasure with Senator Case of South Dakota in 1956 for embarrassing his colleagues by revealing publicly the offer of a campaign contribution by a lobbyist interested in natural gas legislation. This apparently exceeded their annoyance with the lobbyist who embarrassed Senator Case. Much less frequently it is overt, as in the official censure of Senator McCarthy, who, more than one competent observer has suggested, was disciplined finally for continued flouting of the "club rules" rather than for his aggressions on persons outside the Senate which were considered by many of his critics to be more grievous departures from proper conduct.[3]

Incidents of this kind do not carry us far; they substantiate the existence of the norms without telling us much about their content. Learning more about them is not easy. The written rules and official interpretations of them, when they are observed, present no great problem. The norms that are not explicit, the "oughts" that are shared by senators because they are members of the "club," are another matter; perhaps only those members who are in the process of acquiring them understand them at the self-conscious level. They offer quite difficult problems to the non-member student. The kind of participant observation that has revealed the norms of some other groups is neither entirely adequate for, nor permitted by, a group as complex and secretive as the Senate. Perhaps a good beginning for a study of norms would be a series of political autobiographies such as no retired senator so far has seemed willing or able to write. At the present, political scientists and journalists are left to make infer-

[3] See William S. White, "The 'Club' that is the U.S. Senate," New York Times Magazine, November 7, 1954, and Citadel: The Story of the U.S. Senate (New York, 1957); and Richard Rovere, Affairs of State: The Eisenhower Years (New York, 1956), pp. 217–29.

ences about these "oughts" from observations of how senators, as a group, "normally" behave with respect to each other, and, more clearly, from critical instances in which the Senate formally or informally applies sanctions against proscribed behavior, or is in an obvious conflict-of-norm situation among its members.

Political scientists have made some studies of the relative effectiveness of competing claims on political representatives over time, in regard to categories of issues.[4] But the fact that a senator votes more frequently with his party than with a sectional group does not necessarily mean that he puts party allegiance first; it may only mean that the sectional group makes fewer demands on him. Again, it tells us nothing about the kind of situation in which the senator will put the claim of one ahead of the other.

This study rests on two assumptions. The first is that particular conflict situations may furnish clues about the norms that affect behavior and their relative strength among different members of the group. The situation chosen for analysis here is the controversy in the Senate over the assignment of Senator Wayne Morse of Oregon to standing committees after he had bolted the Republican party in the presidential election of 1952. The bare facts of the controversy will be stated, followed by analysis of the relative strength of behavioral norms involved in the contest. The second assumption is that it should be possible to make valid, if crude, inferences about norms for behavior from the printed record which is available to everyone. After all, much of Senate behavior that counts is *public* behavior; whatever their private motives, senators must live with their public records. Accordingly, the study was made, and tentative conclusions reached, wholly from the printed record. After that, persons were interviewed in Washington who had first-hand participant knowledge of the controversy. If the second assumption were correct, no basic alterations should then have been necessary; and that proved to be the case. Some refinements were made, but the conclusions (which are wholly the author's own) did not have to be altered as a result of the interviews.

---

[4] See, e.g., George L. Grassmuck, *Sectional Biases in Congress on Foreign Policy* (Baltimore, 1950), and Julius Turner, *Party and Constituency: Pressures on Congress* (Baltimore, 1951). See also David B. Truman, "The State Delegations and the Structure of Party Voting in the United States House of Representatives," *The American Political Science Review*, Vol. 50, pp. 1023–45 (December 1956).

I. WHAT HAPPENED TO MORSE

Wayne Morse was an early supporter of Eisenhower, but a progressive estrangement from the candidate and his campaign declarations was climaxed by Morse's announcing for Stevenson in the middle of October and resigning from the Republican party a few days later.[5] The break was complete: Morse campaigned for Stevenson and later declined the invitation of the Republican Senate conference to attend its first session. He asked not to be assigned committee seats by the Republicans, now the majority party in the Senate, saying that he would seek his posts as an Independent from the Senate itself. The Republicans accordingly filled their list with party members; the two vacant seats not filled by either party when committee appointments were considered by the Senate on January 13, 1953, were on the District of Columbia and Public Works committees. (By law, a senator must be given a seat on at least two standing committees.) Morse wanted to retain his old assignments to the Armed Services and Labor and Public Welfare committees. A suggestion that unanimous consent be given for Morse and an additional Republican member to be added to each of these committees met the objection of the minority leader. Morse then nominated himself for the Armed Services committe. A written ballot was taken and Morse lost, 81–7. Morse next introduced a resolution which would add himself and one majority member to each of the committees to which he had belonged, for the duration of the 83rd Congress, and asked and received permission from the Senate to postpone his appointment to committees until the resolution could be acted upon by the appropriate committee and the Senate.[6]

The wait was a long one. The Committee on Rules and Administration unanimously reported the resolution adversely in mid-April, but the Senate did not debate it until May 25. The resolution was de-

[5] The New York Times, October 19, 1952, p. 1, col. 7; October 25, 1952, p. 1, col. 4. For Morse's account of his break with the party, see Congressional Record, Vol. 99, pp. 3752–60 (April 24, 1953); and U.S. News & World Report, Nov. 19, 1954.

[6] Congressional Record, Vol. 99, pp. 327–52 (January 13, 1953). The vote is at pp. 346–49. All page references herein are to the bound volumes, not the daily edition.

feated 56–19, whereupon the Senate elected Morse to the vacancies on the Public Works and the District of Columbia committees.[7]

The third vote on Morse's committee assignments came in January, 1954, a full year after the beginning of the 83rd Congress. A resolution changing the committee structure gave Morse's friends an opportunity to offer an amendment which would return Morse to the committees he had served on during the 82nd for the remainder of the 83rd Congress, enlarging them by one member each and reducing by the same number the committees he would leave. Thus it would not be necessary, as it would have been a year earlier when the ballot was taken, to strike anyone from a committee list; but (on the assumption Morse would vote with the Democrats) four committees thereafter would not be controlled by either party. On this proposal Morse mustered his largest vote, but nevertheless lost 59–26.[8]

The bare summary of events gives no indication of the vigor with which Morse fought for his old committee seats. He charged the Republicans with engaging in "terrorism" to enforce conformity, and demanded rights in regard to committee assignments based on eight years seniority in the Senate. The Senate had ample opportunity to become familiar with the argument supporting his case; Morse repeated it frequently in 1953 from January until the end of May in his reports of the "committee of the whole of the Independent party" on Friday afternoons. Morse's argument rested upon the Constitution of the United States and the formal and informal rules of the Senate. Article V of the Constitution states, among other things, that "no State, without its consent, shall be deprived of its equal suffrage in

[7] *Ibid.,* p. 3053 (April 14, 1953); p. 5224 (May 20, 1953); pp. 5421–44 (May 25, 1953). The vote is at p. 5444. See also Sen. Repts. No. 142 and No. 304, 83rd Cong., 1st Sess.

[8] Deaths in the Senate had changed the party ratio to 48–47–1 in favor of the Democrats, but the votes of Morse and the Vice President kept the Republicans in organizational control. The resolution was S. Res. 180, sponsored by the leadership of both parties and reported favorably by the Rules Committee. It provided for the enlargement of two committees (Post Office and Civil Service, and Public Works) from 11 to 13 members. It also established a sliding-scale ratio of majority members who were to be allowed assignment to three (instead of two) committee seats, to minority members accorded the same privilege, a move designed to preserve a one-member margin for the majority party on each committee. The Morse amendment, introduced by Anderson, was sponsored by 12 Democrats and Langer. *Congressional Record,* Vol. 100, pp. 97, 120–21 (January 11, 1954); pp. 218–28 (January 13, 1954). The vote is at p. 228.

the Senate." To Morse, this meant that "to deny any fraction of the normal rights of a Senator, not in his own capacity but as a representative of a State, is to compromise . . . [that] basic guaranty." And what are the "normal rights of a Senator"?—under the Legislative Reorganization Act, to seats on two standing committees, and under a long-standing rule of the Senate, to be appointed to them by ballot by the Senate itself. Furthermore, not just any two committees would do; as Haynes put it: "Once placed upon a congenial committee, a Senator is likely to retain that assignment as long as he remains in the Senate, or until he requests to be excused from further service thereon."[9] Not since 1871, said Morse, had the Senate departed from this practice. If the Senate were in fact a continuing body (and Morse agreed with the majority that it was) its committees likewise had an unbroken life; the parent body need only fill vacancies and assign new members. It was true that Republicans who bolted the presidential candidate in 1924 had lost intra-committee *rank* in the next session of Congress, but Morse was not concerned about that. He believed that committee rank properly should be determined by party seniority, and as the freshman Independent he was prepared to go to the bottom of the list. But committee *assignments,* he argued, depended upon seniority in the Senate, and his colleagues could not deny him his rightful place on his old committees without placing in jeopardy their own rights under the seniority system. Morse therefore declined to request appointment by the conference of either party, insisting that the whole Senate should elect him to committees in accordance with his rights as a Senator.

The Republican leadership denied any wish to discipline Morse. What they wanted was to control the Senate. As Taft pointed out, the Republican margin was paper-thin; with Morse an Independent the Senate division stood at 48–47–1. There were fifteen standing committees. The Legislative Reorganization Act allowed 11 majority members and no minority members to serve on three committees. The Republicans had sought to amend the rule to allow 18 majority and 3 minority members to hold three seats each. The Democrats had scaled down the ratio to 14–3, leaving the majority's margin the same as before. Thus the Republicans could control only 13 committees; Morse and the Democrats would control the other two. The majority

---

[9] Quoted from George H. Haynes, *The Senate of the United States,* 2 vols. (Boston, 1938), Vol. 1, p. 294.

therefore had chosen to lose control of the two least important committees. Case explained that the Republicans had taken Morse at his word and had not assigned Republican seats to him; they had filled Republican requests for committee assignments until only two were left, on Public Works and District of Columbia (Morse contemptuously dismissed this as the "garbage can disposal principle" in committee assignments). If the Democrats had consented to the 15 member margin, it was implied, Morse could have had his old seats.

Lyndon Johnson, the minority leader, thought that Morse was not the responsibility of the minority. In the division of committee assignments between the parties, the Republicans had been given two seats each for 49 members, including Morse. Johnson had expressed the hope that Morse could retain the seats he wanted, but he would not interfere with the majority's assignments. He made clear his intention to vote for the Republican and the Democratic nominees; to break the party lists would invite the majority to meddle with the minority and elect all the committees.

Johnson's determination to respect the other party's committee list was reciprocated by the Republicans. When the resolution adding Morse and a Republican to two committees was debated in May, Johnson opposed it, saying that he was "willing to share the junior Senator from Oregon 50–50 with the majority party, but I am not willing to have the Senator say it will add 4 seats to 2 committees and completely disregard the 47 members who make up the minority party." Knowland, acting for the majority leader, agreed that the minority did not have to accept a change in ratio disadvantageous to them, and the Republicans voted almost solidly against the resolution.

The rebuttal of Morse's arguments was shared by both sides. It was contended that no more was guaranteed the States by the equal suffrage provision in the Constitution than that each should have two Senators. Morse's distinction between the Senate and the majority conference was deemed to be formal only; actually a majority had the right to appoint all committees, and in practice this meant the majority party. Members tended to follow the party leadership simply because that was a practicable way to organize the Senate. The Legislative Reorganization Act, they said, really was designed to reduce the committee load of the Senators, not to guarantee anything new to them. As for that, Morse could have had two committee seats in January, and by election of the Senate, if he had not asked for a postponement. His opponents would agree that he had a right to two seats; what they denied was that he had a right to say which two. There was no mention of seniority in the Constitution nor in the Legislative Reorganization Act; consideration of seniority was a convention of the Senate. Moreover, as Senator George (himself the ranking member of the Senate in seniority) put it, "prior seniority is purely a political matter . . . essentially a matter of party determination, regulation and control." It was party seniority therefore which determined not only rank on committees, but assignment to committees as well.

II. THE APPEAL TO PRECEDENT

The one respect in which little effort was made to rebut Morse on the floor was in his oft-repeated contention that removing him from committees against his will violated the precedents of the Senate. This is curious behavior on the part of a body which ascribes so much importance to precedents. It is useful to an institutionalized group like the Senate to preserve at least the illusion of consistent behavior; it is impressive to the layman, and it makes possible the settling of many problems through appeal to the authority of usage. Precedents that are generally followed are useful to the student of senatorial behavior: they help to identify the working rules of the group, and behavior which violates them is worth investigation.

According to Morse, only one Senator had ever been removed from a committee without regard to his seniority. That was Sumner, chairman of the Foreign Relations Committee, who lost his seat in 1871 because of his opposition to Grant's determination to occupy Santo Domingo. In the only modern instance of such party discipline, the Republicans placed Ladd (who had been chairman of Public Lands), Brookhart, and Frazier at the bottom of their committees in 1925, to punish them for campaigning for LaFollette. But they were not removed from their committees, Morse asserted; that was the point he wanted to make. And against this example of discipline he could and did cite numerous instances when bolting went unpunished. Moreover, when two Farmer-Laborites were elected from Minnesota in 1923 several committees had been enlarged to avoid reducing the ratios of the major parties, as Morse now suggested be done in his case. Thus it seemed to him that the action against him followed an isolated and unhappy precedent, and ignored established practices of the Senate.

We shall not be concerned with the 19th century here. But 1925 is another matter; one member of the Senate today was sitting then, and the party strife which the Republicans sought by Draconian measures to end is by no means ancient history. First we shall look briefly at what happened in 1925; then we shall seek out the party bolters in subsequent presidential campaigns to see what happened to their committee positions. It must be recognized, of course, that there are many degrees of party defection and numerous ingenious modes of effecting it. Morse himself distinguished betwen "bolting" —campaigning for the other party's candidate, which he thought properly should be preceded by resignation from one's old party— and "taking a walk," a matter of campaigning for neither but voting for the opposition's candidate, which he thought does not call for resignation. There are other ways, of course. The politician may "go fishing" (not vote), vote but remain noncommital, avow party loyalty while studiously ignoring the candidate, damn with faint praise, or stage a "sitdown" (announce for the candidate but not help him). The infinite variations on this single theme are worth a study of their own, but we shall be concerned here only with outright bolting— the overt act which cannot be recalled nor misunderstood.

The objects of party discipline in 1925 were bolters. George W. Norris and Hiram Johnson left little doubt that they were for LaFollette, but they did not openly support him; in the formal sense, they remained within the party fold. Ladd, Brookhart, and Frazier, on the other hand, were bolters, whose break with their party's candidate was overt.[10] The Republican conference voted therefore not to invite the three rebels nor LaFollette to the party conference, nor to place them on committees to fill Republican vacancies. Moreover, each of the four was placed at the bottom of the committees on which he served, below the lowest-ranking Democrat. In a word, the Republican conference treated them like independents. But these bolters, unlike Morse, were not willing to consider themselves independents. Brookhart stated flatly: ". . . I did not leave the Republican party.

[10] Kenneth C. MacKay, *The Progressive Movement of 1924* (New York, 1947), p. 195; Alfred Lief, *Democracy's Norris: The Biography of a Lonely Crusade* (New York, 1939), pp. 268–70; George W. Norris, *Fighting Liberal* (New York, 1945), pp. 286–87.

I am a better Republican than is the Senator from Indiana [Watson, chairman of the Committee on Committees] today." They were stoutly supported by Norris and Borah, who raised the old, troubling question: what is a Republican? The Democrats did not know, but they thought it was a problem for the Republicans. Pat Harrison requested and received permission for Senators to vote "present" ("I do not want to enter into the family row over there . . .") on the motion to return Ladd to his chairmanship, and 26 Senators did so vote. Ladd was replaced by Stanfield, a "regular" Republican from Oregon;[11] LaFollette was dropped from the chairmanship of the Interstate Commerce Committee and Watson took his place. But the action of the Committee on Committees went further than demoting the bolters. In a move that today would scarcely seem like chastisement, but obviously ran counter to his preference, Frazier was transferred from Indian Affairs, whose business he understood, to Banking and Currency, whose business he did not. The reason given was forthright. With LaFollette also on the committee, the progressives and the Democrats together would control it; and since LaFollette ranked him, Frazier had to go. The Democrats had been unwilling to increase the committee size to let them both stay. So Morse was mistaken: the action of 1925 provided a precedent for just what was done to him in 1953. But what of the intervening years?

III. OTHERS WHO BOLTED

No presidential campaign in this period has lacked bolters. The disciplinary action of 1925 did not prevent bolting even in 1928. Trouble for the Republicans came once more from midwestern progressives. Norris left his irksome position on the sidelines and actively supported Smith, as did John J. Blaine of Wisconsin.[12] Both sides wooed Robert LaFollette, Jr., his Democratic opponent obligingly dropping out of the senatorial race and Curtis, Hoover's running mate, speaking

[11] The debate is found in Congressional Record, Vol. 67, pp. 15–16, 41–67 (March 9, 1925). The vote is at p. 63. Harrison missed a nice point: if the Republican conference was correct, the bolters were not Republicans and the question of their chairmanships and committee assignments was not a "family row" but the business of the Senate—as Morse made it in 1953 by staying out of the party and away from the conference.

[12] The New York Times, October 25, 1928, p. 1, col. 7 (Norris); October 16, 1928, p. 15, col. 1; and October 21, 1928, p. 21, col. 3 (Blaine).

out for LaFollette in Wisconsin. But LaFollette contented himself with denouncing the Republican platform as "reactionary," praising some of Smith's views, and calling for the election of progressives to Congress.[13] The Democratic rebels were both southerners, but there the resemblance ended. Tom Heflin of Alabama was always a problem to the party, and his campaign against Smith was characteristic of him; he abused Catholics and attacked Tammany Hall in meetings patrolled by his "rangers" (klansmen).[14] Simmons of North Carolina, who called his party's campaign "two-faced and hypocritical," was the senior Democrat on the Finance Committee and had been a regular party leader in his state for a quarter of a century. His single act of rebellion was provoked by Smith's opposition to Prohibition.[15]

The Democratic ranks held in 1932, but not so the Republican. Hiram Johnson declared he would not "taint" his record by supporting Hoover, and campaigned for Roosevelt in California.[16] LaFollette still thought progressive congressmen were the country's best hope, but supported the Democratic candidate because Hoover was "wrong on every issue" and had "a 100% reactionary record."[17] Norris's response to Roosevelt was more positive. Declaring that "what this country needs is another Roosevelt in the White House," he served as chairman of a non-partisan National Progressive League for Roosevelt and stumped for him around the country.[18] Bronson Cutting, a progressive Republican from New Mexico, acknowledged his mistake in ever supporting Hoover and called for universal support for the President's opponent.[19]

By 1936 LaFollette, like Norris, was for Roosevelt as well as against his opponent. In addition to speaking for Roosevelt, LaFollette helped arrange the withdrawal of Minnesota Democratic nominees for governor, senator, and one congressional seat, in favor of the Farmer-

---

[13] *Ibid.*, October 9, 1928, p. 2, col. 3; October 10, 1928, p. 2, col. 4; July 8, 1928, p. 2. col. 5; October 27, 1928, p. 9, col. 1.

[14] *Ibid.*, July 5, 1928, p. 21, col. 4; July 3, 1928, p. 6, col. 2.

[15] *Ibid.*, October 13, 1928, p. 5, col. 3; October 22, 1928, p. 1, col. 4; October 26, 1928, p. 2, col. 2.

[16] *Ibid.*, October 15, 1932, p. 9, col. 1; October 29, 1932, p. 1, col. 7.

[17] *Ibid.*, October 20, 1932, p. 15, col. 2.

[18] *Ibid.*, September 26, 1932, p. 1, col. 7; September 29, 1932, p. 1, col. 6.

[19] *Ibid.*, October 27, 1932, p. 12, col. 5.

Labor candidates, thus effecting a coalition of the two parties.[20] Subsequently, Henrik Shipstead (Farmer-Labor senator from Minnesota) announced for Roosevelt, the first presidential candidate he had supported in twelve years.[21] Norris made a clean break with his party, not only campaigning for the New Deal incumbent in the White House, but also winning his Senate seat as an Independent over nominees of both major parties.[22] Gerald P. Nye said he would stay out of the presidential campaign as a courtesy to Lemke, the North Dakota congressman running as a minor party nominee, but Nye did make two speeches for Norris.[23] The other North Dakota senator, Frazier (who had been disciplined for bolting in 1924), supported Lemke.[24] Two other Republican senators, Couzens of Michigan and Norbeck of South Dakota, bolted their party's nominee, but both were dead before the next Congress convened. No Democratic senator openly left the party fold. Even Rush Holt of West Virginia, who keynoted the first convention of Father Coughlin's National Union for Social Justice, and who also had lunch with Landon, in the end was silent as to whom he would support.[25]

Despite the third term issue in 1940, outright bolting was rare. Burke of Nebraska endorsed Willkie and later joined the Republican party, while Holt sponsored an anti-third term resolution in the Senate; but both had lost in the Democratic primaries in their states. On the other hand, Norris and LaFollette continued their championship of Roosevelt. The Wisconsin senator, in the face of a fight for reelection, announced his position on the eve of the platform conventions of his state's three parties.[26] Norris again headed a nonpartisan group for Roosevelt and campaigned actively for him in Nebraska and the West.[27]

Each party suffered the defection of one senator in 1944. Joseph

20 *Ibid.,* September 29, 1936, p. 23, col. 3; October 4, 1936, p. 1, col. 6.

21 *Ibid.,* October 19, 1936, p. 2, col. 4.

22 *Ibid.,* September 18, 1936, p. 9, col. 1.

23 *Ibid.,* October 2, 1936, p. 9, col. 6.

24 *Ibid.,* October 4, 1936, p. 1, col. 6.

25 *Ibid.,* August 11, 1936, p. 8, col. 2; August 15, 1936, p. 1, col. 4; September 17, 1936, p. 9, col. 1.

26 *Ibid.,* October 1, 1940, p. 15, cols. 7–8.

27 *Ibid.,* October 21, 1940, p. 8, col. 5.

Ball of Minnesota, after hearing Roosevelt's speech to the Foreign Policy Association, announced that he would support the President for a fourth term.[28] The Democratic bolter was O'Daniel of Texas, who was a frequent supporter of Republican policy in the Senate.[29]

What is striking about the election of 1948, in which Truman won despite rebellion from both wings of the Democratic party, is the lack of widespread overt disloyalty in the Senate. Glenn Taylor of Idaho was Wallace's running mate, and at least two southerners—Ellender of Louisiana and Eastland of Mississippi—seemed to have campaigned for the States' Rights ticket;[30] but what confronted Truman in the South apparently was the kind of hostility of which senators are masters, which makes itself plain without committing the irrevocable act.

Party defection in 1952 came in a variety of shades. Morse's was the most complete, ending, as it did, in resignation from his party. Price Daniel of Texas was as forthright in supporting the opposition's candidate, but felt no compulsion, apparently, to leave the Democratic party.[31] Two other Democrats performed equivocal but effective maneuvers within their own states. Harry Byrd, without endorsing the Republican slate, announced that he would not endorse Stevenson, in a speech which doubtless was understood in Virginia.[32] Pat McCarran exchanged mutually uncomplimentary remarks with Stevenson without bothering to oppose him, but in Nevada his organization supported the Republican Malone for reelection to the Senate against the young Democrat who had dared to beat McCarran's man in the primary.[33]

IV. WHAT HAPPENED TO THE BOLTERS

In the record of the twenty year period from 1929 through 1949, which covers assignments to committees of the 71st through the 81st

---

[28] *Ibid.*, October 23, 1944, p. 1, col. 1; October 24, 1944, p. 15, col. 1.

[29] *Ibid.*, October 22, 1944, p. 38, col. 3; November 3, 1944, p. 18, col. 8.

[30] *Ibid.*, November 19, 1948, p. 21, col. 1; November 25, 1948, p. 30, col. 5.

[31] *Ibid.*, October 16, 1952, p. 14, col. 3.

[32] *Ibid.*, October 18, 1952, p. 1, col. 5.

[33] *Ibid.*, October 25, 1952, p. 11, col. 4; October 28, 1952, p. 1, col. 8; October 29, 1952, p. 33, col. 5.

Congresses, there is nothing that remotely resembles punishment of senatorial bolters through loss of seats or rank on committees.

Bolters were treated like other senators when their parties— whether in the majority or not—assigned them to committees. Norris retained his chairmanship of the Judiciary Committee in the 71st and 72nd Congresses, after supporting Smith in 1928. Heflin and Simmons kept their places after opposing him. Bronson Cutting was dropped from the Foreign Relations Committee in 1933, but that was because the Republican quota was reduced from 13 to 8. All those who retained their seats ranked Cutting. Bolters seem to have received normal promotions to better committees. For instance, Robert LaFollette, Jr., went from Post Office and Post Roads to Foreign Relations in 1929. Bolters were regularly advanced in rank on their committees. Not even leaving the party (as Morse did in 1952) hurt them. The 77th Congress in 1941 furnishes an example with two rebels, Norris the Independent and LaFollette the Progressive, listed as the ranking minority members of every committee that either of them served on except one (LaFollette on Foreign Relations). Between them they held the ranking minority position on 7 of the Senate's 33 committees.

Except in the case of Morse, the committee assignments in the 83rd Congress reveal no hint of punitive intent. Daniel of Texas was appointed to the Interior Committee, a choice spot for a solon from an oil-producing state. It need hardly be added that no inconvenience was suffered by Byrd or McCarran.

The contemporary record seems clearly to support the proposition that the Senate norm is that a senator who bolts his party's presidential nominee shall not be punished by loss of what is perhaps his most important senatorial perquisite, his regular place in the committee structure. Any departure from that norm must be regarded as unusual behavior of genuine significance. Why were party bolters punished in 1925 and 1953, and not in the years between?

V. WHY SOME BOLTERS ARE PUNISHED

Some of the variables which might be supposed to have affected the behavior of the Senate appear to have had no influence. Among them are:

(1) *Degree of defection.* Brookhart was demoted on all his committees for little more than criticizing the Republican vice-

presidential candidate, an action that usually is overlooked. Morse campaigned actively for the opposing party's candidate, but so did several bolters who were not punished. Robert La-Follette, Sr., took the field himself against his party's candidate and was punished; his running-mate on the Progressive ticket, Senator Wheeler, was not.

(2) *Degree of estrangement* (formality, conclusiveness of break). The 1924 rebels stayed in the party and were disciplined; Norris and the young LaFollette, like Morse, left the party but were not penalized.

(3) *Frequency of defections.* The 1924 bolters were old trouble-makers, but so were Norris, young LaFollette, and Heflin. Morse, on the other hand, left the party fold only once.

(4) *Strength and importance of the bolters.* The four senators who were disciplined in 1925 represented a stubborn and not in-consequential wing of the party, with a long tradition. Morse did not. Among the senators not disciplined, Norris and the junior LaFollette were formidable individuals. Ball and O'Daniel, to mention only two, were not.

The variable which does prove out is the *ideological division* of the committee to which the bolter belonged. Thus where such a com-mittee is not divided along lines of interest group ideology, or where it is divided but the majority group has a workable margin, it is not necessary to penalize an insurgent member. On the other hand, where the dissident element holds the balance of power, the defec-tion furnishes a pretext for securing effective control of the committee for the majority.

That is what happened in 1925. The Republican party was split between east and west; the east had the White House but the west had the seniority in Congress. With the party ratio in the Senate 55–40–1 the Republican margin looked better than it was. Five Re-publicans (LaFollette, Brookhart, Ladd, Frazier, and Norris) and the Farmer-Labor member (Shipstead) would vote with the progressive Democrats and at least five other Republicans (Borah, Johnson, Mc-Masters, Howell, and Schall) were generally undependable.[34] A year

[34] "Purging the Republican Ranks," *Literary Digest,* Vol. 84, pp. 7–8 (March 21, 1925). See also George Creel, "What Do These Senators Want?", *Collier's,* Vol. 71, pp. 9–10 (March 10, 1923), and "Non-existent Republican Majority," *Outlook,* Vol. 142, p. 350 (March 10, 1926).

earlier a coalition of Democrats and insurgent Republicans had made Smith, a Democrat from South Carolina, the chairman of the Interstate Commerce Committee. In this political climate, the Republican leaders in the Senate were determined not to lose control of any committee, however unimportant, if they could help it. The bolt of 1924 gave the leadership an opportunity to gain ground. LaFollette and Ladd were relieved of their chairmanships of otherwise manageable committees. Frazier was shifted from Indian Affairs, where he and LaFollette could team up with progressive Democrats to control it, to Banking and Currency, where his vote was not needed. The party leaders' strategy was explained bluntly by Reed of Pennsylvania, who said that an effort had been made to effect a similar change on Manufactures (which he thought had "gone to the devil" the last two years) where LaFollette and Brookhart held the balance, but it had failed.[35] The bolters were allowed to keep their other committee assignments, with loss of rank, because they did not endanger conservative Republican control of those committees.

In 1953, one of Morse's assignments as a Republican presented no problem of control. Though not free from group conflict, the Armed Services Committee was not divided into two camps either by partisanship or by interest group ideology. Control of the committee did not turn on any one member's vote. This was freely admitted in the debate. Morse pointed out that the Armed Services watchdog subcommittee chaired by Lyndon Johnson (successor to the Truman-Mead subcommittee) had submitted 41 reports, all of them unanimous.[36] There was a rumor at one stage that Morse would be reassigned to the Armed Services Committee, but not to the Labor and Public Welfare Committee; but Morse, by declining the invitation to the Republican conference and announcing that he would seek his seats from the Senate, made it easy to drop him from both committees without precipitating a fight along lines of interest group ideology or raising an intra-party punishment issue. The question put was the "rights" of a senator *qua* senator.

The Labor and Public Welfare Committee presented a quite different case. At the beginning of the 84th Congress it was the most sharply divided committee, along both party and interest group lines, in the Senate. The split extended even to the professional staff, who

[35] *Congressional Record,* Vol. 67, p. 67, (March 9, 1925).
[36] *Ibid.,* Vol. 99, pp. 342–43 (January 13, 1953).

did not work for the whole committee but were divided between the majority and the minority.[37]

The character of the Committee split could be demonstrated by ranging all Senators at the beginning of the 83rd Congress along a "liberal-conservative" continuum to find where the Committee members would fall. For the purposes of this study that was done by preparing a table which ranked members of the Senate according to the percentage of times each cast a "liberal" (or "progressive") vote over a six-year period on a series of issues selected by *The CIO News*. Eighty senators were ranked; the other sixteen were new and so had no voting record for this period. Similar computations were made for votes selected by two other organs of "liberal" opinion, the AFL Labor's League for Political Education, and *The New Republic*. Correlations with the percentages based on the votes selected by *The CIO News* were so high, however, that only the latter were used in the table. In addition to correlating closely with the other two, the selection made by *THE CIO News* covers more roll-call votes spread more evenly over the six years.[38] A senator who voted "liberal" at least half the time on the issues so chosen will be referred to here as "liberal." It is not argued that a ranking of senators according to this criterion measures the "liberalism" of senators in a philosophical sense. What *is* assumed is that it gives a fair approximation of the relative acceptability of senators to the urban-labor interests who were loyal to the New Deal-Fair Deal and who would be extremely concerned about the work of the Labor and Public Welfare Committee. Presently, data from the table will be used to mark the people who eventually supported Morse in his fight to regain his committee seats, and to raise the question why they did not vote for him at first. At this point it may be used to show the split on the Labor and Public Welfare Committee.

[37] George B. Galloway, *Congressional Reorganization Revisited* (College Park, Md., 1956), p. 6. Morse, Douglas, and Humphrey, in arguing for Morse's resolution in May, all admitted there was a "philosophical division" on the committee, which would not be affected if a conservative Republican were added along with Morse.

[38] Sixty-nine votes selected by *The CIO News* are found in the issues of August 11, 1947; July 19, 1948; January 2, 1950; August 14, 1950; December 17, 1951; and August 18, 1952. Duplications were eliminated. Thirty votes selected by Labor's League for Political Education may be found in their booklet, *Voting Records of Senators and Representatives, 1947 Through 1952*. Sixty votes selected by *The New Republic* are shown in the issues of September 27, 1948, pp. 28–30; November 14, 1949, pp. 24–25; October 9, 1950, pp. 14–15; and September 22, 1952, pp. 16–17.

As the 83rd Congress convened, the four Republican holdover members on the 13-member committee ranged from the moderate liberalism of Tobey and Ives through the moderate conservatism of Smith (of New Jersey) to the strong conservatism of Taft. The five Democrats (Lehman, Douglas, Neely, Murray, and Hill), on the other hand, were all of a piece; they could be counted on to support the "liberal" side 90 per cent or more of the time. And the new Democratic appointee, John Kennedy, was their kind; in his six-year tenure as a member of the House of Representatives, Kennedy's voting record was substantially like theirs.[39] The new Republican appointees (Goldwater, Purtell, and Griswold) could be counted on to strengthen the conservatives, but two of them would not be enough. With the Democrats voting as a bloc, the best they could get was a tie. Morse, with his voting record like the Democrats', would decide the outcome. When it is remembered that the Republicans in 1953 controlled both White House and Congress for the first time in twenty years, and that both parties had promised to revise the Taft-Hartley Act, it is clear why the Republicans were reluctant to allow Morse to occupy the "swing position" that Ives accused him of wanting.[40] As it turned out, the partisan division on the committee, even with a dependable Republican margin of one vote, was so sharp that the committee accomplished little in the 83rd Congress.

VI. THE CONFLICT OF LOYALTIES

Morse's support, first and last, came from the liberal Democrats. The CIO selection of roll calls shows 33 senators who cast "liberal" votes at least half the time. Twenty-seven of these were Democrats, one

[39] In a similar selection of votes in the House of Representatives, Kennedy voted "right" 93 per cent of the time on 30 votes in *The CIO News*, and 100 per cent "right" on 20 votes in the AFL's tabulation and 12 votes in *The New Republic*.

[40] *Congressional Record*, Vol. 99, pp. 343–44 (January 13, 1953). A note of caution, however, should be added. The Committee on Rules and Administration recommended in January of 1953 (S. Res. 1) that nine committees, including Labor and Public Welfare, be increased by two members, and six others be reduced by two; as amended and passed (S. Res. 18), Labor and Public Welfare remained the same size. (*Congressional Record*, Vol. 99, p. 233, 279–81, January 7 and 9, 1953). In May 1954 two lesser committees were increased by two members each (see n. 8, above), but the motion to enlarge Labor and Public Welfare again was defeated. Failure to increase the committee's size, which would have strengthened Morse's claim to a seat, strongly supports the argument that there was indeed an element of punishment in the majority's attitude.

(Morse) an Independent, and two (Langer and Tobey) relatively independent Republicans. Three (Aiken, Ives, Smith) were more regular Republicans—and none of them ever voted for Morse. In January of 1953 Morse got his own vote, five liberal Democrats, and Tobey. In May he was supported by 19 of the 27 liberal Democrats. Among the eight who did not support him were Lyndon Johnson, the leader; Clements, the whip; Kerr and Hennings, members of the Policy Committee; and Smathers, close to the leadership group though not formally a member of it. Others who supported him were Tobey, Langer (paired for), and Cordon, his Oregon colleague. A year later he added the votes of Hennings, in the leadership group, and two other liberal Democrats, plus a handful of others not easily explained.[41]

It is evident that the Republicans generally, and the conservative Democrats, suffered no very strong cross-pressures in casting their votes. It was the liberal Democrats who were torn between the line adopted by the party leaders and their loyalty to a friend and ally. This may be inferred from their voting behavior, and it is supported by persons who shared their experience. This was especially true in the case of a group of about a score of them who met regularly in a biweekly informal meeting (their administrative assistants meeting on alternate weeks) for program planning. They were Morse's friends, and they received support from the same kinds of groups that helped him. It was because Morse shared their convictions that he left the Republican party. It was their aid that Morse could and did expect. It was they who failed him the first time, in Morse's view, but who eventually rallied to him handsomely. What explains this contradictory behavior?

It is not the last two votes that need explaining, but the first; there is no reason to believe that Morse's friends were not sympathetic with him in January, as they were later. But Morse could hardly have posed the issue that first time in a less palatable way—a way which was only partially of his own choosing. He did not himself know very early what the Republicans planned to do about his committee assignments. Then after announcing that he would seek appointment directly from

---

[41] Jackson (D. Wash.) also voted for Morse in May 1953 and January 1954; he was a freshman senator. A similar selection of votes cast in the House of Representatives showed that in his six years in the House Jackson's percentage on a total of 61 votes selected by The CIO News was 92, on a total of 26 votes selected by the AFL's LLPE was 100, and on a total of 59 selected by The New Republc was 97.

the Senate, Morse stood aloof from his friends, neither asking nor receiving their counsel or support. Through a tactical error Morse failed to give the Senate the customary notice at least one day in advance of his resolution to increase the size of two committees to include himself and an additional Republican, so that the resolution had to go to committee. As a consequence he had to nominate himself, request a written ballot (a maneuver that took his friends by surprise), and ask that his supporters strike from the ballot a party-nominated member, Republican or Democrat.

This is what most of Morse's friends declined to do—to interfere with the committee selections of the other party. The position of the Democratic party leadership never changed; it opposed Morse every time. Nevertheless three members of the Policy Committee voted for Morse the second time, despite a Policy Committee decision to make it a party issue, and four the third. But to vote for him in January 1953 involved more than going counter to the leadership of their party.[42] It would also violate a *Senate* norm of long standing and general acceptance. The principle had been stated by Henry Cabot Lodge in 1919 when the Democrats had tried to reduce the Republican margin on four committees. Said Lodge: "We feel that the makeup of your committees is your business and your responsibility, and that the makeup of our committees is our business and our responsibility. That is the ordinary rule of courtesy and good manners which I have never before seen violated in the Senate."[43] The Democrats accepted his statement of the rule and voted for his list intact. This was the rule which prevented the majority party from making all the committee selections, as it had the power to do; and this rule proved stronger than the ties of friendship and interest group ideology which bound liberal Democrats to Morse in 1953.

Heavy pressures bore upon the liberal Democrats between January and May of 1953, and not the least of them from Morse himself. It

[42] The authority of the leadership in January 1953 was strengthened by two other actions in regard to committees. First, Lyndon Johnson went against ancient usage in the Senate by insisting that each freshman Democratic senator be given one good committee place. It is significant that Jackson was the only freshman Democrat ever to vote for Morse and that he did not do so the first time. Second, the enlargement of the more important committees made possible some attractive transfers. Eight Democrats who did not vote for Morse in January 1953 but ultimately did so, were beneficiaries of transfers to better committees.

[43] Quoted in Haynes, *op. cit.*, Vol. 1, p. 290.

is hard to convey a sense of the bitterness with which Morse attacked the liberal Democrats and their party leader.[44] His heavy defeat had placed him in an untenable position; "even the liberal Democrats have deserted him" taunted the Oregon newspapers, and Morse's harsh cry of pain filled the chamber. His position improved in the spring of 1953; labor rallied to his support, and his filibuster against the Tidelands bill won prestige for him with many liberal groups. Yet no better reason for the behavior of his friends comes to mind than the one they insistently gave themselves: a vote for Morse in January 1953 required that a committee member chosen by the opposing party be struck; four months and again a year later, it did not.

VII. CONCLUSIONS

From this study some tentative conclusions regarding norms for behavior in the Senate may be suggested as hypotheses for further testing:

(1) Bolting the party ticket in a presidential election is not usually punished in the Senate by loss of rank or membership on committees. Senators who bolt are most likely to be deprived of committee rank or membership when the deprivations will affect a close ideological division on one or more committees in a way that is favorable to the majority. Paradoxically, discipline is most likely to be applied when it is least likely to be effective—i.e., when a close division of power gives the disciplined member maximum leverage. Thus the two examples of punishment did not seriously hurt the victims. The bolters disciplined in 1925 regained their committee rank in the next Congress. Wayne Morse received better committee assignments from the Democrats in 1955, just before he joined their party, than he had lost two years earlier. Discipline has not seriously inhibited bolting; the 1924 bolters repeated their offense and there have been party defections in every presidential election since 1924.

(2) The response of senators under cross-pressures of claims of friendship or ideological allegiance, on the one hand, and loyalty to the party leadership on the other, will depend on the structuring of the situation:

[44] See, e.g., the colloquy on March 6, 1953, *Congressional Record,* Vol. 99, pp. 1679–86. Morse said he had refused the apologies of the liberal Democrats and he threatened to campaign against them in 1954.

(a) The requirements of party regularity are generally binding on questions pertaining to the organization of the Senate, which include the working arrangement that each party will accept without question the committee list of the other. This norm is generally stronger than the claims of friendship or ideological allegiance. Senators who supported the proposal to add Morse and a Republican to two committees apparently believed they had not violated this norm when their vote would not deprive any senator of his regular committee assignment nor the majority party of its control of a committee, even though their vote was opposed by their party leaders.

(b) Unless other interests can be exploited to reenforce an appeal to party loyalty, it will probably prove weaker than strongly pressed claims of friendship or ideological allegiance. This may be true even with members of formal party leadership groups. The apparent weakness of the appeal to party loyalty may be deceptive, however; when the outcome is not in doubt it may not be strongly pressed.

THREE
DEMOCRATIC PARTY LEADERSHIP
IN THE SENATE

PARTY leadership in Congress has been one focal point for the sustained attack on the structure and performance of the American party system that has gone on for a decade and a half. Academic critics and members of Congress, individually and in committees, supplemented by a wide array of interested citizens and groups, have laid out blueprints for institutional reorganization. While there is some variety in their prescriptions, it is not hard to construct a composite model of

The author is grateful to the Fund for the Advancement of Education for a Faculty Fellowship in 1953–54, which made possible the beginning of this study, and to then Senator Lyndon B. Johnson for the privilege of serving for part of that time as a member of his staff. Among the many people whose assistance is greatly appreciated are Senators Scott W. Lucas and Ernest W. McFarland, former Democratic Leaders; George B. Galloway, Legislative Reference Service, Library of Congress; Pauline R. Moore, Chief Clerk, and Gerald M. Siegel and Roland Bibolet, formerly professional staff members, of the Democratic Policy Committee; Felton M. Johnston, Secretary of the Senate; Robert G. Baker, Secretary for the Majority; and Emery L. Frazier, Chief Clerk of the Senate. I am especially indebted to George E. Reedy, Jr., formerly Staff Director, Democratic Policy Committee and now a special assistant to the Vice President, whose friendship and counsel have been literally invaluable. No responsibility for any statement of fact or opinion in this paper should attach to the Fund for Advancement of Education or any of the individuals named here.

This is a revised version of a paper read at the Annual Meeting of the American Political Science Association at New York City on September 9, 1960. The article originally appeared in *The American Political Science Review*, LV (June 1961), 331–344.

party leadership in legislation on which there has been a fairly wide consensus among the reformers.[1]

The fount of party policy would be a reformed national convention, meeting biennially at the least. The obligation of the majority party in Congress, spurred by the President if he were of the same party, would be to carry out the platform put together by the convention. For this purpose frequent party conferences would be held in each house to consider specific measures. Some would be for the purpose of discussion and education, but on important party measures the members could be bound by a conference vote and penalized in committee assignments and other party perquisites for disregarding the will of the conference. Party strategy, legislative scheduling, and continuous leadership would be entrusted to a policy committee made up, in most schemes, of the elective officers of the house and the chairmen of the standing committees. Some have suggested a joint policy committee, made up of the policy committees of the respective houses, which might then meet with the President as a kind of legislative cabinet. The committee chairmen would not be exclusively, and perhaps not at all, the products of seniority. Power to override or disregard seniority, regularly or in exceptional cases, has been suggested for the conference, the policy committee, or the principal elective officer of each house. Individual chairmen would be expected to push the program of the conference and policy committee through their respective committees, that being the principal justification for their membership on the policy committee.

The same kind of organization would obtain in the minority party, though of course it would not bear the same responsibility for legislative program and scheduling.

---

[1] Some representative selections from the voluminous literature are: *Organization of Congress*, Hearings, Joint Committee on the Organization of Congress, 79th Cong., 1st sess., pursuant to H. Con. Res. 18 (1945), pp. 28, 77–8, 334, 801, 805, 822–23, 846, 851, 872, 931; *Legislative Reorganization Act of 1946*, Hearings, Senate Committee on Expenditures in the Executive Departments, 80th Cong., 2d sess. (1948), pp. 38–9, 66, 118–19, 210–11; *Organization and Operation of Congress, ibid.*, 82d Cong., 1st sess. (1951), pp. 276–78, 287–90, 460; Committee on Congress, American Pol. Sci. Assn., *The Reorganization of Congress* (Wash., D.C., 1945), pp. 53–54; *Toward a More Responsible Two-Party System*, Report of the Committee on Political Parties, Amer. Pol. Sci. Assn., 1950, pp. 50–65; R. Heller, *Strengthening the Congress* (Wash., D.C., 1945), pp. 6–9; George B. Galloway, *Congress at the Crossroads* (New York, 1946), esp. ch. 4; Estes Kefauver and Jack Levin, *A Twentieth Century Congress* (New York, 1947), pp. 96–142.

Despite the frequency with which this model (with some variations) has been sponsored by informed and respected persons, precious little of it has made any headway in Congress. Policy committees have been created, it is true, first by both parties in the Senate and later by the Republicans in the House of Representatives. But they are not composed of committee chairmen nor do they perform the functions hopefully suggested for them. Beyond that Congress has not gone. The reason can not be simply congressional hostility to change; other reforms proposed at the same time (notably professional staffs for committees and individual senators, and a reduction in number and simplification of jurisdiction of committees) have been successfully carried out.[2]

A basic premise of this paper is that the reformers' model has failed to attract support in Congress because it does too much violence to the political context in which members operate—that is, to the relationships of the members with the constituencies which they serve and must please, and to the internal power systems of the respective houses. An attempt will be made briefly to establish this point. A second premise is that the preoccupation with reform has obscured the fact that we have no really adequate model of party leadership as it exists in Congress, and that none can be constructed because we lack simple descriptions of many of the basic working parts of the present system. The major portion of the paper will be devoted therefore to an attempt to describe some of the operations of the principal elective officer of the Democratic party in the Senate, the floor leader, especially in the eight-year period that Lyndon B. Johnson of Texas occupied that position. The description will be based primarily on personal observation and on interviews with men who have served as Democratic leader or worked on his staff, and secondarily on the small store of scholarly and journalistic material available. The description is only a partial one. Leadership in the Senate is highly personal and exceedingly complex. People who know a great deal about it are prevented from describing it by the heavy work loads they bear and the restrictions of confidentiality. The justification for a study

[2] George B. Galloway, "The Operation of the Legislative Reorganization Act of 1946," *The American Political Science Review*, Vol. 45 (March 1951), pp. 41–68; *Congressional Reorganization Revisited* (College Park, Md., 1956); "Congressional Reorganization: Unfinished Business," in Earl Latham (ed.), *The Philosophy and Policies of Woodrow Wilson* (Chicago, 1958), pp. 214–27.

with obvious limitations is the importance of the subject and the possibility that it will stimulate others to add to it.

It should be understood that the paper makes no value judgments about the actual operations of Senate leadership nor the many proposals for change.

I. THE POLITICAL CONTEXT

One of the most durable notions in commentaries on American politics holds that the national convention is the supreme organ of the party and so the platform it draws up ought to have strong moral claims on the leadership in Congress. The advocates of party responsibility (who support the proposition) are too sophisticated, to be sure, to defend the convention out of hand as it now exists. It should be made smaller and more representative, they say, and its sessions should be longer so that more deliberation may occur.

The prognosis for these reforms, it must be said, is poor; the dominating influence of television runs in the other direction. Conventions get larger and noisier and their sessions shorter, and largely successful efforts are made to prevent them from deliberating at all. But what no amount of reform can change is the central fact that the convention's main business is to nominate a presidential candidate who has a chance to win; and a presidential candidate, like a man running for Congress, has a constituency to think about. It is fashionable to say that a member of Congress has a local constituency, the President a national one, but both statements, while technically true, are only partially correct in a political sense. Either man is free to be as national in his concerns as he pleases so long as he does not neglect the overriding importance of the people who can elect or defeat him. In the President's case these are primarily the voters in populous two-party states of the industrial North, and especially (because of the unit rule in the electoral college) the minority blocs within them which may swing a close state, and perhaps a close election.

The member of Congress recognizes the convention for what it is, a device of the presidential party, and the deliberations of the platform committee for what *they* are, a forum in which the party determines the maximum program which can be stated without shattering the party. The platform is a useful instrument for gauging the extent to which one wing of the party can go in meeting its constituent problems without alienating irrevocably another wing of the party which has opposing constituency interests; indeed, it is the only party device which provides quite this test. But not all party members can support all parts of such an instrument with equal fervor. The attitude of the member of Congress toward the platform is precisely the same as that of the President: he uses it, condemns it, or ignores it as it suits him in dealing with *his* constituency. This suggests then one of the insuperable (at present) obstacles to powerful central party leadership in Congress: the member's relationship to his constituency is direct and paramount. The constituency has a virtually unqualified power to hire and fire. If the member pleases it, no party leader can fatally hurt him; if he does not, no national party organ can save him.

Arguments for responsible party government fall before the lessons of life. The most powerful effort to advance party responsibility in this century was made not by political scientists but by Franklin Roosevelt when he tried to purge intransigent Democrats in 1938. Every politician in the country knows how that came out—just as he knows that the prestige of national party leadership was not enough to save Senate Democratic leaders Scott Lucas and Ernest McFarland, nor Republican Policy Committee Chairman Homer Ferguson, nor Senate Foreign Relations Committee Chairmen Tom Connally and Walter George. He knows that the efforts of popular Presidents to help favorite candidates have been generally unsuccessful and that, on the other hand, senators like the senior LaFollette (one of five chosen from its history by the Senate for special honor), Borah, Langer, Byrd, and many others have made careers of party dissidence. He knows how much his own success has turned on his knowledge of constituency interests and prompt service to them. When constituents demand that he follow national party leadership the member responds quickly; in the early months of Franklin Roosevelt's regime many congressmen boasted that they voted "down-the-line" with his program. That kind of regularity would be permanent if voters wanted it. In the long haul they neither want nor respect it, and members of Congress act accordingly.

This is not to say that the member's identification with a national party is meaningless to him. Far from it. His attachment is intensely practical and probably deeply sentimental. Without its label he would have almost no chance to win. Party victory enhances his chances and adds to the sweetness of triumph the solid perquisites of the majority. Within the legislative body he depends on it for services and for almost indispensable cues for voting on a wide range of technical issues. But the legislative party, as David Truman has put it, "is mediate and supplementary rather than immediate and inclusive in function."[3] It is important, but not crucial.

The second immovable object in the way of legislative party leadership is the system of specialized standing committees. The establishment of standing committees with preemptive jurisdiction over categories of legislation is more than a division of legislative labor, it is an allocation of political power. The committee chairmen, especially when they are clothed with the immunity of a seniority rule, are chieftains to be bargained with, not lieutenants to be commanded. A party leadership of formal power, as distinguished from one of persuasion and accommodation, is incompatible with specialized committees.

The direct relationship of representative to constituent, and the specialized committee, are not the only hindrances to central party leadership, but they are formidable. It is significant that the politicians who operate the two great representative systems which are most often compared, the British and the American, are acutely aware of these basic elements in their respective power structures. British governments have rigorously suppressed everything likely to enable the individual member to build up independent support—residence requirements, private bills, services to constituents, personal expertise. And they have made their parliamentary committees small editions of the House of Commons, few in number, large in size, and unspecialized (except for Scottish business).[4] The Americans have done just the opposite. The persons least enthusiastic about a policy committee made up of committee chairmen probably were the committee chairmen themselves, who had no wish to trade sovereignty for a vote in council. Moreover, some standing committees of Congress have with

[3] David B. Truman, The Congressional Party: A Case Study (New York, 1959), p. 95. His chapters 4 and 8 are especially valuable for their analysis of Senate leadership.

[4] Ivor Jennings, Parliament, 2d ed. (Cambridge, 1957), pp. 268–79, 355–80, 454–72; R. T. McKenzie, British Political Parties (London, 1955), pp. 241–53, 546–58; Leon D. Epstein, "British Mass Parties in Comparison with American Parties," Political Science Quarterly, Vol. 71 (March, 1956) pp. 97–125.

good logic resisted dividing into subcommittees, which inevitably stake out their own claims to preemptive power.[5]

II. THE FLOOR LEADER'S JOB

The elective party officer in the Senate upon whom, more than any other, falls the burden of central leadership is the floor leader. Needless to say, it is not the same job at all times. Much depends upon the leader's objective situation *vis-a-vis* the White House and upon his subjective view of his relationship to the presidency.

One situation is that of a majority leader with a popular and aggressive President of the same party in the White House who makes strong demands on Congress. Good examples would be John Worth Kern in Woodrow Wilson's administration,[6] and Joseph T. Robinson in that of Franklin D. Roosevelt. The support of that kind of President gives the leader great leverage with his colleagues so that he can accomplish much, but his power (however personally skillful he may be) is essentially derivative. The President may push him into unwelcome adventures, perhaps without consultation or even warning.

A second situation, perhaps the most difficult of all, is that of a majority leader with a President who is legislatively aggressive without being able to muster adequate popular support for his program. This was the position of Senators Scott Lucas and Ernest McFarland with President Truman. Lucas especially was in sore straits. Truman regarded his remarkable reelection victory as a mandate, particularly for the civil rights pledges he had made. Lucas shared Truman's goals and believed it was his job to advance them, but he was not so optimistic about what could be done. Taking from the President's long list of legislative demands a few upon which Democratic senators might unite, he hoped to make a legislative record before hopelessly splitting the legislative party over civil rights.[7] Nevertheless he loyally put the civil rights legislation first, with the results he had predicted.

[5] An example is the House Committee on Banking and Currency which has only recently, with reluctance, established subcommittees and has tried, without much success, to avoid specialization by numbering (not naming) them after the British fashion.

[6] See Claude Bowers, *The Life of John Worth Kern* (Indianapolis, 1918), ch. 17.

[7] William S. White, "Rugged Days for the Majority Leader," *New York Times Magazine*, July 3, 1949, p. 14 ff.

Other situations carry their own problems. The least difficult relationship perhaps is that of the majority leader with a President of his party who is not legislatively aggressive, the relationship enjoyed by Senators Taft and Knowland with Eisenhower. Not unlike it perhaps was the situation of majority leader Johnson, who had to carry the programming responsibilities of the majority without a Democratic President.

The leadership of the congressional minority, with the opposition's man in the White House, offers opportunity as well as problems. It is a good position from which to rally the troops; the initiative rests with the opponent, but there is no compulsion for the minority to take party stands on divisive issues. The leader of a minority with a President of his party would seem to have the worst arrangement possible. His relationships with the White House and his senatorial colleagues deserve close study.

The job of the majority leader obviously will be affected by his notion of his responsibilities toward a President of his party. William S. White contends that the Senate expects that a floor leader of a party occupying the presidency "will not so much represent the President as the Senate itself," and that the image of him as the President's man is a popular heresy born of the days of Roosevelt's enormous prestige. David B. Truman argues that "the fundamental complexity and subtlety of the role lie in the fact that the elective leaders are, and probably must be, both the President's leaders and the party's leaders."[8] They may both be right, without affecting the proposition that the perception of the leader's role may vary considerably with the incumbent.

Alben Barkley, for instance, regarded himself as responsible for Roosevelt's program, but he resigned his leadership when the President sharply criticized and vetoed a tax bill passed by Congress. Congress considers revenue legislation to be peculiarly within its own domain and the veto was bitterly resented. Barkley was promptly reelected unanimously by his colleagues and the President made amends as gracefully as he could.[9] Senator Lucas shared Barkley's general view. He believed that if a leader could not agree with his President 80 percent of the time, the leader should resign. In constant

---

[8] William S. White, Citadel: The Story of the U.S. Senate (New York, 1956), pp. 96–98; Truman, op. cit., pp. 298–99.

[9] Alben W. Barkley, That Reminds Me (Garden City, N.Y., 1954), ch. 12.

touch with the White House over a direct telephone, Lucas put Truman's program ahead of his own health and his political career. His successor, Ernest McFarland, had no direct telephone and wanted none. His relations with Truman were good, but he liked the long mile between the Hill and the White House; it was not too far for the Senate's ambassador to travel. His general view seems to have been shared by two other leaders very unlike him and each other, Senators Knowland and Taft.

Lyndon Johnson, as majority leader, did not work with a Democratic President, and it would be presumptuous to speculate about hypothetical relationships. But he *did* work with a Republican President for six years, and this relationship is illuminating. Johnson regarded the presidency as the one office in the American system which can give national leadership. He scoffed at the notion that his own initiative, in the absence of presidential leadership of Congress, made him a kind of "prime minister." His own description of his activity was that "we prod him [Eisenhower] into doing everything we can get him to do, and when he does something good we give him a 21-gun salute." He consistently refused to turn the Democrats in the Senate loose to attack Eisenhower at will, believing that no President can be cut down without hurting the presidency itself—with the American people the losers. Johnson worked with Eisenhower with dispassionate professionalism, supporting or differing with him as he believed he should.

Needless to say, Johnson was very far from regarding the Senate as a rubber stamp for any President, or even as a body which waits to deliberate upon what he sees fit to initiate. It is doubtful that any leader was ever more consciously proud of the Senate as an institution, nor more determined to preserve and expand the unique and independent role which the Constitution and its history have made for it.

III. THE LEADERSHIP OF SENATOR JOHNSON

Lyndon B. Johnson was Democratic leader in the Senate from 1953 through 1960. With Robinson and Barkley, he is one of only three men in recent times to hold the position for an extended period, and he was by general agreement the most skillful and successful in the memory of living observers. What accounts for his success?

How did he perceive his job? What powers had he and what stratagems and tactics did he employ?

Philosophy and approach

Johnson was a legislative pragmatist. He believed it possible to do anything that was worth the effort and the price, and so considered every problem from the standpoint of what was necessary to achieve the desired objective, and whether the objective was worth the cost. He learned early and never forgot the basic skill of the politician, the ability to divide any number by two and add one. But to find a ground on which a majority could stand, he did not regard as "compromise." "I always seek the best and do the possible," he said. "I have one yardstick that I try to measure things by: Is this in the national interest? Is this what I believe is best for my country? And if it is we outline it to these fellows of various complexions . . .", Democrats as different as Byrd and Morse, Republicans as far apart as Case and Dworshak. Johnson respected these differences: "The thing you must understand is that no man comes to the Senate on a platform of doing what is wrong. They will come determined to do what is right. The difficulty is finding an area of agreement . . ." To do that, "first you must have a purpose and an objective and the vision to try to outline what the national interest requires, what the national need is. Then you lay that on the table, and are as reasonably patient and as effective as you can be, from a persuasive standpoint."[10]

This is the way to "do the possible" and pass bills—the pragmatist's test of legislative achievement. More than that, he wanted the bills to become laws. Johnson consistently declined to pass strings of bills he knew Eisenhower would veto. "What do you want," he demanded, "houses [or farm legislation, etc.] or a housing issue?"

Johnson's emphasis on persuasion was crucial. He said the "only real power available to the leader is the power of persuasion. There is no patronage; no power to discipline; no authority to fire Senators like a President can fire his members of Cabinet."[11]

His formal powers certainly were not impressive; as Truman says, the majority leader must build his influence "upon a combination of

[10] "Leadership: An Interview with Senate Leader Lyndon Johnson," U.S. News & World Report, June 27, 1960, pp. 88–93, 89.

[11] Ibid., p. 88. Cf. Richard Neustadt's argument that the President's power, too, is essentially the power to persuade. Presidential Power (New York, 1960), ch. 3.

fragments of power."[12] The office of Democratic leader, it is true, combines all the most important elective positions—Chairman of the Conference, of the Steering Committee, of the Policy Committee. (The Republicans fill these positions with four different men.) Each position adds something to his influence and to the professional staff he controls. The Steering Committee handles committee transfers and assignment of new members, and Johnson's voice as chairman was highly influential, to say the least. One of his most successful political acts was his decision in 1953 to put all Democratic senators, even new ones, on at least one important committee. As Chairman of the Policy Committee he had substantial control over legislative scheduling (in close collaboration with the minority leader), which gave him not only the power to help and hinder but an unequalled knowledge of legislation on the calendar and who wanted what and why. A tactical power of importance was what Johnson called the "power of recognition"—the right of the majority leader to be recognized first when he wanted the floor. He exploited this right with great skill to initiate a legislative fight when and on the terms he wanted.

The "power of persuasion" may be abetted by some favors Johnson was in a position to perform. He could help a senator move his pet legislation, not only in the Senate but, through his friendship with Speaker Rayburn and other crucially influential leaders, in the House as well. The senator, it should be added, did well to observe a "rule of prudence" and not ask for too much. Because there were always members who would help him on legislation of little interest to themselves, Johnson could muster a respectable vote for a senator's bill or amendment that was bound to lose—a substantial boon to a man who wants his constituents to take him seriously. Johnson had largesse to bestow in the form of assignments to special committees, assistance in getting appropriations for subcommittees, and appointments as representatives of the Senate to participate in international meetings. Because intelligence flowed in to him and he was the center of the legislative party's communication network (in a system

[12] Truman, op. cit., p. 115. For the formal powers and relationships of the floor leader, see Floyd M. Riddick, The United States Congress: Organization and Procedure (Manassas, Va., 1949) pp. 86–100; for historical accounts, George H. Haynes, The Senate of the United States: Its History and Practice (Boston, 1938), pp. 480–483; and Lynn Haines, Law Making in America (Bethesda, Md., 1912), ch. 3; for a personal account, Alben W. Barkley, "The Majority Leader in the Legislative Process," in Amry Vandenbosch (ed.), The Process of Government (Lexington, Ky., 1949).

which lacks formal, continuous communication among the specialized committees which do the work), a cooperative member could be enormously better informed through the leader's resources than his own. A master of parliamentary technique, Johnson could tell a senator how to do what he wished or untangle the Senate from a procedural snarl, instructing senators what motions to make and bringing them and the chair in on cue.[13]

Nevertheless persuasion was, in Johnson's case, overwhelmingly a matter of personal influence. By all accounts, Johnson was the most personal among recent leaders in his approach. For years it was said that he talked to every Democratic senator every day. Persuasion ranged from the awesome pyrotechnics known as "Treatment A" to the apparently casual but always purposeful exchange as he roamed the floor and the cloakroom.[14] He learned what a man wanted and would take, and he asked for help. He did not hesitate to "cross the aisle"; Republican votes saved him more than once, sometimes to the surprise and chagrin of *their* leadership. Although he had, as Stewart Alsop said, "a real talent for friendship, and that talent is the final weapon in Johnson's huge armory," some of his colleagues undoubtedly found his overpowering personality somewhat trying to live with.[15] Johnson sometimes approached those senators he was not "easy" with through the Democratic Whip, Senator Mike Mansfield, or the Secretary to the Majority, Robert G. Baker. Always the goal was the same: the combination that would yield one more than half the votes. Because he so often found it, because he spurned the hopeless fight, he was able to fashion a myth of invincibility which was itself mightily persuasive: when he moved, it was taken for granted that "Lyndon's got the votes."

Johnson always actively cultivated a close working relationship with the Republican leader, except for rare and calculated clashes. This served to broaden his leadership to include the whole body, adding

---

[13] See, as one example, the Senate debate on H.R. 5836, a postal rate bill, on February 28, 1958. Many of the "cues" have been edited from the *Record,* but enough remains to suggest Johnson's domination of an intricate parliamentary process. *Congressional Record,* Vol. 104, pp. 3105–3148.

[14] Stewart Alsop, "Lyndon Johnson: How Does He Do It?" *Saturday Evening Post,* January 24, 1959, pp. 13 ff., 43; W. S. White, "Two Texans Who Will Run Congress," *New York Times Magazine,* Dec. 30, 1956, p. 5 ff.

[15] Alsop, *ibid.,* p. 43.

to his control over it and his ability to obtain the magic majority. This relationship moreover made "the leadership" more nearly invulnerable to incipient rebellion. It also satisfied the Senate's historic sense of its role as the conservator of minority rights, and greatly improved the temper of the proceedings.

Strategy and tactics of influence

Although it is not likely that he ever quite used these terms, Lyndon Johnson's legislative strategy frequently reflected an acute awareness that senators must play many different and often conflicting roles, and that one task of leadership is to structure a situation so that a member can select a role which will allow him to stand with the party.

One evidence of this awareness was the care with which he tried to keep his own roles straight. As a senator from Texas, for instance, he had to give the oil and gas industry the same kind of support that other senators give the principal industries in their states.[16] Before he became leader, he did not hesitate, as a Texas senator, to lead the attack on Leland Olds' reappointment to the Federal Power Commission.[17] In the submerged oil lands controversy of 1953, on the other hand, Johnson voted as a Texas senator but stayed carefully in the background, leaving spokesmanship for the states' rights position to his Texas colleague, Price Daniel, and to Florida's Senator Holland. As a consequence, northern Democrats were able to make an issue of Republican support of the bill and of President Eisenhower's signing it. Likewise, when the annual attempt was made to reduce the depletion allowance granted in the tax code to producers of oil and gas, Johnson carefully stayed out of the floor debate. The so-called natural gas bill (to forbid the Federal Power Commission to regulate the sales by independent producers of natural gas to interstate pipe line companies), which comes up periodically, caused more trouble. Johnson could leave its sponsorship to other oil state senators until he came to announce a legislative program at the beginning of a session. Failure then to include the natural gas bill simply could

[16] For a sympathetic statement of Johnson's problem by a northern liberal senator, see Richard L. Neuberger, "Making a Scapegoat of Lyndon Johnson," *New Republic*, July 4, 1955, pp. 9–10.

[17] Joseph P. Harris, "Senatorial Rejection of Leland Olds," *The American Political Science Review*, Vol. 45 (September, 1951), pp. 674–92.

not have been explained away in Texas. Again, when liberal Democrats staged a filibuster against the Dixon-Yates contract in 1954, Johnson stood aloof for two weeks while the issue was made, then stepped in as leader to end the filibuster when the point of diminishing returns was reached. The timing was well calculated. Majority support for anti-monopoly and rural electrification provisions in the Atomic Energy Act had been achieved by the filibuster and they were promptly voted when it ended.

Even more important as a leadership technique was the manipulation of the role perceptions of other senators. This was an important part of Johnson's major effort as minority leader to reunite his then bitterly divided legislative party. He exploited every opportunity to get his colleagues to think, not as northerners or southerners, liberals or conservatives, but as Democrats. A homely illustration is suggestive. In 1954 when some Republican orators came close to accusing Democrats of disloyalty, many southern Democrats tended to shrug it off as attacks on Harry Truman and northern liberals. But each time Johnson talked to a southern colleague he produced a freshly typed copy of some of the statements about Democrats made by Republican wavers of the "bloody shirt" after the Civil War. The parallel was striking and the lesson plain.

A better illustration perhaps was furnished by the appointment in the same year of one Albert Beeson to the National Labor Relations Board.[18] The Democratic minority on the Labor and Public Welfare Committee was strongly opposed to Beeson, whom organized labor accused of anti-labor bias, because they said his failure to sever his relations completely with a California corporate employer constituted a conflict of interests. This left conservative Democrats unmoved; they recalled many years when the NLRB had been frankly stacked in favor of labor. The Senate vote on Beeson seemed sure to provide yet another occasion for a sharp division between northern and southern Democrats.

Then a careful reading of the committee testimony showed that Beeson's statements had shifted from one hearing to another. Immediately Johnson saw the way: Beeson should be opposed not for conflict of interest, but for flouting the dignity of the Senate. The

[18] *Congressional Record,* Vol. 100 (1954), pp. 1049–51 (February 1), 1970–2005 (February 18).

key man he perceived to be Senator Walter George: as a conservative southerner, he was almost sure to support Beeson; but as a *senator*, proud of the Senate and sensitive about its dignity, he would vote against a man he believed guilty of misrepresentations to its committee. Either way, he would take most southerners with him.

The Democratic Policy Committee decided to rally Democrats against Beeson, not on conflict of interest but for false statements to its committee. The minority report was written that way. Speeches were written for Democrats, stressing the theme that the Senate's dignity had been flouted. Lister Hill, a southern Democrat, dominated the presentation. A Republican senator detected the shift in emphasis; had the conflict-of-interest objection been dropped? The Democrats assured him it had not, but said no more about it. The strategy called for delay over the weekend, to rally more votes, but when Johnson knew George was convinced the speeches were cancelled and a vote taken. Beeson was confirmed, but the Democratic minority had stood solidly together on the kind of issue which usually divided them. The Beeson incident, multiplied many times in their two years in the minority, taught the Democrats once more the habit of voting together.

The concentration on Senator George illustrates two other tenets of Johnson's strategy of leadership. One is that in most situations a single man holds the "key" to it. The problem is to know how to turn the key. A second is that a highly esteemed senator may be used as an "umbrella" on a controversial issue, for other senators who feel they can safely vote with him. Thus a southern senator could feel secure in the explanation that he voted "just like Mr. George."

Both were strikingly demonstrated in the enactment of two bitterly controversial labor bills in 1958. The first came in April when Senator Kennedy's Labor and Public Welfare subcommittee reported a welfare and pensions plans disclosure bill.[19] The principal hazard to the bill was the prospect that far-reaching amendments to the Taft-Hartley Act might be piled on it, killing any chance it had to pass the House— a threat which materialized when minority leader Knowland announced his intention to do just that. But the move was anticipated. For three days the Senate stalled while Johnson conferred almost continuously with Kennedy, Lister Hill (chairman of the full committee) and John McClellan. Senator McClellan was the "key" to the

19 S. Rept. 1440 (on S. 2888), 85th Cong., 2d sess., April 21, 1958.

situation. His Select Committee on Improper Activities in the Labor or Management Field had issued an interim report in March urging many of the amendments which Knowland intended to offer.[20] An agreement was reached: Hill and Kennedy pledged that they would offer a labor reform bill by June 10, and McClellan promised to vote against his own amendments until they had received proper committee consideration.[21] The Senate thereupon was thrown into 12-hour daily sessions until the bill was passed.[22] Fourteen amendments (six by Knowland) were beaten down, 12 by roll-call votes. Only one Democrat voted against his party consistently, and only two others voted against it even once. Only one amendment (prohibiting convicted felons from serving in the administration of pension and welfare funds) was adopted.[23]

When the general labor reform bill was reported promptly on June 10, it too had the united support of Johnson, Hill, Kennedy and McClellan.[24] Consequently, only one relatively insignificant amendment (continuing Taft-Hartley's non-communist oath for labor leaders and extending it to employers) was adopted over the opposition of the bill's sponsors, while 20 amendments were defeated. Once again most Democrats stood firmly together. Senator McClellan furnished the "umbrella" for conservative Democrats; when he publicly and repeatedly urged support for the bill as "the best that can be passed in this Congress," he made it safe and respectable for them to vote for it.[25]

Parenthetically, these bills also illustrated Johnson's strategy of alternately riding with loose reins while the Senate handled miscellaneous business and rested from its exertions, then keeping it in early and late on a major bill. The long, driving sessions undoubtedly reduced the Senate's notorious tendency to waste time.

There was a place in the Johnson scheme of things for floor de-

[20] S. Rept. 1417, 85th Cong., 2d sess., March 24, 1958.

[21] See Joseph Alsop's syndicated column, "Matter of Fact," for April 28, 1958.

[22] Welfare and Pension Plans Disclosure Act of 1958, P.L. 836.

[23] For the extended debate, see *Congressional Record*, Vol. 104, 85th Cong., 2d sess., for April 23–26, 28, 1958.

[24] S. Rept. 1684 (on S. 3974), 85th Cong., 2d sess.

[25] S. 3974, The Labor-Management Reporting and Disclosure Act of 1958. The debate is in *Congressional Record, ibid.,* for June 12–14, 16–17. McClellan's statement is at p. 11087.

bate. It furnished a forum for senators who love to talk; it registered positions and who held them; it kept the Senate in session while the serious business of legislation was going on somewhere else. Johnson knew how to make skillful use of the versatile Democratic "bench." But what emerged from Johnson's own statements and from examples of his work was the view that good legislation is not the product of oratory and debate but of negotiation and discussion, designed not to make issues but to find common ground that equal, independent and dissimilar men could occupy.

A small-scale model of a typical operation was the amendment of the Fair Labor Standards Act in 1955. Labor and liberals wanted to increase the number of workers covered and to raise the minimum wage from 75 cents to $1.25 an hour. Eisenhower supported a 90-cent minimum wage. Southern Democrats would go no higher than that and opposed any increase in coverage. Johnson found the formula: $1 an hour with no additional coverage. Both sides were warned that amendments might be dangerous to it. The issue was settled with less than an hour of debate.[26] This procedure, with all factors intensified, explains how two civil rights bills were got through the Senate.

IV. OTHER AGENCIES OF PARTY LEADERSHIP

The roles appropriate to other agencies of party leadership—the Conference (or Caucus), the Policy Committee, the Steering Committee (committee on committees), and standing committee chairmen—have been the subject of recurring controversy within Congress as well as outside it, as they probably will continue to be. No attempt will be made to settle it here. Instead we shall show how Democratic leaders generally and Senator Johnson in particular made use of these agencies, and then consider some criticisms and suggestions made recently by Democratic senators.

The party conference theoretically is the supreme organ of the legislative party, as the national convention is of the national party. Actually, its influence on policy has waxed and waned. Democrats historically have been more willing than Republicans to be bound by its decisions. Beginning in 1903, the Senate Democratic Conference could bind its members by a two-thirds vote, though there were oc-

---

[26] "Democratic Strategy," New Republic, June 20, 1955, pp. 3–4.

casional individual rebels. Conference discipline reached its peak in Woodrow Wilson's administration. It was so effective (or oppressive) that Nebraska Senator Gilbert M. Hitchcock introduced, during the 1915 ship-purchase bill debate, a resolution requiring senators "to vote in accordance with their own convictions and judgments"; and open rebellion broke out against it after World War I. An even more stringent rule binding Democrats to support an Executive measure on a majority vote in conference was adopted at the beginning of the New Deal era, but a member was excused if he had conscientious objections to a bill or if it ran counter to pledges made to his constituents.[27]

The principal function of the Democratic Conference in recent years has been the selection of party leaders at the beginning of a Congress. Senator Johnson also used it at the beginning of a session to present his own "State of the Union" speech on the legislative program. (Developments in the second session of the 86th Congress will be discussed later.) His frank opinion was that "not much" can be accomplished in conference. Issues which really divide the legislative party cannot be settled that way; indeed, differences are exacerbated and new rifts may be opened. For example, in 1954 (his second year as minority leader) Johnson responded to criticism of the infrequency of conferences by calling one. Two issues were carefully selected for discussion because the legislative party seemed to be united on them, the contested election of Senator Dennis Chavez and the question of tying together the Alaska and Hawaii statehood bills. The party united happily behind Chavez and agreed on the statehood issue, but a member's speech on the latter almost upset the concord. Party members frequently stand together for different reasons, but talking about those reasons may only open old wounds and drive them apart. Floor debate may do the same, but it is not so likely, since many members are usually absent and arguments are not made directly to each other.

More than any other party agency, the Policy Committee has become what the floor leaders have chosen to make it.[28] Senator Barkley —Democratic leader in 1947, when the policy committees were estab-

[27] Haynes, op. cit., pp. 474–78.

[28] For a detailed analysis of both party policy committees in the Senate, see Hugh A. Bone, Party Committees and National Politics (Seattle, Wash., 1958), pp. 116–96, and his "An Introduction to the Senate Policy Committee," The American Political Science Review, Vol. 50 (June 1956), pp. 339–59.

lished in an appropriation for the legislative branch—determined the method of selection. To sit with three *ex-officio* members (Leader, Whip, Secretary to the Conference), he chose six members on the basis of geography, deliberately omitting the older party leaders (at the cost of some resentment) and committee chairmen. He knew that men of established power would be hard to control. He wanted younger men, more pliable, willing to work hard to make reputations, who should be easier for him to work with. His method of selection prevailed—though in time, because succeeding leaders only filled vacancies, Policy Committee members gained in personal power and some became committee chairmen. Some leaders have thought privately that members should resign when they assume chairmanships, but this is not the practice. But the dominant consideration in filling vacancies still is the one Barkley established: the new member should be a man the leader *wants* on the committee. Senator Lucas left a seat vacant two years rather than take a man he did not really prefer to have. McFarland, too, in honoring geographical and ideological considerations, nevertheless chose men he considered friends. Senator Johnson tended to appoint older men with established positions of leadership. But in the 86th Congress he added the members of the Legislative Review Committee to the Policy Committee meetings, which gave wider geographical representation and assured that there would always be three freshman senators present.[29] Like Barkley's inclusion of the Whip and Secretary to the Conference, this practice is likely to become custom.

Their use of the Policy Committee has varied with the leaders. Barkley set out to have weekly meetings but seldom did; his leadership was personal, intuitive, and informal. Both Lucas and McFarland held weekly meetings. Lucas used it to select bills for Senate consideration, make the legislative schedule, and help plan floor strategy. Vice President Barkley was invited to attend the meetings, which he often did, and after committee discussion to add his comments. Discussion led to general agreement; no votes were taken and no decision was considered binding on the party. McFarland considered

[29] The Legislative Review Committee in the 86th Congress consisted of Senators E. L. Bartlett (Alaska), Clair Engle (California), and Philip A. Hart (Michigan). The function of the Legislative Review Committee is to keep up with the objections of Democratic members to bills on the calendar and to voice them on calendar call, so that the legislation will not pass "without objection."

the Policy Committee a kind of "cabinet." He too cleared the legislative program with the committee, but he used it primarily for discussion, to give him a sense of what was possible.

When Senator Johnson chose new members of the Policy Committee he tried to balance considerations of geography, seniority, ideology, and influence in the Senate. He wanted men he could work with, but each also should represent a power group in the legislative party. They were men he would have to deal with if there had been no Policy Committee, though in that event he probably would have chosen to work with them individually rather than as a group. A Policy Committee meeting therefore was like a conference of chieftains. Each man had independent power; each unofficially represented a group. He brought more than intelligence on Senate attitudes; he brought influence also, since other votes were almost sure to go with his. The Policy Committee was far from being "the Johnson organization" in the Senate, although some of its members sometimes helped with tactical operations.

The meetings were for discussion, to thrash out ideas on an issue. Few votes were taken, and the minutes were brief and confidential. The Policy Committee made few decisions or announcements, although a statement sometimes was issued through the Committee to suggest broad party support. Thus the Policy Committee's declaration that the McCarthy censure vote was not a party issue probably was more effective than a statement by the leader alone. But Policy Committee decisions committed no one, not even the members of the committee themselves.

Johnson's employment of the Conference and the Policy Committee was criticized by some Democratic senators in the 86th Congress, with the result that more frequent conferences were held in the second session. The first public criticism came from Senator William Proxmire of Wisconsin in three Senate speeches in the Spring of 1959.[30] Proxmire called for "regular caucuses with specific agendas proposing consideration of our legislative program," a strengthened Policy Committee which would "find and express the party position on vital over-all issues," and closer adherence to the party platform. He was supported, in whole or in part, by Senators Clark, Morse, McNamara, and Douglas.

[30] *Congressional Record*, Vol. 105, pp. 2814–20 (February 23), 3559–78 (March 9), 5956–59 (April 15).

A motion was made at the first conference of the second session (January 7, 1960) to hold conferences every two weeks or whenever 15 Democrats requested it, but this was withdrawn when Johnson reiterated his willingness to call a conference on any Democratic senator's request.[31] Five days later, at a second conference, Senator Gore's motion that the Policy Committee be made into "an organization for evolving a coherent party policy on legislation," with its membership increased to 15 and selected by the Conference, was defeated 51–12. A motion to confirm Johnson's power to fill vacancies on the Democratic Steering Committee was adopted 51–11. After that, several conferences were held. Senator Gore has said that one of them "paid off in Democratic unity in the passage of the first aid-to-education bill in 11 years" on February 4 by a 51–34 vote after only two full days of debate.[32] Another conference on February 15 discussed the report of the Joint Economic Committee and the Administration's proposal to remove the ceiling on federal bond interest rates.[33]

Without a systematic survey of Democratic senatorial reaction to the conferences, it is safe to say only that sentiment has been mixed. Much can be and is said in favor of more frequent conferences. They provide a good way for members to learn about broad problems beyond the scope of their committee work. Younger members may find it easier to talk there than on the floor of the Senate, and may prefer an institutionalized procedure for expressing their views to the leader and learning his plans. Perhaps the strongest argument is simply that it seems like a better, more democratic way to run a party.

The critics of the conference say that so long as members are not bound it is futile and this is quickly reflected in the attitudes of senators toward it. Those not in favor of the policy under discussion tend to stay away; their votes have to be corralled in the traditional manner, through individual conferences with the leader. More senior members may not come because their opinions can be made effective where decisions are actually made. Other members avoid them simply because of business more pressing than a non-binding caucus. Furthermore, no real division of sentiment is likely to be reflected in candid discussion in a party conference. Aside from the danger of intensifying

[31] *Congressional Quarterly Weekly Report*, January 8, 1960, p. 43.

[32] *Ibid.*, January 15, 1960, p. 91.

[33] *Ibid.*, February 12, 1960, p. 224.

differences, there is the likelihood that views stated in confidence will be "leaked," probably in distorted form, to the press. The result of all these factors, say the critics, is a rather academic discussion, poorly attended, which was not requested in 1960 by any member after the middle of February.

From the lively senatorial discussion of party leadership three pertinent points might be emphasized. One is that the proponents of change do not want increased party discipline. As Senator Proxmire put it: "I will follow the dictates of my conscience against the decision of a caucus as readily as a decision of any leader, if I believe my course to be right and theirs wrong."[34] The goal is discussion, not decision. The problem of putting together a majority remains. A second is that the Policy Committee could be changed in size, composition and method of membership selection without increasing its influence. This seems to be the history of the Republican Policy Committee. There is no tradition of leadership in the Policy Committee. Its influence depends upon the use the leadership makes of it. A third is that Johnson did not believe (and his view apparently was shared by most Democratic senators) that either the Conference or the Policy Committee was a proper agency to make policy. That function belongs to the standing committees. Johnson has said that if members want to influence policy "the first place to make it is in committees of which they are members. . . . If they expect me to get a majority vote there, how do they expect me to get a majority vote out here?"[35]

Johnson's acceptance of the standing committees as the primary source of legislative policy did not deny to their chairmen the benefits of his friendly persuasion. What they had in committee, what they could get out and when ("Give me a bill!"), what could pass the Senate—these were the topics of repeated personal conferences.

One of the most important and least generally appreciated arms of party leadership was the group of people Stewart Alsop called "the biggest, the most efficient, the most ruthlessly overworked and the most loyal personal staff in the history of the Senate," most of whom had been with Johnson for many years.[36] Lucas and McFarland tried to keep staff members assigned to them for the party separate from their state offices. Johnson used the best man for the job, whether it

[34] *Congressional Record,* Vol. 105, p. 2817 (February 23, 1959).

[35] *Ibid.,* p. 9260 (May 28, 1959).

[36] *Op. cit.*

was state or party. Because he took ideas from anyone and used those he liked, Johnson got a steady flow of them from his staff. They had much to do with his ability generally to move first with the best information.

V. CONCLUSION

Suggestions for change in the leadership structure of the Senate seem to fall into two classes. The first class, which has had strong academic sponsorship, has sought to strengthen central leadership through conference and policy committee, looking toward the party responsibility of the British for their model. These suggestions have failed because they do not fit the character of the American representative system, with its direct responsibility of representative to constituent, nor the internal power system of Congress, with its specialized committees presided over by senior officers. They have sought to impose party coherence through organizational devices, and to take power from those who have it and assign it to those who do not. The second class of suggestions has aimed not at a more disciplined party but at additional leverage for a minority group within the legislative party. These have so far had small success because their sponsors *are* a minority.

What should be fully exploited by academic writers on the Senate is the insight which can be gained from studies of strong leadership which *has* emerged there from time to time. Whether it is exercised by a formal leader or some other person, it reveals much about the structure of the Senate as a social system precisely because it is indigenous to the Senate.

Systematic analysis of Lyndon Johnson's tenure as Democratic leader should be especially rewarding. As a majority leader without the leverage furnished by a President of his party, he had to make the best use of purely senatorial tools of influence. In this he succeeded to the point that he could manage the enactment of two laws on the most divisive domestic issue of our time. This brief description of some aspects of his leadership suggests that the successful senatorial leader is one who (1) can and does help individual senators to maximize their effectiveness in playing their personal roles in the Senate, and (2) structures roles and alternatives so that a maximum number of senators can join in support of the proffered solution of an issue.

FOUR
THE OUTSIDER IN THE SENATE: AN ALTERNATIVE ROLE

T HE growing concern of students of politics with the social structure of official bodies and the behavior expected of their members promises to make the Senate of the United States a prime
target of research. Two recent books make notable contributions
and suggest the trend. One is William S. White's *Citadel: The
Story of the U.S. Senate*,[1] an "insider's" impressions based on
years of close observation; and the other is Donald R. Matthews'
U.S. Senators and Their World,[2] the work of a political scientist. One (though not the only) concern of both books is the
system of norms for behavior of members of the Senate.[3] Although reached through different routes (White's largely inferred from observed behavior, Matthews' principally from
interviews) their statements of Senate norms and the way they
work have much in common. The norms (or "folkways," as
Matthews calls them) are viewed as cultural "oughts" upon

The author gratefully acknowledges his indebtedness to Senator William
Proxmire of Wisconsin for invaluable assistance in the preparation of this
paper, and to the Rockefeller Foundation for a grant which made possible
the theoretical work on it. The author is, of course, solely responsible for
all statements of fact and judgment.

This article originally appeared in *The American Political Science Review*,
LV (September 1961), 566–575.

[1] New York, 1956.

[2] Chapel Hill, 1960.

[3] See especially White, chs. 5–10, and Matthews, ch. 5.

which there is a high degree of consensus. The members who conform most closely to the norms are, generally speaking, the most
influential and effective members. This general view is almost certainly correct, as it would be for any stable human group; in this
the Senate is not unique (as White sometimes seems to suggest it is)
but typical.[4]

But what about the senator who does not conform? What is his
place in the Senate and what happens to him there? This study will
explore these questions through a case study of such a senator. But
first it may be useful to try to restate the relevant parts of the analysis
of White and Matthews (without holding them in any way responsible
for the restatement) in terms of role theory, which will provide the
conceptual framework for the analysis of the senator's experience.[5]
In this the senators will be seen as actors in a political sub-system
called the Senate, vested with an official position (or status) called
"senator." The analyst's problem then is to describe the "senator"
role—the dynamic, behavioral aspect of the official position. The
new senator, with different motivations, faces much the same problem: he must learn or be taught the norms which define the rights
and obligations of his position in order to take the actions which
will validate, poorly or well, his occupancy of the position. White
and Matthews, in effect, describe the senator role by stating the
norms which prescribe how persons who occupy the senator position
are expected to behave. Needless to say, it is essential to identify
whose expectations are meant—who, that is, prescribes the appropriate behavior. For White the expectations apparently emanate from
a powerful elite he calls the "Inner Club" whose members, appropriately referred to as the "Senate type," most nearly fulfill the

---

[4] George Homans, The Human Group (New York, 1950), pp. 147, 169–170, 426–28.

[5] "Role" and related concepts are defined in a great variety of ways by social
scientists, depending upon the discipline of the definer and the special problems
which engage his interest. For an excellent clarification of the definitional problem
see Neal Gross, Ward S. Mason and Alexander W. McEachern, Explorations in Role
Analysis: Studies of the School Superintendency Role (New York, 1958), ch. 2. Because the purpose of the present study is not to refine role theory but to employ
it rather crudely to gain some insights into the behavior of senators, concepts are
stated with as little elaboration as possible. For the theoretical formulation principally relied on see Theodore Sarbin, "Role Theory," in Gardner Lindzey (ed.), Hand-
book of Social Psychology (Cambridge, Mass., 1954), Vol. I, pp. 223–58.

requirements of the role, and who wield the internal sanctions. Matthews suggests that the expectations are widely shared by the membership as a whole.

What is the "senator" role (White's "Senate type" or "Senate man," Matthews' effective senator) which emerges from these two books? It is one of a prudent man, who serves a long apprenticeship before trying to assert himself, and talks infrequently even then. He is courteous to a fault in his relations with his colleagues, not allowing political disagreements to affect his personal feelings. He is always ready to help another senator when he can, and he expects to be repaid in kind. More than anything else, he is a Senate man, proud of the institution and ready to defend its traditions and perquisites against all outsiders. He is a legislative workhorse who specializes in one or two policy areas, says Matthews. He has a deep respect for the rights of others, says White, making his institution the last citadel of individualism. In this composite, the senator as an ideal type is a man of accommodation who knows that "you have to go along to get along"; he is a conservative, institutional man, slow to change what he has mastered at the expense of so much time and patience.

But what of the man who does not play by the rules? What sanctions, if any, does the system impose? White suggests small inconveniences: the formal rules, for instance, may be closely applied to him.[6] But the Senate is disinclined to proceed against any senator; the "great ones" do about as they please and the others, except for a few who are not acceptable at all, can get away with almost anything so long as it is not directed against a member of the Inner Club.[7] The whole thrust of his book nevertheless suggests that the non-Senate type who does not make the Inner Club never amounts to much in the Senate. This is essentially Matthews' point, too, which he arrives at through some ingenious measurements showing on their face, that the senator who violates the folkways is less effective in getting his bills passed.[8] Neither is bothered much by the cases of spectacularly successful senators who do not altogether fit the type—the talkative Humphrey, whom White firmly locates in the Inner Club; the dom-

[6] Op. cit., p. 82.
[7] Ibid., pp. 122, 126.
[8] Op. cit., pp. 114–17. More will be said about this later.

ineering Taft and Johnson, who leapt immediately to leadership. White explains them simply as "authentic geniuses among Senate types,"[9] which indeed is consistent with his emphasis on sentiment and feeling rather than overt behavior. In Matthews' collective profile they cause hardly a wrinkle.

This study is a participant-observer analysis of a single case of presumptively deviant senatorial behavior, that of William Proxmire, Democrat of Wisconsin, in his first year in the Senate. The observer was legislative assistant to Senator Proxmire that year. The observer's assumption was that one way to gain insights into the structure and working rules of a social system is to learn what the neophyte has to learn during his "initiation" period. Senator Proxmire was an ideal subject. He went to the Senate keenly aware of the importance of learning its norms and constructing with care the role he should play there. His interest was theoretical as well as practical; as a person trained in the social sciences he was self-conscious about his learning experiences and determined to rationalize them in order to develop a consistent view of the Senate and his place in it.[10] More than that, he was willing to share his experiences and discuss them regularly with the observer.

Because this is a study of an individual in his relations with an institution, an attempt will be made first to suggest some of the relevant personality factors. Then Proxmire's choice of role will be recounted. After that some inferences will be drawn and hypotheses suggested about the role systems of the Senate.

I. PERSONALITY FACTORS

A complex human being like William Proxmire cannot be psychologically categorized by a layman. Nevertheless, analysis begins with simplification; from the whole man must be abstracted some elements which shape him as a political personality, which identify him as a political type. In Proxmire's case, the first would seem to be a driving ambition to succeed, to which almost everything else in his life is

[9] *Op. cit.,* p. 82.

[10] Proxmire has a B.A. degree from Yale, an M.B.A. from the Harvard Graduate School of Business Administration, and he carried his doctoral program in government at Harvard to the dissertation-writing stage.

subordinated, coupled with a puritan's belief in the sanctity of unremittent work.

Only a man with Proxmire's bottomless ambition and faith in the efficacy of effort would have believed he had any prospects at all in Wisconsin politics. His disabilities were perhaps best summed up in an apocryphal story given wide currency in the state in 1952, when he first ran for governor. It relates a conversation between his opponent, Governor Walter Kohler, and, say, Driscoll of New Jersey, at the governors' conference that year.

"Have you an opponent, Walter?" asks Driscoll.

"Yes," replies Kohler. "He's the son of an Illinois Republican. He graduated from Yale and Harvard, worked for J. P. Morgan and married a Rockefeller, and just moved into Wisconsin three years ago."

"My God, Walter," explodes Driscoll. "Did you pick him yourself?"

The presumed liabilities bear closer inspection.[11] The Illinois Republican father was a physician who worked long hours seven days a week until his death at 79, who taught his son that it is morally wrong as well as inefficient to be awake and not at work. At Yale Proxmire learned the rewards of perseverance: too light for football, he nevertheless made every practice, spring and fall, for four years and finally got his letter by participating in one play in a "letter" game. His experience at the Harvard graduate school confirmed what Proxmire had suspected while working for Morgan, that the financiers no longer made the decisions that mattered; the politicians did. The public life therefore offered the largest opportunities for a man who would make his mark. There also his political values crystallized. ("I didn't raise my son to be a Democrat," said Dr. Proxmire. "Harvard did it to Bill.")[12] To decide to be governor of his newly adopted state did not seem preposterous to Proxmire; experience had taught him that he could reach his goals because he wanted to more than most people and would pay a higher price.

Another lesson of experience, reenforced by temperament, was that he did better alone. The second personality trait—and I think the decisive one—which affected Proxmire's choice of role in the Senate is his compulsive independence. No group can contain him

[11] See the sketch of Proxmire's life and personality by Godfrey Sperling, Jr., in *The Christian Science Monitor*, August 31, 1957; or the Chicago *Sun-Times*, August 25, 1957.

[12] Chicago *Daily News*, August 8, 1957, p. 22.

long; he does not trust it to take care of him nor make his decisions, and he cannot abide the restrictions on his actions which would go with truly belonging. Claims upon him which would limit his freedom of action, even those of friends and supporters, are onerous. His position in the Democratic Party of Wisconsin is a case in point.

The value of Proxmire's winning a Senate seat in 1957 to a party which had won only one other statewide race in 25 years can hardly be overstated.[13] Nevertheless, before the election an astute political reporter said in his syndicated column that it was no secret that there were "some pretty substantial Democrats who would not mind Proxmire's defeat in the senatorial election, considering their personal feeling alone and not the welfare of the party to which they owe their allegiance."[14] Some understanding of this estrangement is crucial to an explanation of Proxmire's political personality.

After World War II a group of Wisconsin Democrats, many of them Madison intellectuals, undertook the seemingly impossible task of rejuvenating their moribund and reactionary party. Their success, after a decade of effort, was spectacular; in 1958 the Democrats captured the state Assembly, all statewide offices but one, and half the congressional seats. These organization people naturally would like a dominant voice in party affairs, and at the minimum they expect to be consulted. Proxmire has not done much consulting, the plain fact being that if he had he almost surely would never have gone to the Senate. He had barely qualified to vote in the state when he won his first office—from a Democratic assemblyman who had lived all his 65 years in one Wisconsin county. After that Proxmire ran as he pleased (three times for governor before going to the Senate) without heeding pointed suggestions that he had "had his chance."

His indefatigable campaigning undoubtedly did much to rebuild the party, but as usual he made his own calculations along the way. He discovered very early that time spent hunting up a county chairman is, on the average, enough to shake two hundred hands downtown. Whether the chairman would get him any votes was problematical; not so with the handshaking. With Democratic politicians at that time virtually ignored by communication media in large areas of this Republican state, direct personal contact through continuous

---

[13] Proxmire was elected in August, 1957 to the unexpired term of Senator McCarthy, and to his first full term in 1958.

[14] John Wyngaard, August 17, 1957.

campaigning seemed the one sure way to make himself known. This piece of practical wisdom, acted upon, did not endear him to the organization but it made him unbeatable in a primary.

More important, a strong hold on the electorate, which can control him only in the most general sense, enables him to resist any group (including his staunch supporters) which might seek to exercise specific influence. Two incidents will illustrate. The morning after his first election to the Senate Proxmire stood with his wife before daybreak in the rain at a plant gate in Milwaukee, thanking the workers for their help. A couple of weeks later, when a labor leader dared to suggest that he was the union's man, Proxmire chose a state CIO convention as the place to declare his independence of labor. One act was as significant as the other and they were not unrelated.

II. THE FIRST STAGE OF SOCIALIZATION

Throughout the spring of 1958, for roughly half his first session in the Senate, Proxmire strove earnestly to be a model freshman senator. He worked hard on his committees and took care of his constituents. He accepted cheerfully a mammoth portion of the burden of freshmen of the majority party, presiding over the Senate. He did much more than his share; an unofficial tabulation midway in the session showed that he had sat in the chair longer than anyone else and about sixteen times as long as Vice President Nixon. The club apparently approved of him. No senator can ask his colleagues how he is doing, but his staff members can and do check with *their* peers. The reports at first were always the same: He's doing fine; he hasn't made a single mistake.

But Proxmire had not satisfactorily answered the question that mattered most to him: How much could he talk on the floor? Ordinary prudence, as well as Senate practice, counsel a neophyte to bide his time before exercising very freely his undoubted right to speak at any time. But to a man like Proxmire the life of the Senate is the debate on the floor. Not to be there and participate is to deny himself equal membership in the Senate. Proxmire said of a freshman colleague who seldom spoke: "He might as well not be a senator!"

Nevertheless he forbore, trying to find socially acceptable ways to take some part. The "morning hour," that period at the beginning of each day when senators introduce bills and insert material in the *Congressional Record*, seemed safe enough so he quickly became a regular contributor to the *Record*. He entered colloquies on the floor only when specifically invited to do so by senior members. He cautiously scheduled his first major speech for the day before the Easter recess when most members would be gone, having been assured that this was an appropriate time for a freshman to talk. Only two members heard him through, the presiding officer and Senator Douglas (who canceled an appointment in order to give Proxmire an audience).[15]

But almost as if he could not help himself, Proxmire became steadily more active in debate until he was one of the busiest men on the floor. Then came the first warnings that he was "talking too much." The warnings were characteristic of the operations of the Senate. None of them was direct. They came in friendly tips: someone heard an unnamed person say it; the report was passed on to a Proxmire staff man for what it was worth. Or a very senior senator in the chair would pointedly overlook Proxmire standing at his desk, to recognize other members ahead of him out of turn.

Proxmire retired, brooding, to his office. He was puzzled and frustrated. He believed that he *had* exercised great restraint. He had kept his speeches short, except when asked by a party floor man to help kill time. So he sat mute. Not even a debate on unemployment compensation, in which he was deeply interested, could make him speak.

Then the dam broke. In the first week of June Proxmire offered six amendments to the Mutual Security Act and pressed them to a vote.[16] Inasmuch as Proxmire was not a member of the Foreign Relations Committee, and four of his amendments were first introduced on the floor so the committee had no chance to consider them, the performance was hardly a demonstration of modesty and withdrawal. Criticism was sharp and immediate (though indirect, as always), and it spurred Proxmire to a decision: he would "be a senator like Wayne [Morse] and Paul [Douglas]"; he would talk when he pleased on whatever he chose and would not worry about his influence in the Senate. He had found his role.

The Senate soon learned what that meant. In mid-July, for instance, Proxmire served notice that "I intend to rise every day, from now on

[15] *Congressional Record*, Vol. 104 (April 3, 1958), pp. 6200–14.

[16] *Ibid.* (May 26, 1958), pp. 9424–25; (May 28), p. 9655; (June 4–5), pp. 9868–69, 10157–63, 10260–62, 10266–70.

until social security improvement is adopted, to plead for it,"[17] which he did, on 27 consecutive occasions. But if the club was unused to being lectured by a freshman member, it must have been wholly unprepared for his threat to hold them beyond adjournment by the very antithesis of freshmanlike behavior, a filibuster.

The provocation was a bill to allow the Metropolitan Sanitary District of Chicago to increase the amount of water it may withdraw from Lake Michigan by a thousand cubic feet per second for a three-year test period.[18] Similar bills had been passed by both houses twice before (by the Senate in the closing hours of a session with scant debate) only to be vetoed by the President because of objections raised by Canada. Once more it appeared that the bill would come up in the flood of last-minute legislation, and with committee and leadership support it seemed sure to slide through the tired Senate. Moreover, because the Canadian position was now ambiguous the President might sign the bill.

But the pressure for adjournment which was the greatest factor in favor of the bill's passage could also be its doom—if its opponents had sufficient nerve. Their hope was to stall consideration as long as possible, then make it clear that the cost of passage was extended debate. It was a simple, time-proven strategy, but not one designed to make friends.

Proxmire was by no means the only man fighting the bill—there was a militant bipartisan coalition on each side—but he was probably the most determined and certainly the most conspicuous. It was he who blocked unanimous consent to allow any deviation from the rules in handling the bill. Thus he objected to a meeting of the Public Works committee while the Senate sat, and to the bill's being reported to the Senate after the expiration of the morning hour—tactics which brought sharp rebukes from two senior members but delayed the bill a day.[19] And it was he who held the floor from nine till midnight the last night of the session, until the water-diversion bill was put aside for other business;[20] and he who sat through the early morning hours, armed with a score of amendments and great piles of materials, ready to

[17] Ibid. (July 18), p. 14187.

[18] H.R. 2, 85th Cong. See S. Rept. 2482, Congressional Record, Vol. 104 (August 20, 1958), p. 18606.

[19] Ibid. (August 19), p. 18457.

[20] Ibid. (August 23), pp. 19464–66, 19469–78, 19522–39, 19554–55.

resume the debate. When the session ended at 4:11 A.M. the unfinished business of the Senate was a Proxmire amendment to the bill. It is not likely that anyone on the floor that night doubted that Proxmire was ready to talk on through Sunday if need be, but probably few present realized how eager he was to do just that.

III. THE CHOICE OF ROLE

What may be suggested about the "senator" role from this summary statement of the first stage of Proxmire's socialization in the Senate?

First, at a certain point in his first session, Proxmire selected the role he would play. He did not play badly the role associated with the member of the Inner Club; he rejected it. He did not fail in an effort to· make himself acceptable to the Inner Club; he decided he did not want to try to be one of them. The role he chose was one suited to his personality and temperament, one he had played before.[21] In his opinion it offered him the best opportunities to attain his goals in the Senate. Conformity with the folkways would not have allowed him, for instance, to associate himself so persistently with expansion of social security nor to make his Horatio-like stand against the water-diversion bill. Moreover, the independent role clearly was congenial to his constituency—Proxmire's seat had been held successively by "Old Bob" LaFollette and his son and by Joe McCarthy—and Proxmire was up for reelection. But it is important that his performance was not simply a bid for votes; it was rather a deliberately adopted legislative style which he has followed consistently since reelection.[22]

Second, he had a model to go by. He mentioned two senators and

[21] In his first press conference after winning the special election in 1957, Proxmire shunned labels such as "liberal" and "Douglas Democrat," but mentioned approvingly that some labor leaders had described him as a "maverick." Chicago *Daily News*, August 29, 1957.

[22] Representative actions are not hard to find. In 1959 Proxmire made three speeches criticizing the Democratic party leadership in the Senate, with support from four other senators. *Congressional Record*, Vol. 105 (February 23), pp. 2814–20, (March 9), pp. 3559–78, (April 15), pp. 5956–59. In 1960 he opposed the judicial nomination of a Wisconsin man who had massive support from within and outside the state, with no one else from Wisconsin in opposition. (Proxmire said: "I have had more visits and phone calls in connection with this nomination than with any other matter I have dealt with since I came to the Senate.") Hearings, Senate Judiciary Subcommittee, 86th Cong 2d sess., *Nomination of James R. Durfee; Congres-*

could have named others. The norms for his behavior were furnished by a small group within the Senate, just as the norms of the "Senate type" are likewise furnished by another, perhaps much larger, group within the Senate. The model, moreover, is rooted in Senate history. There have always been members of the Senate labelled variously as "independents," "mavericks," and the like. They have come from all sections of the country, although the midwest seems to have produced more than its share. It is not necessary to try to establish a roster of such senators; a voluminous popular literature and common knowledge support the contention that the "loner," the man who conspicuously walks his own way, is a familiar figure in the Senate.[23] What is more important is to try to sharpen the description of the role and to distinguish it from its opposite, the "Senate type" which makes up the membership of the Inner Club.

Because the most significant characteristic of the role is its conscious rejection of the behavior associated with belonging to the Inner Club, we might tentatively label it the "Outsider." The term is not meant, however, to apply indiscriminately to all members of what White calls the Outer Club (*i.e.*, all senators not in the Inner

---

sional Record, Vol. 106 (January 25), pp. 1027–1033, (April 19), pp. 7577–78, (April 20), p. 7750. In 1961 he was the first to make a fight against a Kennedy nominee. *Ibid.* (daily edition, January 23, 1961), pp. 1086–1100.

[23] "Borah and Johnson, Disturbers of the Senatorial Peace," *The Literary Digest* (August 23, 1919), pp. 52, 55; Austin Haines, "Smith W. Brookhart, Dissenter," *Nation* (November 1, 1922), pp. 465–7; Richard Barry, "A Radical in Power: A Study of La Follette," *Outlook* (November 29, 1922), pp. 564–7; Chester H. Rowell, "LaFollette, Shipstead, and the Embattled Farmers," *World's Work* (August, 1923), pp. 408–20; F. E. Haynes, "LaFollette and LaFollettism," *Atlantic Monthly* (October, 1924), 536–44; Bruce Bliven, "Robert M. LaFollette's Place in Our History," *Current History* (August, 1925), pp. 716–22; Charles Merz, "Androcles and the Lion: The Silent President and the Roaring Borah," *Century* (April, 1926), pp. 698–703; Richard Washburn Child, "He Rides Alone," *Saturday Evening Post* (May 21, 1927), pp. 6–7, 187, 189; Dixon Merritt, "Four Senators," *Outlook* (December 28, 1927), pp. 531, 534; Ray T. Tucker, "Those Sons of Wild Jackasses," *North American Review* (February, 1930), pp. 225–33; Frederick R. Barkley, "The Voice of the Corn Belt: Senator Norris—Square Peg in the G.O.P.," *Outlook* (January 14, 1931), pp. 52–4, 74–5; Louis H. Cook, "Brookhart, Insurgent," *North American Review* (February, 1931), pp. 178–84; Oswald Garrison Villard, "Borah Goes on the War Path," *Nation* (July 25, 1934), p. 91; "Borah: Political History-Maker," *Literary Digest* (February 1, 1936), p. 9; Richard L. Neuberger, "Wayne Morse: Republican Gadfly," *American Mercury* (July, 1947), pp. 16–24; Robert L. Riggs, "Wayne Morse: The Peril of Independence," *The New Republic* (March 2, 1953), pp. 10–12; Robert L. Riggs, "That Maverick Morse," *Nation* (May 5, 1956), pp. 380–2.

Club), who may simply have failed somehow to be taken into the inner communion, but to the man who does not *want* to be in.

If the "Senate type" who belongs to the Inner Club is distinguished by his sensitiveness to Senate moods, his regard for Senate traditions and norms, and his spirit of accommodation, the Outsider is notable for his determination to speak out whenever he pleases on whatever subject he chooses without regard to whether he can get any vote but his own. And if the "Senate type" cares more for the esteem of like-minded colleagues than any other kind of approval, the Outsider typically looks elsewhere—to his constituents and to his ideological allies across the nation, perhaps more than to those other members of the Senate whose norms he shares.

The difference between the Outsider and the Senate type is not so much in ideology or issue orientation (although the Outsider is more likely to be liberal, as his opposite number is apt to be conservative) as in legislative style. The popular literature of forty years has drawn a sharp picture of that style. The Outsider feels impelled to stand for principle absolutely, preferring defeat on those terms to half-a-loaf. He likes to tell people what they should and frequently do not want to hear. He is never so confident of the soundness of his opinions as when he holds them alone. He is as comfortable alone against the crowd as the Senate type is in the bosom of the club; indeed he is probably happiest when he stands by himself against powerful and wrong-headed foes. As a consequence few people, in the body or outside, are lukewarm toward him; they tend to like or dislike him strongly. He is like the "sons of the wild jackasses" who came out of the midwest thirty years ago, of whom it was said that "theirs is not a compromising spirit, and this lack of the give-and-take philosophy may, with their want of a sense of humor, be their strength."[24]

The characterization is not really adequate. For one thing, it is undoubtedly too harsh. Many who helped shape it were deeply unsympathetic with the goals and tactics of the men they described, among whom there were, then and now, attractive as well as powerful personalities. Nevertheless there is more than a suggestion that unpopularity was not unknown to them and they were not dismayed by it. Even if it were wholly fair, the description obviously would not apply in all its details to any individual. What we have sketched

[24] Tucker, *op. cit.*, pp. 226–27.

here is an "ideal type"; real people are only more or less like it.[25] Its relevance is that it suggests what I shall argue here, that the Outsider is not a deviant at all but a person playing a recognizable and recognized role, a legitimate alternative to some others which he might select.

Deviant behavior has been defined as "behavior which violates institutionalized expectations—that is, expectations which are shared and recognized as legitimate in a social system."[26] My argument is that the Outsider role has been accepted and esteemed by a considerable part, at least, of the general public and by the specialized publics of close students of the Senate and that within the Senate itself it is recognized as legitimate whether it is popular with a majority or not. Most theories of deviant behavior postulate an effort (even if ineffective) by the social system to eliminate or at least control the offending behavior. The Senate has proved that it can and will take telling measures against what it considers deviant behavior, but the kind of behavior associated with the Outsider role is remarkably free of institutional inhibitions.

One piece of evidence supporting the assertion of widespread public acceptance of the role is the long tenure in office usually enjoyed by the established maverick. Approval by the special publics is suggested by the frequency with which close observers rank men noted for their independence at or close to the top of lists of outstanding senators. Thus a group of political scientists who specialized in legislation (presumed to be able to make informed judgments largely free from provincial, partisan or emotional bias) were asked in 1950 to "grade" all members of the Senate; they consistently put Douglas first, and the next three in order were Kefauver, Morse and Lehman.[27]

[25] This should be emphasized. No classification of individuals is intended. Where individuals are mentioned it is only to illustrate a characteristic in the construction of a type.

[26] Albert K. Cohen, "The Study of Social Disorganization and Deviant Behavior," in Robert K. Merton et al. (eds.), Sociology Today (New York, 1959), pp. 461–84, 462. Robert A. Dentler and Kai T. Erickson argue that deviants are functional to the group, testing and tracing its boundaries, as opposed to the notion of deviance as a dysfunctional aspect of group or society; but they accept Cohen's definition and it is clear that they are talking about behavior which is regarded as illegitimate by the group. "The Function of Deviance in Groups," Social Problems, Vol. 7 (Fall, 1960), pp. 98–107.

[27] Byron L. Johnson and W. E. Butt, "Rating the Senators," New Republic (March 3, 1952), pp. 10–11.

The same year *Time* included Douglas among the "Senate's most valuable ten," calling him, among other things, a "maverick liberal."[28] *Collier's* congressional award for 1946 went to Robert LaFollette, Jr., "as notable an independent as the Senate has known since his fiery father, Wisconsin's famous Old Bob . . ." who always "has been free to do his stuff as he thought it should be done."[29] One of two awards made by the American Political Science Association in 1959 to outstanding members of the Senate went to John J. Williams of Delaware, who is noted for his lone-wolf assaults on wasteful spending, subsidies, and tax privileges.[30]

More than that, the Senate itself has in a sense put its *imprimatur* on the role. In 1955 the Senate set about selecting "five outstanding persons, but not a living person, who have served as members of the Senate" whose portraits would be painted in oval spaces left blank for that purpose when the Reception Room was decorated a century earlier.[31] A committee of five senators chaired by John F. Kennedy considered nominations for two years with advice from many people.[32] The senators finally selected were Webster, Calhoun, Clay, Taft, and the senior LaFollette. The names fall almost automatically into slots—the nationalist, the sectionalist, the compromiser, the arch Republican, the maverick liberal.[33] Was the committee—

[28] "Senate's Most Valuable Ten," *Time* (April 3, 1950), p. 20.

[29] James C. Derieux, "For Distinguished Congressional Service," *Collier's* (April 26, 1947), pp. 78–79. The awards, made each year for four years to one member of each house, consisted of a $10,000 cash prize and a gold medal presented by the President of the United States. Other senators chosen were Arthur H. Vandenberg (1945), Alben W. Barkley (1947), and Vandenberg again (1948). Young Bob's style in the Senate was not his father's; indeed, by the time the *Collier's* award was made he probably was a valued member of the Inner Club. But the point is that his independence was stressed in the article announcing the award.

[30] *Congressional Record*, Vol. 105 (September 11, 1959), pp. 19085–86. See also William Benton, "For Distinguished Service in Congress," *New York Times Magazine* (July 24, 1955), pp. 14 ff.

[31] New York *Times*, May 5, 1957, IV, p. 2.

[32] The original committee was made up of Lyndon B. Johnson, chairman; Richard B. Russell, Styles Bridges, Mike Mansfield, and Eugene D. Millikin. *Congressional Record*, Vol. 101 (August 2, 1955), p. 12967. Johnson later was replaced by Kennedy and Millikin by John W. Bricker. For a description of the selection process, see John F. Kennedy, "Search for the Five Greatest Senators," *New York Times Magazine* (April 14, 1957), pp. 14–18.

[33] See S. Rept. No. 279, 85th Cong., 1st sess., *Congressional Record*, Vol. 103 (May 1, 1957), pp. 6206–8.

perhaps consciously—filling historic roles? The choice of LaFollette is striking. It is doubtful that any man ever aroused more bitter antagonisms in the Senate or was ever more reviled by his colleagues than he.[34] That LaFollette was selected as a prototype seems more likely from the fact that his closest competitor was George W. Norris, a man not like any of the other "outstanding persons" but the most like LaFollette.[35]

What happens inside the Senate to the Outsider? Not much; as White observed, the Senate is not a body disposed to impose sanctions on any behavior but the most outrageous. The point is important. A group may be expected to punish deviant behavior, and the Senate has proved that it can and will do so with dreadful finality.[36] Calculated and continued flouting of the dignity and good order of the Senate, easier to recognize than define, is deviance which compels sanctions. It will be punished finally, as Huey Long and Joe McCarthy learned, by a spiritual banishment more conclusive than formal censure and more galling, in its daily erosion of ego, than physical expulsion. But the Senate is of all official bodies (again, as White remarked) perhaps the most tolerant of individualistic, even eccentric, behavior.

Institutional arrangements, both formal and informal, encourage tolerance. An external system determines who shall be members and confers upon them an equal official status, and the seniority system softens the contest for status and preference internally. The Senate is a relatively large group (though its smallness has always been emphasized); it *does* have a hundred members, and the staff people who share intimately in the work of the body multiply that number several times. Differences in style, temperament and goals therefore may be

---

[34] This was frankly acknowledged in the committee report, *ibid.*, p. 6205, which says of LaFollette, in part: "Ceaseless battler for the underprivileged in an age of special privilege, courageous independent in an age of partisan conformity, he fought memorably against tremendous odds and stifling inertia for social and economic reforms which ultimately proved essential to American progress in the 20th century. . . . The bitter antagonisms stirred by his unyielding opposition to international commitments and conflict were ultimately submerged by widespread admiration for his dedicated life-long fight against political corruption and corporate greed." An editorial criticism of the selections characterizes LaFollette as "the champion of lost causes." "What Makes These Senators Great?" *Christian Century* (May 15, 1957), p. 612.

[35] *Congressional Record, ibid.,* pp. 6212–13.

[36] White, *op. cit.,* pp. 121–35.

softened by simple avoidance if not by the sharing of committee tasks, or by the temporary alliances of mutual interest which account for much legislation. And because the Senate agenda is managed largely by unanimous consent a majority judiciously refrains from employing against irksome behavior the small sanctions which serve merely to irritate the offending member. The imposition of censure or ostracism is a rare and traumatic action reserved for really deviant behavior usually borne a long time.

The evidence is strong that the Senate accepts as legitimate a wide range of behavior. Its members advance without hindrance to the perquisites of seniority, and some of the most powerful committees have had rather odd chairmen. Relations among subgroups appear to be easy; an Outsider who fights with only a handful of friends on one issue may, because of personal expertness on the subject, be chosen by the leadership to lead the party on a crucial measure the next week. Proxmire has said that no sanctions have been imposed on him; on the contrary, the leadership gave him substantial help in 1960 in the passage of a dairy price support bill which was helpful to his constituents.[37] Proxmire, like other Outsiders, readily joins subgroups in support of common interests and frequently votes with the majority. The behavior associated with the Outsider role seems to fall well within the bounds of what most members of the Senate regard as tolerable.

If this analysis is correct, an assumption of role consensus in the Senate is incorrect; there is variability not only in the behavior of occupants of the senator position but in the expectations—the "ideal patterns"—of behavior to which members may conform.[38] The Outsider therefore is not a deviant but an alternative role. It would be a mistake also to assume, without empirical justification, a bimodal distribution of acceptable behaviors—the Inner Club member and the Outsider. What is more probable is the existence of several legitimate "senator" roles. One thinks, for instance, of the persistence of the pure service type, the "Errand Boy," who eschews controversy and distinguishes himself neither in committee nor on the floor, but renders himself unbeatable by causing his beneficence to fall like

[37] S. 2917, S. Rept. 1592, 86th Cong., 2d Sess.; P.L. 86–799. See *Congressional Record* (daily edition, August 19, 1960), pp. 15594–600.

[38] See the discussion of "the postulate of role consensus" in Neal, et al., *op. cit.*, ch. 2.

gentle rain on all his constituents, Democrats and Republicans alike. The identification and conceptualization of alternative roles will in turn provide important clues to strains and conflicts, or to the existence of subsystems, within the body.[39]

It should be emphasized, however, that the successful performance of this task would by no means exhaust the sets of role orientations in the Senate which are worth analysis.[40] What we are dealing with here—the way the senator relates himself generally to his colleagues and the obligations of his office, or better, the *style* of his performance in chamber, committee room and office—is concerned with only one set, albeit an important one. Externally it is the image of himself as senator which he projects to his publics. Within the Senate it is the cluster of attitudes and modes of behavior toward other members which identify him to them and stimulate and shape their attitudes and behavior toward him. The choice of this role among available alternatives is therefore crucial to the successful performance of his other roles and to his self-esteem, and its importance is heightened by the fact that, once adopted, it is not easy to change.

IV. ASSESSMENT OF THE ROLE

The disability usually supposed to be associated with the Outsider role is that the senator who chooses it is thereby doomed to be less effective in the Senate. White puts it indirectly: the Inner Club runs the Senate;[41] the Outsider would be then, by definition, not of much consequence. Matthews goes further, attempting to test the proposition that the more effective member abides by the folkways. He constructs an index of "Legislative Effectiveness" by calculating the propor-

---

[39] *Ibid.,* pp. 25–26.

[40] The most perceptive and elaborate statement of the interrelated sets of roles within a legislative sub-system is found in the comparative study of four state legislatures by Heinz Eulau, John C. Wahlke, LeRoy C. Ferguson and William Buchanan, "The Role of the Representative: Some Empirical Observations on the Theory of Edmund Burke," *The American Political Science Review,* Vol. 53 (September, 1959), pp. 742–56; "The Legislator as Specialist," *Western Political Quarterly,* Vol. 13 (September, 1960), pp. 636–51; and especially their mimeographed working paper, "The Role Concept in the Comparative Study of State Legislatures," pp. 3–17. See also my "The Congressional Committee: A Case Study," [see pp. 77–112 of the present book—Eds.]

[41] *Op. cit.,* pp. 86–87.

tion of all public bills and resolutions introduced by each senator in two successive congresses that were passed by the Senate, arguing that "to the extent that the concept as used on Capitol Hill has any distinct meaning, 'effectiveness' seems to mean the ability to get one's bills passed." He then plots the effectiveness index against indexes measuring conformity with two Senate folkways and concludes: "The less a senator talks on the Senate floor, and the narrower a senator's area of legislative interest and activity, the greater is his 'effectiveness.' "[42]

It should be said at once that Matthews is as modest in his claims for his statistical test as he is resourceful in constructing it. Nevertheless the effectiveness index raises questions too important to ignore. To the individual senator, to whom being a senator is part of a professional career, the ability to get reelected might be considered a fair test of effectiveness and any behavior judicious which helps him pass the test. From the point of view of society, the conception of the Senate as a bill-and-resolution factory where the individual members are paid on a piece-work basis seems both too narrow and contrary to fact. To take the last point first, the passage of a bill is a collective process in which the introducer may have played a very small part, if indeed his bill was not changed beyond recognition.[43] Conversely, bill introduction may be no more than a form of advocacy, or a way to state a personal platform, or simply a bid for publicity. Or again, a senator may persistently sponsor legislation he knows can pass only well in the future, if at all, as George Norris did the TVA.[44] But more important, the enactment of legislation is but one and perhaps not the most important function of either house of Congress, let alone of all members individually. An adequate assessment of the effective-

[42] *Op. cit.,* pp. 114–17.

[43] In determining standards for the selection of the five outstanding senators, Kennedy rejected the notion of choosing those whose names are prominently associated with legislation. He pointed out that the senator whose name a bill bears may not be for the bill and may not even have read it, while a senator whose legislative efforts fail may find that later on someone else will take up his bill and succeed. John F. Kennedy, *op. cit.*

[44] Stephen K. Bailey and Howard D. Samuel, *Congress at Work* (New York, 1952), ch. 8; Henry C. Hart, "Legislative Abdication in Regional Development," *The Journal of Politics.* Vol. 13 (1951), pp. 393–417.

ness of alternative Senate roles or individual role-takers must await an analysis of the political functions performed by the Senate.[45]

Suppose, for instance, that one function of the legislature should prove to be "the institutionalization, crystallization and resolution of conflicts."[46] Might not then the Outsider's outspoken championship of minority, perhaps unpopular, views contribute to the process? The analysis would have to take account of the latent functions—the unintended and unrecognized consequences—as well as the manifest functions.[47] A latent function of the legislature might be to provide catharsis for fringe views which never will prevail.[48] If so, what better agent than the lone fighter against hopeless odds (regardless of his motivations or what he fights for) who, as he afflicts the mighty, may serve as the psychological representative of all the Outsiders in the great society?[49] To turn the questions around, is it likely that certain modes of legislative behavior should persist over long periods of time *without* having relevance for the political functions the legislature is called upon to perform?

It may be that Senate role and Senate function are directly linked and either may be approached through the other. The "ideal pattern" of behavior which we have called "role" may embrace one or more basic functions of the Senate, performed in greater or less degree by all the members, writ large and personified in the "ideal" role-taker. Thus the Errand Boy, if we may assume there is such a role, simply is performing to the virtual exclusion of everything else a function which by all accounts has always consumed a great deal of

[45] Robert K. Merton, *Social Theory and Social Structure* (Glencoe, Ill., 1957), pp. 19–84.

[46] In their comparative study of four state legislatures, Eulau, Wahlke, Ferguson and Buchanan use this phrase to define the legislative process (cited in note 40).

[47] *Op. cit.*, pp. 60–84. Merton makes "the distinction between manifest functions and latent functions; the first referring to those objective consequences for a specified unit (person, sub-group, social or cultural system) which contribute to its adjustment or adaptation and were so intended; the second referring to unintended and unrecognized consequences of the same order."

[48] David B. Truman suggests this as one of the functions of the public hearing of the congressional committee. *The Governmental Process* (New York, 1953), pp. 327–77.

[49] This is suggested by Proxmire's mail from all over the country when, for instance, he criticized his party's leadership in the Senate.

energy and time of senators and (especially since the Legislative Reorganization Act) their staff. In any event, what is important is that a functional analysis be made, and that it take into account what the legislators actually do and not just putative functions ascribed to them. Not until such an analysis has been satisfactorily performed can anyone say what senatorial role is "effective" and what is not.

Any sophisticated assessment of Senate roles, moreover, must recognize that any role, or even a single item of behavior, may have "diverse consequences, functional and dysfunctional, for individuals, for sub-groups, and for the more inclusive social structure and culture."[50] Thus the behavior of the Senate type who is in the Inner Club may be functional for groups which benefit from preserving the status quo, dysfunctional for those seeking change; functional for the preservation of harmony within the body, dysfunctional for conflict resolution in the larger society. The behavior associated with the Outsider may be functional for protest groups seeking a spokesman, dysfunctional for groups needing leverage inside the legislative body. It may even be functional for the leadership, to the degree that it makes more persuasive the middle position usually taken by the leaders. A given role may be functional in some respects for the role-taker, dysfunctional in others. Proxmire, for example, unquestionably has paid a price for choosing the Outsider role (as he would if he had chosen another) which he believes to be justified by the increased freedom of action it gives him. The important thing would seem to be not what role is chosen but what the role-taker uses it for, what goals are served by it. The Inner Club member may get little more than the personal satisfaction of belonging, the Outsider no more than personal publicity. Either may, on the other hand, choose his role self-consciously with the probable consequences clearly in mind, in order to maximize the advantages to be gained toward legislative goals he has set himself.

[50] Merton, *op. cit.*, p. 30.

FIVE
THE INTERNAL DISTRIBUTION
OF INFLUENCE: THE SENATE

T HE Senate of the United States is a small and special world. The chamber is quiet. It must be, because there is no public address system and business is conducted in conversational tones. It is dignified: somber-suited men, a few quite old, move in the perpetual twilight of its high ceiling lights. There is a feeling of continuity; in the bottom drawer of the Victorian desks the men who sat there have signed their names and some, at least, must stir the least imaginative newcomer.

It is the place of the states, as the Founding Fathers meant it to be. No teeming state may override the constitutional guarantee of perfect numerical equality, and no man is bigger simply because he comes from a big state. Indeed, men from small states have walked this floor with a heavy tread: Borah of Idaho, Norris of Nebraska, LaFollette of Wisconsin. It is the place of the individual; most business is done by unanimous consent, and one man with ruffled feelings must be pacified, if he knows the rules.

It is a small world, ingrown and not wholly immune from narcissism, yet its nerve ends are in the great world outside, and its reaction to events can be instantaneous. It does not forget, nor does it let the Executive forget, that it has unique

Ralph K. Huitt, "The Internal Distribution of Influence: The Senate" in *The Congress and America's Future*, David B. Truman, ed., © 1965 by The American Assembly. Reprinted by permission of Prentice-Hall, Inc., Englewood Cliffs, New Jersey.

powers over and responsibilities for the conduct of foreign policy.

Its members are accustomed to deference; their elevators carry them where *they* want to go while the public waits. Nevertheless all of them must return, sooner or later, to account to the people who sent them, and not one may be absolutely sure he will come back.

The small and special world of the Senate is not easy for the outsider—nor all the insiders—to understand. Prestige outside and inside the body are not necessarily equated, and prestige both outside and inside does not necessarily mean influence inside. Formal powers are less important than the brains and self-confidence to assume a large role, tempered by the sensitivity to internal controls necessary not to overplay it. The tranquil outer surface is deceptively simple: the complex and largely unstated rules of its inner life may be missed or misunderstood even by men who live with them a long time.

Sober and sophisticated men have fallen in love with the Senate, and some of them have betrayed their infatuation in print. Others, including some members of the body, have excoriated it in harsh despair.

All this seems worth saying, or trying to say, at the beginning of what is intended as a dispassionate analysis of some of the elements of power in the Senate. It is a way of saying that the Senate is not easy to write about with confidence. Some familiarity with senators and their world brings with it a hesitancy to say very much with certainty. Nevertheless the Senate *does* have a public life, and some insights may be gained from it.

I. FORMAL PARTY LEADERSHIP

In the House of Representatives the chair is more than a symbol of authority; it is the seat of the most powerful man in the body, the Speaker. He is there when great business is afoot and many other times besides. Not so in the Senate. The Constitution says the Vice-President (a man of prestige if not much power) should preside and sometimes he does—during the opening prayer, perhaps, or when a tie vote (which he can break) seems likely. His surrogate technically is the President *pro tempore,* a venerable majority member who may spend more time in the chauffeured limousine the office provides than in the chair itself. Presiding is the special burden of the freshman senators of the majority party, who among them do it most of the time. Their staff people like to send constituents over to the gallery (with a pardonably deceitful hint of pride in his quick success) "to see our senator preside." It is a good joke but a small one—poor pay indeed for hours spent at the most tedious and least influential job in the Senate. Nevertheless their chore underlines a basic truth about the Senate, that power is not where rules say or appearances suggest it should be, but where it is found.

The men who sit in the front seat on either side of the aisle, the floor leaders of the respective parties, have much influence, as have the chairmen of the standing committees in varying degrees. Besides these incumbents of formal positions there are senators who exercise influence in informal groups which set the tone and shape the norms of the body. The relative effectiveness of these extra-constitutional power-wielders depends upon a combination of personal aggressiveness and sensitivity to the climate of the Senate, of time and circumstance and external influences, which makes generalization hazardous indeed. Generalizations must be tried just the same. Political power of the magnitude of that exercised by and within the Senate demands that repeated attempts at analysis be made.

The floor leaders: some stable elements

There are elements of the floor leader's power in the Senate which are relatively stable and permanent, others which are variable; among the variable elements there are some about which he personally can do much and others about which he can do little.

The most important stable element by far is the character of the American political system. Governmental power is divided between the national government and the fifty states, and at the national level it is shared in a shifting balance by the Executive, Congress, and the courts. These are basic constitutional arrangements about which the leader can do almost literally nothing. He can do little more to change the kind of political parties these arrangements have helped to produce. The leader is the principal officer in the Senate of a national political party. What does this mean? If his party has captured the White House, he can expect some policy guidance from the President; but if he is in the minority, he would be hard put to it to find anyone with a claim to national party leadership superior to his own. "National" party in America is an ambiguous concept: ideologically, it is a cluster of ideas, symbols and associations which its "members" share more or less; operationally, it is an agglomeration of state and local parties, interest groups, and temporary associations which want for one reason or another to elect a President. Its quadrennial platform, compounded of principle and expediency, may be ignored or even denounced by the presidential candidate himself. The most astonishing thing about this remarkable organization, the party, is that it *does* command considerable loyalty from its members, inside and outside public office.

But it is not a loyalty which binds a congressman to a party line, no matter who enunciates it, when it goes contrary to his own convictions or strongly held wishes his constituents appear to hold. Party identification may be the strongest influence on voters without meaning the same thing to all voters; so a high score on party votes will not necessarily get a campaigning senator in free. Survival in office rests ultimately on his relations with his own constituency. The leadership cannot help him or hurt him very much, and he knows it. Great careers have been built on party dissidence, and he has seen party giants go down. The leader understands this, too, because his party office gives him no immunity. What leader did more than John Worth Kern, who put Woodrow Wilson's massive legislative program through the Senate virtually intact? And what was his reward but to be retired by Indiana voters in 1916? What else happened to Scott Lucas in Illinois and Ernest McFarland in Arizona, both Democratic leaders, in successive elections? For each man defeat closed his senatorial career; there is no device in American life by which a party may restore a defeated leader to office. Moreover, congressmen know that a trip to the party woodshed may smart but is seldom fatal; not even Franklin Roosevelt could purge intransigent Democrats. No member of Congress can escape the lonely awareness that he is essentially on his own. This explains a basic fact of life in the Senate: no one finally can make anyone else do anything.

A second element affecting the leader's situation which changes little is the relative paucity of formal powers attached to this position. He is not a national officer in the government. He is not a national officer in his party. He is not even an officer in his house, as the Speaker is in the House of Representatives. He must put together "fragments of power," as David Truman has said, combining them with great personal skill and tenacity, if he is to succeed.[1] The majority leader has, for instance, the right to be recognized first when he pleases, which gives him substantial parliamentary advantage. Through the Policy Committee he may control the scheduling of floor consideration of bills; through the Committee on Committees (or the Democrats' Steering Committee) he may influence his party's committee assignments. If he is a Democrat both are made easier, because he is also chairman of the two committees. Because he is the center of the senatorial party's communications network and has access to the President if they are of the same party, the leader knows more than other senators and can share what he knows as he chooses. He may use these advantages, with some small favors he can bestow, to help other senators get what they want and expect them, in return, to help him. Democratic leader Mike Mansfield certainly was too modest when he said he had no more power than any other senator. On the other hand, there is no reading of these formal powers which will support the notion that they amount to much.

The converse of the leader's powers is the very considerable freedom of action reserved to the members themselves. This freedom is tenable only because it is exercised in the main with moderation and good sense. The Senate transacts most of its business through unanimous consent; debate is limited, schedules agreed to, rules set aside without objection because leaders respect the rights and interests of individual senators, who in turn go along with reasonable arrangements proposed by their leaders. But nothing is surrendered. One man may object and slow business to a halt. The ultimate expression of a latent institutionalized anarchy in the Senate is, as everyone knows, the filibuster—the privilege of unlimited talk—which permits a determined minority, and under certain circumstances a single member, to impose a negative on the entire body.

The Senate has never been entirely easy with its rule of "unlimited debate." Henry Clay tried unsuccessfully in 1841 to get adoption of a one-hour rule to limit debate. Nearly a century later the Senate accepted a cloture rule after a "little group of willful men" had, in Woodrow Wilson's opinion, "rendered the great government of the United States helpless and contemptible" by successfully filibustering

---

[1] David B. Truman, The Congressional Party: A Case Study (New York, 1959), p. 115.

his proposal to arm merchant ships. Cloture has gone through several variations since then, but it has always been hard to invoke and slow to take effect. Sixteen senators must sign a petition for limitation of debate, which brings the question to a vote two days later. At times the votes of two-thirds of the whole membership have been required to adopt cloture, but in 1959 this was reduced to two-thirds of those present and voting. After adoption of cloture each senator still may talk an hour on the measure.

Cloture undoubtedly is difficult to achieve. It has been employed successfully only six times since 1917, and four of these came in the first ten years of the rule's existence. Perhaps it will be easier in the future; the last two times have come close together. In 1962 a cloture motion was adopted 63–27 to overcome a liberal filibuster against the creation of a private corporation to develop and manage communications satellites such as Telstar. In 1964 every member of the Senate was present to adopt cloture 71–29 on a civil rights bill. But this is a relative matter; there is no prospect that the present rule ever will make it simple to terminate debate on a fiercely controverted matter, and the filibuster (or the threat of it) will remain a potent weapon.

Should cloture be made substantially easier to attain? The question seems to be one of the relative importance of majority will and minority rights. The argument for a more liberal rule is that the majority always should be able, finally, to prevail. After extended debate— long enough to correct imperfections, effect all possible compromises, and provide catharsis for the losers—the majority should work its will. The defenders of the conservative rule point out that the majority can in fact have its way; what is required is the mustering of more than a simple majority. They argue that a special majority should be required to override a determined minority which is not open to being converted by debate. Otherwise resistance and nullification are encouraged and enforcement is made more difficult. The rule of the special majority is a familiar one in the Constitution; it is required for approval of treaties, impeachments, constitutional amendments, expulsion of members, and overriding presidential votes.

What is more important than the leader's powers—and more will be said about this later—the leader cannot control the vast delegations of power parceled out by the Senate to those feudal chieftains, the chairmen of the standing committees. Nor is there any prospect that the delegations can be recalled; the Constitution has seen to that. The separation of powers means that to the Executive and the legislature the other must always be "they." The British House of Commons may rely upon the bureaucracy for assessments as well as facts; the departments are controlled by ministers who also sit as leaders of Parliament. If they do not like what they get, the Honourable Members have sanctions which ministers heed. Not so Congress; vigilance in the committees is the alternative to the forfeit of that equal status to which Congress is entitled and may, in the rough fashion in which such sums must be calculated, actually have.

The leader is a man of great influence nevertheless. The basic reason is that the Senate must be led, and the need will grow more compelling, not less. It is significant that when the senatorial party chooses a man to bring a measure of coordination to this body of specialists, it often abandons the strict seniority principle. Election by his peers is a mark of confidence in him which is bound to strengthen his hand.

The floor leaders: important variables

Some elements of the leader's power potential are variable; of these the situational probably is the most crucial. Perhaps some illustrations will support the point.

The two most productive bursts of congressional energy in this century came in the early years of the administrations of Woodrow Wilson and Franklin Roosevelt. Congress worked continuously the first 567 days of Wilson's first term (April 7, 1913, to October 24, 1914) and was *not* in session only eleven months in four years. Working through Washington summers without air conditioning, Congress passed the most impressive array of constructive legislation perhaps in its history. The New Deal's beginning, with its fabulous "hundred days," needs no retelling; why labor a legend? The two periods, in many ways dissimilar, had this in common: Congress felt the hot breath of the country. Wilson's Democrats had been long out of power; his progressivism had brought them back. They bent willingly to his imperious leadership—so much so that Senate Democrats allowed themselves to be dominated by twenty progressives with no more than two years' seniority (including their leader, Kern), eleven of whom were newly elected! Kern, serving his only term, failed to muster his majority on only one bill Wilson really wanted.[2] Twenty years later, Roosevelt's legions were as eager to go along. Joseph T. Robinson put the emergency banking bill through the Senate in seven hours—including committee and floor consideration—using the only copy of the bill in existence. (The House of Representatives had passed a folded newspaper, accepting the fiction that it was the bill.[3])

It is not necessary to define "normal" times to say that these were not normal, nor that Kennedy's years were more nearly so. When a newsmagazine asked majority leader Mike Mansfield in 1962 "why Kennedy's program is in trouble with Congress," Mansfield replied that Congress responds to sentiment in the country; he believed the country would support the President but there was no sense of urgency yet.[4]

Lucas and McFarland had a Democratic President with a program; they shattered the senatorial party trying to enact the Fair Deal. Johnson had two precious years in the minority to put it together again; he literally sought issues on which the Democrats could be got to vote together. Taft and Knowland, his opposite numbers, could do little with their bare majority and small help from the White House. Johnson's six years as majority leader with Eisenhower raise the question: what difference would a Democratic President have made? Mansfield faced a reaction to Johnson's demanding leadership; a respite of some duration was in order.

The list could go on, but the point is clear: a leader is not free to be any kind of leader he pleases. His alternatives are framed for him by the situation in which he must operate.

At the same time he is not the creature of his situation. The second variable is his own perception of the role of leader. The sharp contrast between Johnson and his successor, Mansfield, is in point. Because he did not drive the Senate as Johnson did, Mansfield was accused (even publicly by a colleague) of being a weak leader. The charge missed the mark: Mansfield had not failed to be like John-

[2] Claude G. Bowers, *The Life of John Worth Kern* (Indianapolis, 1918). See Chapters Fourteen, Seventeen for Kern's record as leader.

[3] Joseph Alsop, Jr., and Turner Catledge, "Joe Robinson, the New Deal's Old Reliable," *Saturday Evening Post* (September 26, 1936).

[4] "Why Kennedy's Program Is in Trouble with Congress," *U.S. News and World Report* (September 17, 1962).

son, he did not *want* to be like Johnson. He was not a weak leader but a deliberately different kind of leader. This is made obvious by interviews held by *U.S. News* with Johnson, in 1960, and with Mansfield in 1962.[5] The men agreed that the majority leader has few real powers, but that is superficial. Johnson made it plain that he meant to use his "only real power," persuasion (by which he meant the employment of every resource he had), to the utmost. Mansfield called Johnson "the best majority leader the Senate ever had," but Johnson would not recognize Mansfield's description of the job. Mansfield did not want the leadership; he was drafted. He was "one among my peers." He had no instruments of authority. He would not use legislative scheduling for leverage nor influence a committee assignment. He would not "think" of telling a senator how to vote. Implicit in his comments was his basic philosophy that all senators are equal, that there is none, not even the leader, who is "more equal" than the others.

How does the leader perceive his relationship with the President? This is bound to affect his performance. There is the President's man; Robinson is an example. Unquestioning fidelity to Roosevelt came easy. He had been successively an ardent Wilsonian, a conservative vice-presidential candidate with Al Smith, an "Old Guardsman" in Congress, a gubernatorial candidate in Arkansas on a strict economy platform. He took the New Deal in stride; party loyalty bridged all ideological chasms. Then there is the man who represents each—the Senate and the President—to the other, but places high value on loyalty to the President. This is the Mansfield view; he said it was easy to follow Kennedy's leadership because they saw eye-to-eye, but he would resign if there was a serious difference. Kern, Barkley, and Lucas felt much the same way. Other leaders have regarded themselves primarily as the Senate's agent to the White House. This was McFarland's view. Taft seemed to regard his relationship with the President as something like a partnership; and Knowland drew a sharp distinction between the leadership and senatorial roles, stepping back several rows to speak in support of the Bricker amendment, which Eisenhower opposed. Again, it is tempting to speculate how Johnson would have worked with a Democratic President. No man ever had more pride in the Senate, but he venerated the Presidency and cor-

[5] "Leadership: An Interview with Senate Leader Lyndon Johnson," *U.S. News and World Report* (June 27, 1960). The Mansfield interview is cited in note 4.

rectly assessed its unique importance to the successful working of the American system. Despite criticism from the liberal wing of his party, he would not oppose Eisenhower just to make issues nor encourage his Democratic majority to attack the President.[6]

Still another aspect of the leader's perception of his role involves the relations between majority and minority leaders. Ideally, there should be two points of view at a time, which complement each other. Sometimes a leader thinks he must fight all the time; this seems to have been the general notion of Kenneth Wherry, who apparently behaved more as a senator from Nebraska than as the minority spokesman, even siding consistently with a minority bloc in his own party. Other opposing leaders have seen their respective roles much as might contending trial lawyers whose professional obligation is to expedite the business of the court. More than that, some pairs of leaders have been able to make clear distinctions between their partisan roles and their partnership in promoting the general welfare, and these relationships make attractive chapters in the history of the Senate. Johnson with Taft, with Knowland, and with Dirksen, as well as Mansfield with Dirksen, fit this pattern.

Perhaps the variable in the leader role which is easiest to identify and hardest to assess is leadership style. The range of behavior has been broad indeed. The contrast between the highly successful leaders of the New Freedom and the New Deal, whom we mentioned earlier, is relevant. Kern was modest, conciliatory, a man of "infinite patience and never-failing tact." A colleague said of him: "He was a strong partisan, but there was a kindness about him that turned aside all feelings of ill will or animosity."[7] Of his New Deal counterpart, contemporary observers said "President Roosevelt uses him to push and pull, butt and bludgeon his ideas into legal existence. . . ." Robinson was a man who

. . . loves a fight, and when it is necessary to make enemies, he never exhibits the usual politician's soft unwillingness to offend. He cheerfully steps on toes that require to be stepped on, and sometimes on some that don't, and he can read the riot act with complete authority.[8]

[6] Ralph K. Huitt, "Democratic Party Leadership in the Senate," *American Political Science Review,* 55 (June 1961), 333–344 [pp. 136–158 of the present book—Eds.]; William S. White, *The Professional: Lyndon B. Johnson* (Boston, 1964), pp. 171–177.

[7] Bowers, *op. cit.,* p. 374.

[8] Alsop and Catledge, *op. cit.,* p. 7.

If these are extremes, Johnson might occupy a middle ground. His determination to "persuade" included everyone who might be got to go Johnson's way. The tactics ranged from the casual but pointed remark in his restless roaming of floor and cloakroom to the saturation bombardment known as "Treatment A," in which the whole gamut of emotions—patriotism, loyalty, selfishness, fear, pride—might be played upon. Johnson's persuasive talents were universally respected but not invariably loved.

Wise leaders have used other men for jobs not quite in their own line. Robinson was not a man for a sensitive situation; when persuasion was needed he called on "fixers" like James Byrnes and Pat Harrison; or at the second level, Vice-President Garner; or as a court of last resort, Jim Farley. One of Johnson's prime skills was his manipulation of the versatile Democratic "bench," fitting men to precise jobs he wanted them to do.

Much has been said here about the leader, particularly the majority leader, because he is the most influential and promising figure in the strongest centralizing agency in the Senate, the party. In his study of party operations in the Eighty-first Congress, Truman found the majority leader in both houses to be a middleman ideologically who sought positions on which a majority could be put together. He worked with the committee chairmen and tended to support committee bills, but when he and the chairman were in opposition on a committee bill the leader tended to carry with him a majority of the committee and the party as well.[9]

There is a limit to what party in the Senate can carry, but it is not a negligible force. Truman has said that the congressional party is "mediate and supplementary rather than immediate and inclusive in function," meaning by "mediate" that "its members' fortunes are not identical with those of the legislative party, but at the same time they are not completely independent of it."[10] The party emerges as the most often-heeded cue-giver in the Senate. A senator may vote with it because there are no competing cues; that is, on an issue he may hear no clear voice from home and may have no strong sentiments of his own. But it goes farther than that: on administration measures in the Eighty-first Congress even the dissident Southern wing voted

[9] Truman, op. cit., pp. 140, 242.
[10] Ibid., p. 95.

with the Democratic majority more than the Republicans most likely
to vote with the administration. This unifying tendency is more evident in the majority party. Lacking the recognized leadership furnished the majority by the President, the minority may lack the capacity to organize a stable majority of its members around a program
of opposition.[11]

Other party agencies

Some students and practitioners of American politics have had a
dream—an oft-recurring dream—about how the American political
system might work. The dream is called responsible party government.
There are variations in its details, but the basic notion is always the
same, that the parties will perfect machinery through which they will
keep the promises they make. The solemn pledges would be made in
frequent conventions. The President and his congressional majorities
would work together closely. The elected leaders in the two houses
would formulate programs through policy comittees made up of the
chairmen of the standing committees and ratify them in conferences
of all the members of the party in the respective houses. Members
would be bound, formally or in honor, to support the party position.
The chairmen of the standing committees would push through their
groups the bills they agreed to in the policy committee. The minority
in turn would provide a constructive and loyal opposition through
similar party machinery. The majority would bear responsibility for
its program, the minority would offer a genuine alternative, and the
voter would have a chance to make an intelligent choice.

This is not an idle dream. All the parts of it exist in real life. Some
of them are old and some relatively new. All of them work, more or
less, but not quite the way the dream would have it.

The conference (or caucus, as it was called) is as old as the republic. Congressional caucuses nominated presidential candidates before
there were conventions. The conference can indeed be an effective
party instrument; Kern used it regularly in the enactment of Wilson's
legislation. Members were bound and loyalty was expected. It is
significant, however, that a substantial bloc of Kern's Democrats were
themselves progressives, deeply committed to Wilsonian pledges
which they also made. But ideological dedication is not the norm
in Congress. Most members chafe at efforts to bind them. They seek

[11] *Ibid.*, p. 192.

that blend of policy positions which they individually can comfortably defend at home. Johnson was bitterly criticized for not holding more conferences, but his critics made clear they did not mean to be bound by conference decisions; they wanted only to advise and be informed. Johnson responded with some conferences, and Mansfield began his tenure with several. Both parties have found them useful in recent times primarily as means to pass the word.

Policy committees by that designation are relatively new. The Joint Committee on the Organization of Congress recommended in 1946 that policy committees be created to formulate legislative policy of the parties, but the House struck them from the Reorganization Act passed that year. The next year the Senate independently established its own policy committees. The two committees have proved useful without having much effect on policy. They have developed differently in each party.

The Republican committee began with nine members but grew until, in 1955, all Republican senators up for reelection were made members. In the Eighty-eighth Congress the number was fourteen, eight of them ex officio as party officers, the other six elected by the conference. (The Republicans have a different man for every party job; the Democratic leader is also chairman of the conference, policy committee, and a committee on committees called the Steering Committee.) The practice of inviting other Republican senators interested in issues under discussion was expanded in the late years of the Eisenhower Administration to an open invitation to a weekly luncheon meeting where all members could be informed of the President's views. The practice has persisted, although attendance dropped off with the loss of the White House. In the Eighty-eighth Congress, nevertheless, the Republicans still could go from committee meeting to conference simply by switching chairmen, making the meeting a convenient platform for announcing a Republican consensus on an issue.

The real utility of the Policy Committee to the Republicans has been the research staff it has made available to them. In the Eighty-eighth Congress there were generally eighteen staff members, about a dozen of them professional. Their importance was magnified by the fact that the rich professional resources of standing committee staffs were largely the possession of the majority, while the parties divided equally the policy committees' appropriation. The staff resources of the Policy Committee were available to individual Republicans as well as the leaders, and most took advantage of them. Sometimes work done for a single member later was distributed to all, along with a series of position papers of general usefulness.

The Democratic Policy Committee has been what the successive leaders have chosen to make it. There are nine members, three ex *officio* and six chosen by the leader—but the latter serve as long as they are in the Senate. Barkley chose this mode of selection. Some effort has been made to keep an ideological and geographical balance on the committee, but there are liberal Northerners who would say it has been unsuccessful. The principal test in filling a vacancy is whether the leader *wants* him. Johnson made regular use of the committee to counsel with him. He liked to put friends on it who were men of power in their own right. No announcement of decisions was ever made except for tactical reasons. Mansfield apparently made small use of the committee except for legislative scheduling, which seems reasonable in light of his perception of the leader's role. The staff has also done useful research, but this is less crucial to the Democrats, who have controlled the committee staffs.

The other party agencies of importance are the committees on committees and the campaign committees. The Republican committee takes its committee selections to the conference, where consideration may be heated and prolonged. The Democratic leader may have critical influence over committee assignments if he wants it; he chairs the committee and the conference usually goes along. Johnson used his power deliberately and frankly. One of his first acts as leader was to give all Democrats at least one good committee, a revolution which won the support of freshmen members. He arranged shifts which would put members facing reelection on committees advantageous to them. Mansfield said that he let the Steering Committee freely decide committee assignments, but the makeup of the committee itself came under attack. The most vocal critic was Senator Joseph Clark of Pennsylvania, who charged that the "Establishment" —those senior members who "control the institutional machinery of Congress" (about whom more will be said)—dominates it, to the benefit primarily of the southern minority. He has contended that in 1963 new assignments and transfers went heavily against senators who had voted to liberalize the cloture rule.[12] It is not necessary to decide whether he is right to say that the matter is crucially impor-

---

[12] Joseph S. Clark, *Congress: The Sapless Branch* (New York, 1964), pp. 125–127, and *The Senate Establishment* (New York, 1963), pp. 40 ff., 100–103.

tant. The work of the Senate is done in committees; the careers of senators turn on committee assignments. The ability to control committee appointments is power indeed.

The senatorial campaign committees are designed to help senators of their party who are in close races with a chance to win. The committees are in continuous existence, with staff help and substantial assistance to give. They are mentioned here only because of occasional charges that the money and other help at their disposal are dispensed unfairly to penalize partisan colleagues with whom the committee majority are not sympathetic. Whether the charges are true or are merely attempts to get leverage with the committee, an outsider cannot decide.

II. THE LITTLE GOVERNMENTS OF THE STANDING COMMITTEES

The ultimate check on party government in the United States is the system of standing committees in Congress. This is another way to say that the ultimate check is the coordinate status of the legislature and the executive branches, so long as Congress is able roughly to hold its own. Because a coordinate legislature must have some way to gather and assess information on its own, if it is not to be a ward of the bureaucracy, the most efficient, practical way is to divide up in committees which specialize and develop a measure of expertise. Committees which specialize and have exclusive jurisdiction over certain kinds of legislation become little legislatures themselves, with power largely independent of the elected leadership of the parent body. Centralized power and dispersed power are contradictions; to the degree that the latter exists the former is limited.

It is necessary, therefore, to see the committees both as organs of investigation and deliberation, indispensable to Congress, and as subsystems of power, crucial both to the interests which seek access to government and to the work satisfactions and career aspirations of their members.

Internal life of the committees

The chairman of a major standing committee in the Senate is an influential and important man indeed. He usually is in virtual control of his committee. He calls committee meetings, decides what bills will be considered, appoints subcommittee chairmen, controls the selection of witnesses, and, excepting bills of overriding importance, determines which bills favorably reported by his committee really will be pressed for floor consideration. He probably will lead the floor fight for it or designate the man who will. In practice, he chooses committee members who will go to conference with the House on committee bills and may choose to lead the group himself. The chairman decides whether the staff will be as large and expert as money will buy or funds will be returned to the Treasury; whether the staff will be encouraged to be aggressive or passive; and whether a real fight will be made to carry the bill through floor and conference as the committee wrote it or the effort will be halfhearted.

That is why the mode of selection of the chairman is so important. Certainly the seniority system, which moves the ranking member of the majority on the committee automatically to the chairmanship, provokes hot debate. The principal points are clear. Seniority is good because it settles out-of-hand the most disruptive organizational problem Congress ever faced, which sometimes took months to settle. Seniority is bad because it gives a margin of influence to those states and sections which regularly return the same men—if one happens not to like their point of view. These obvious aspects of seniority obscure others as important, on which not much is known. What is the effect on committee operations and policy when a new chairman drastically different in style or ideology takes over—such as happened to the Senate Judiciary Committee when liberals Kilgore and Langer served as chairmen between conservatives McCarran and Eastland? Are there institutional devices for cushioning the change? What can committees do when the chairman becomes incompetent, perhaps from senility, or especially if he has enough wit and obstinacy to hold on to the committee reins? Occasionally the leadership is forced to intervene, as the Democrats had to do with the Foreign Relations Committee chairmanship in Johnson's tenure as leader, but there must be cases which have not been pushed that far. When a seniority chairman is out of step with a majority of his committee, what happens? Can he tyrannize over them and does he, or are reasonable accommodations made? These are questions to be answered if an intelligent assessment of the seniority system is to be made.

These questions lead to more basic ones. What are the patterns of relationships between chairmen and their committees? Or put somewhat differently, how do individual incumbents perceive the chairman's role? It should be obvious that elements discussed earlier which affect the floor leader's performance should be equally pertinent here. A chairman assumes a job that is fairly narrowly defined by the institutional history of his house. He confronts certain situational aspects: the size of his majority and its temper, the urgency at the moment of his committee's business, the attitudes and demeanor of his party's congressional and executive leaders. But within the limits of this institutional and situational frame he surely is as free as the floor leader to try to behave as he pleases.

Unfortunately, the behavior of chairmen has not been subjected to much scholarly or even journalistic scrutiny. It is not safe or fair, therefore, to try to offer examples. Even so, some "ideal types" of chairmen can be suggested. There is the chairman who successfully dominates his committee. He may use his dominion to make an empire, grasping all the legislative business he can claim title to, or he may suppress committee activity because he is out of sympathy with the majority; either way, he is the boss. A different kind of chairman may not be especially interested in his committee's subject matter, but may see his job as a facilitator of whatever its members want to do. He is a genuine chairman, the servant of the group's goals. Still another may be unsympathetic with what the majority wants but conscientiously helps them; he is a "service" chairman, reinforcing the majority sentiment with assistance only a chairman can give. Still another may regard his committee as a stage for his own performance, an extension of his own personality. He is not so much concerned with what it does as he is with the setting it provides for him. Undoubtedly the list could be extended. What matters, of course, is to discover through comparative studies the *range* of behavior open to chairmen, the patterns it commonly falls into.

The chairman's notion of his own role will probably determine how he reacts to that grievous problem, the need for subcommittees. The Legislative Reorganization Act of 1946 reduced the number of Senate committees from thirty-three to fifteen. What it did not and could not do was reduce the volume of committee business. The result was a steady proliferation of subcommittees, each of which tends to carve out for itself some specialized part of the full committee's jurisdiction. The subcommittee chairmen thus parcel out to a degree the chairman's power, as he and his colleagues have parceled out the power of the leadership. Some chairmen we have described do not care; at least one has given a subcommittee to every majority member of his committee (although he *did* later abolish one because he did not like what its chairman did with it). But to the man who hoards the power he has waited so long to get there must be other alternatives. He may eschew subcommittees entirely, putting the whole burden on the full committee. He may make himself chairman of every subcommittee. He may try to prevent specialization by the subcommittees, numbering instead of naming them and referring bills of all kinds to each of them. Needless to say, the subcommittee chairmen understand the game; they trade bills around until they have established *de facto* jurisdictions.

A problem faced by every member is what to do about transferring from one committee to another. Not many senators can at once get the committee they most want, and there definitely is a status system among committees. Donald Matthews studied gains and losses of membership on Senate committees over a period of a decade (1947–57) and found a discernible pecking order, with committees tending to lose members to committees above them and to gain from those below.[13] Foreign Relations, Appropriations, Finance, and Armed Services headed the list; the District of Columbia Committee was a predictable last. A transfer, regardless of his *Senate* seniority, is last in *committee* seniority; the agonizing question then is: better junior on a good committee or senior on a less prestigious one? The problem is complicated by the impossibility of calculating the rate at which senior members will die or retire.

Like other institutionalized human groups, committees tend to become small local systems in their own right, reflecting the norms of the larger system but developing nevertheless a group life of their own. Richard Fenno's study of the House Committee on Appropriations is a brilliant pioneering effort to explore the life of one such small system.[14] He found the principal norms to be a dedication to work and a passion for protecting the Treasury. Junior members were

[13] Donald R. Matthews, *U.S. Senators and Their World* (Chapel Hill, 1960), pp. 148–152.

[14] Richard F. Fenno, Jr., "The House Appropriations Committee as a Political System: The Problem of Integration," *American Political Science Review*, 56 (June 1962), 372.

socialized to respect these norms, and those who conformed best gained committee status earliest. It is probable that committees with great turnover do not develop a highly integrated group life, but the stable groups with great prestige surely must. If so, the character of that internal life, the norms that shape it, should be of great concern to bureaucrats, interest groups, and party leaders whose success may turn on their ability to placate and influence the committee.

But the balance must be kept: a committee is an institution of Congress; it exists to serve the purposes of congressmen. These are individual purposes as often as they are institutional or partisan. No one who has ever looked seriously at the committee's public activity, the hearing, can doubt that. David Truman has said that there are three functions or purposes of public hearings.[15] The first is to provide "a means of transmitting information, both technical and political, from various actual and potential interest groups to the committee." The second function "is as a propaganda channel through which a public may be extended and its segments partially consolidated or reinforced." The third is "to provide a quasi-ritualistic means of adjusting group conflicts and relieving disturbances through a safety valve." These purposes or functions relate to the performance of the committee as a working unit of the legislature, carrying its share of the work load, representing groups and reconciling their conflicts, reinforcing the authority of the political system. But the committee also affords the member a chance to get *his* job done. He may wish to make himself a national leader, build a reputation as a subject-matter expert, advertise himself to the constituency, do a favor for a supporter, discharge some of his own aggressions—the list could be a long one.[16] What is important is to see that in every aspect of congressional life it is necessary to satisfy both the system needs and the largely personal needs of the member who must keep himself solvent in a free-enterprise politics.

External relations of committees

Like every other human group, the Senate committee lives in an environment which affects and is affected by it, with which it must

---

[15] David B. Truman, The Governmental Process (New York, 1953), p. 372.

[16] Ralph K. Huitt, "The Congressional Committee: A Case Study" [pp. 77–112 of the present book].

somehow get along. Its environment is both congressional and non-congressional—and the latter may extend around the globe. In the congressional environment there are the other committees. The relationship seems to be largely live and let live, which the party leadership, overlapping memberships, frequent transfers, the smallness of the body and the frequent testimony of members before committees not their own, all make easier. Some tension between the legislative committees and the Appropriations Committee seems to exist beneath the surface, because what the former authorizes the latter may reduce or even deny, but this seems less sharp in the Senate than in the House. Undoubtedly friction is lessened by the Senate Committee's practice of inviting senior members of the legislative committee to participate when appropriations for their programs are discussed. Apparently little attempt is made generally for committees with the same jurisdictions in the two houses to work together; sometimes their staffs collaborate a bit, but the committees seem to work independently and meet in conference. The two taxing committees are an exception. Their senior members belong to the Joint Committee on Internal Revenue Taxation, through which they share an expert staff and collaborate effectively.[17] The separateness of the parallel committees reflects the separateness of the two houses, whose majority leaders probably meet only at the White House unless they are personal friends, as Johnson and Rayburn were. It is indeed true that "two houses do not make a home."

In the non-congressional environment, the most frequent and immediate relations of senatorial committees are with the administrative agencies. This usually is called "legislative oversight of administration," a term which is more misleading than not because it suggests a clear legislative mandate to the agency which the committee is determined to see carried out. Undoubtedly there is some of this in the relationship, and committees are directed in the Legislative Reorganization Act of 1946 to supervise the work of the agencies which fall within their jurisdiction. But unfortunately the mandate often is left unclear, sometimes deliberately so, and problems come up not dreamed of when the legislation was passed. Again,

[17] Ralph K. Huitt, "Congressional Operations in the Field of Money and Credit," in W. Fellner, et al., Fiscal and Debt Management Policies (Englewood Cliffs, N.J., 1963), pp. 446–457.

the relationship between committee and agency sometimes more nearly resembles a partnership than master and servant.

If oversight is the relationship the committee *does* want, there are traditional tools available to it. The appropriations committees in either house can guide and direct, under the threat of reduced funds. The committee may investigate the stewardship of the agency. The principal agency officers have to come before the committee before confirmation by the Senate. Congress can legislate in detail, telling the agency precisely what is desired. These formidable-seeming tools should be enough, but in practice they raise questions. Can the spending committees actually get to the heart of the matter in the enormous budgets they report, or are they limited to granting an increment, more or less, over last year? After the committee has terrorized the agency, does anything change or do the bureaucrats go back to business as usual? Is confirmation before assumption of office much of a check? How much effect on actual agency operations does the political officer have anyway? How can Congress effectively legislate in detail when the last century of administrative history has been that of increasingly large delegations of legislative power because of the legislature's inability to cope with the bewildering details of modern industrial life?

Moreover, despite a dearth of analysis of the oversight exercised by individual committees, there is enough to show that it varies widely from committee to committee. One may interfere with administrative detail outrageously, another may simply try to keep informed through its professional staff, and a third may decline to supervise at all. A single committee may bear down hard on one agency and be indifferent to another, and its militancy may wax and wane over time. Some variables might be suggested. The first, obviously, is the chairman: one aggressively suspicious of bureaucrats may be succeeded by another who thinks they should be let alone. A second is the character of the agency: a senator who would be horrified at the thought of congressional interference with the Federal Reserve Board may attempt to retry a National Labor Relations Board case in committee. Still another is the character of the program: one with wide interest and visibility will get more attention than others requiring expertise and secrecy. Again there is the closeness to the constituency: the State Department obviously does not affect as many people directly as the Department of Agriculture does. Finally, there is the quality and size of the professional staff: this may in fact be an *index* to the intentions of the chairman. What matters once again are *patterns* of recurring relationships, the *range* of behavior open to committee and staff.

These considerations are not unrelated to the question of power structure within the Senate; far from it. When committee and agency can work out something resembling a partnership, there is advantage in it for both sides. The committee adopts the agency; it protects the agency from other agencies and from executive control to the limit of its (perhaps considerable) ability. On the other hand, if the agency controls what senators (and their constituents) want, the senator with preferred access to the agency has far less need to get legislation. As a man with access to scarce services, he is in a bargaining position with legislator and bureaucrat alike. He can perform services which may make him unbeatable. These are power relationships—perhaps the most important of all and the least understood by outsiders.

III. THE INFORMAL SYSTEM

It is unlikely that there is an absolute correspondence in any institutionalized human organization between the formal structure of authority and the actual distribution of influence. Human groups develop "norms"—cultural "oughts" which prescribe proper behavior for their members on which there is a high degree of consensus. The most influential and effective members usually conform most closely to the norms; in their own behavior they represent, in effect, what the group values. Perhaps the formal leaders are these persons, but they may not be; they may instead be members without official power ascriptions who nevertheless exercise a measure of control over what the group decides and does. This is recognized in many groups by the labels attached to this informal influence structure—the "inner clique," the "old guard," the "king-makers."

It would seem highly probable, therefore, that such an informal structure exists in the Senate—but who are they, what do they control, and how do they exercise their influence? Two commentators on the Senate have confidently asserted the existence of such an influence group without agreeing on any of these questions. One is

William S. White, an experienced journalist and sympathetic observer of the Senate.[18] The other is Joseph S. Clark, a senator who is, it may fairly be said, an unsympathetic participant-observer. White calls his influentials the "Inner Club," Clark his dynasts the "Establishment."[19]

White asserts that "the inner life of the Senate . . . is controlled by the Inner Club." Its members are the "Senate type" (or the "Senate man"). The Senate type is a prudent man. He serves a long apprenticeship before he begins to talk but even then speaks little. He is courteous and forbearing, never allowing the business of the body to affect personal relations. He is helpful to other senators and expects reciprocity. More than anything else he is devoted to the institution; he "speaks to the Senate," not to the country or the world or anyone outside. It does not matter what his political views are; wealth, popularity, social status, intellectual power, party affiliation, or national reputation are not determinants. "At the core of the Inner Club stand the Southerners . . ." but it is not a matter of geography; others may and do belong. Southerners are in because they "express, consciously or unconsciously, the deepest instincts of the 'Senate type' . . ." who is "a man for whom the institution is a career in itself, a life in itself and an end in itself." He is a man who has "tolerance toward his fellows, intolerance toward any who would in any real way change the Senate, its customs or its way of life." How do they operate? Certainly not in conventional ways: ". . . one day the perceptive onlooker will discover a kind of aura from the Inner Club that informs him of what the Senate is later going to do about such and such." In 1956 a proposal to establish a joint committee to oversee the work of the Central Intelligence Agency failed. "Under their bleak and languid frowns the whole project simply died; a wind had blown upon it from the Inner Club and its erstwhile sponsors simply left it." But White admits that the Inner Club members may not have nearly so much influence on what the Senate does that affects the outside world as men who are not truly Senate types at all; they are guardians of the "inner life."

Senator Clark is not talking about that kind of thing at all. His

[18] *Citadel: The Story of the U.S. Senate* (New York, 1956). All the quotations used here are taken from Chapter Seven.

[19] Clark, *Congress: The Sapless Branch* (op. cit.). The quotations are taken from Chapter Six.

"Establishment" consists of "those Democratic chairmen and ranking Republican members of the important legislative committees who, through seniority and pressures exerted on junior colleagues, control the institutional machinery of Congress." The official leadership group "are usually captives of the Establishment, although they can some- times be found looking out over the walls of their prison, plotting escape." "Establishment" members have specific ideological commit- ments: the bonds which unite them are "white supremacy; a stronger devotion to property than human rights; support of the military establishment; belligerence in foreign affairs; and a determination to prevent Congressional reform." Clark gives names; among seventeen Democrats, only two are not Southerners; among eleven Republicans, only two or three would not be included among hard-core con- servatives. This informal structure therefore *is* selected by ideology: Clark's ultimate tests are these: "So long as a Democrat stands firm against civil rights and cloture, or a Republican against cloture only, his (or her) Establishment status remains unquestionable." Clark clearly is not talking about White's Inner Club; Hubert Humphrey was specifically named as a member of it, but he could only be a captive of the "Establishment." Clark is a liberal and the "Establish- ment" is the conservative opposition. They are the people who oppose the President's program. Yet the record adduced by Clark does not make them seem so formidable; on three important record votes men- tioned, the "Establishment" lost 80–19, 57–35, and 61–26.

For the student of influence in the Senate these formulations are not much help. White's empathy for the Senate is uniquely his; how does one learn how to discover an aura, to interpret a frown? How does one translate the influence of the inner life of the Senate on the public discharge of its constitutional responsibilities? Clark's "Establishment" certainly is concretely conceived, but how seriously can one take a senatorial power elite which would not include John- son, Humphrey, or Mansfield? Moreover, the strength of the "Estab- lishment" comes largely from certain advantages they hold under the rules, a condition Clark devoutly wishes to change. The in- formal structure of power in the Senate remains a legitimate prob- lem of research, but it seems reasonable to agree with Truman and Matthews "that the 'real' leaders of the Senate are, for the most part, those in positions of formal authority."[20]

[20] The quotation is from Matthews, *U.S. Senators and Their World, op. cit.,* p. 253. Also see Truman, *The Congressional Party, op. cit.,* pp. 285 ff.

Senate staff

One dimension of power in the Senate which is subtle and complex but largely unexplored is the influence on their principals of members of professional staffs. There can be no doubt that this provision of the Legislative Reorganization Act of 1946 has profoundly changed and vastly improved the performance of the Senate. Like the President of the United States on an appropriately smaller scale, a senator is an institution. He is what he is plus what he can add to himself by the considerable array of brains and skills the law allows him to buy. The work load now carried by the typical Senate office would be unthinkable without the division of labor among roughly a score of people. Similarly, committees would lose their cutting edge if they lost their staffs. But first-rate professionals do more than carry out assignments. In the offices of individual senators they learn to think like the boss; they determine to some degree who sees him and what importunities reach him. In the committee rooms they identify the problems and provide the facts and questions. The product of the Senate is to some unmeasured and perhaps immeasurable degree their product. Their influence probably would be very easy to overstate, but it does exist.

It is unlikely that staff power has a structure apart from the relationships among senators themselves. A case in point is the loose grouping of the principal assistants of about a score of liberal senators who held regular meetings for a while during the Eighty-second Congress. The membership shifted somewhat in accordance with the issue under discussion. Needless to say, these caucuses had the approval of the participants' principals, and indeed were no more than an extension of senatorial activity.

The most important staff positions in the senatorial office are administrative assistant (the top job) and legislative assistant. Other professionals may be called legal counsel, press secretary, or other titles. These jobs attract some very bright and able people, who sometimes remain with a senator for years, serving him with sacrificial devotion. They are men capable in most cases of achieving successful, perhaps distinguished, individual careers in their own names if they chose to do so. Yet they will submerge their own ambitions and identities in those of a senator, seeing another take credit for their best work, coming in time to think and even talk like him, to exult and suffer with him. Why do they do it?

No one can say with confidence. There is no systematic research into the motivations and satisfactions of these senators' men. Surely the possibility of sharing the power and glory of the supreme office must sustain some of them. Kennedy, Johnson, Nixon, Lodge, and Goldwater all were or had been senators when their parties chose them, and Kennedy and Johnson took their senatorial staffs into the White House with them. But some of the most faithful staff people toil for men who never will be notable beyond state boundaries, and there is a veritable parade of professionals through the offices of some senators with great expectations.

Whatever is revealed by systematic research, one hypothesis may be ventured: the principal staff men share significantly in the exercise of their senators' power or they would not stay. A bankrupt in a millionaire's club is no more contemptible than a man without power in a political system. It is the power over mens' lives and fortunes exercised by the national government that attracts ambitious men to the hazards of elective politics, and the prospect of sharing it which enlists and holds the gifted auxiliaries.

How big should senatorial staffs be? Perhaps much larger than they are, in the case of a few populous states. Perhaps not so large as they are, in the case of the smaller ones. But the indispensability of professional staff should not lead to the easy assumption that there is no limit to the number of staff persons who can be properly employed. Few senators are competent (and some not at all, in fact) to operate a small bureaucracy of their own, and that is not their job anyway. Furthermore, the cushion staff provides between the senator and those who want to see him can become impenetrable, thus destroying the sensitivity to group demands which makes him useful to the system. Finally, any increase in staff beyond what is imperative to keep the work moving probably would be used to court the constituency, making the burden of the non-incumbent opponent—who already must run against the Post Office and the Government Printing Office—quite unbearable.

IV. ARE REFORMS NEEDED?

More than any other governmental institution in American life, Congress is under continuous criticism and demand for reform. The Senate shares in the general criticism of Congress and comes in for some directed especially at it. It is not easy to summarize what is said and what has been proposed. *Congressional Quarterly* devoted sixty-two double-columned pages to such a summary in the summer of 1963, with hardly a wasted word. It is possible, however, to suggest some categories of criticism and reform which are relevant to a discussion of power in the Senate.

One is concerned with leadership. Changes are included which would strengthen the hand of elected leaders and encourage them to work more closely with the national leadership, especially the President, and which would weaken the feudal baronies of the committee chairmen. The seniority system is a special target; if it cannot be destroyed, at least chairmen might be required to relinquish their authority at a certain age or the committee majority might be given some choice among the ranking members.

A second category which is more modest includes proposals to bring some coordination to the spending and taxing programs of Congress. The Legislative Reorganization Act required a joint budget committee composed of the four revenue and appropriations committees of the two houses to meet and set a legislative budget by February 15 of each year, but the provision was unrealistic; it still is law but it has never worked. The two taxing committees have proved that coordination is possible just the same. Their senior members, working through a joint committee and a joint staff, have eliminated duplication and conflict between the committees. Once the House Appropriations Committee successfully produced and passed an omnibus appropriation bill, and the redoubtable chairman of the committee, Clarence Cannon, never ceased to think it was an improvement over a dozen different bills. The critics argue that a government which spends $100 billion a year of its citizens' money should attempt, at least, to relate income and outgo and bring a measure of planning to the process.

A third category relates to the effectiveness of individual members. Congressional business characteristically lags through the early months of a session and begins to pick up when other people are taking their families on vacation. The hardest work months come in the summer. Congress adjourns, if it ever does, when children are back in school. This result of poor scheduling is typical of a host of small irritations. Only two trips back home each session are paid for by the government; many members go nearly every week. In the case of a senator from the State of Washington, say, this is a major drain which may require steady "moonlighting" if he is not rich. Salaries are raised infrequently because members dread the catcalls from home. Allowances for office help and materials are wholly inadequate for senators from populous states. These are nagging nuisances which reduce a senator's efficiency.

A fourth category of reforms is aimed at the conduct of individual members which brings discredit on the whole body. This is not so much unlawful conduct—senators are punished for that like other citizens—but behavior which falls in a kind of twilight zone where the ethics of the individual must be the regulator. A senator belongs to a law firm, makes well-compensated speeches to interest-group audiences, owns securities in businesses dealing with the government. He makes trips abroad at government expense with no public audit of his accounts. He intercedes with government regulatory agencies on behalf of constituents. No one of these activities is necessarily wrong; indeed many are essential to the discharge of his duty. Most members carry them out with scrupulous regard for what is proper. But some members do not, and there's the rub.

The prognosis for reform varies sharply with the categories. The first two involve a restructuring of power arrangements, a matter of taking power from those who have it and assigning it to those who do not. Several observations might be made. One is that there does not exist a model of a legislature as it ought to be. Political institutions grow in the soil of national experience. It is unlikely that one can be proven to be abstractly better than another, but even if it could that would not make it a practical alternative; people simply do not choose their institutions that way. Second, altering the power structure is no cure for inability to muster a majority, because more political force is needed to make the alteration than to win on any single issue. A successful reform is a demonstration of effective massing and use of political power, not a prelude to it. National party leadership may dominate Congress one day—when the concern of people with national problems overrides their parochial interests. Third, there may be unanticipated consequences to any change. Reducing the number of committees and clarifying their jurisdictions was regarded generally as one of the unqualified successes of the Legislative Reorganization Act. But the party leader no longer has his choice of several committees for referral of a particular bill; if a chairman is hostile, the leader must try the dubious business of by-passing the committee. Again, when the tyranny of the Speaker was overcome in the session of 1910 and 1911, a strengthened Rules Committee was the chosen instrument. But who is hero, who the villains, in the 1960s? The successful joint operations of the taxing committees provide another illustration: they have resulted in effective domination of federal taxation by the conservative senior members. The liberal members of those committees are not eager to see power over both spending and taxing put in the hands of a single joint committee. They have learned that a coordinating device works for those who control it.

Measures designed to make the congressman's life easier and his workday more efficient ought to be matters better left to the members themselves. This would seem to be true also of standards of ethical conduct, but unfortunately it is not. It is very well to say Congress should police its own members, but self-regulation is a shibboleth which practically is not within the competence of most groups. What group in American society really disciplines its own members? Doctors? Lawyers? Professors? The public may think so, but the members know better. Perhaps criminal groups do, but adequate documentation is not available. Outside controls are better, and Congress really has none. The electorate obviously should provide them, but just as obviously it does not.

The problem remains and it is a serious one. The effectiveness of a political institution turns in part on the respect in which it is held. Whatever subjects it to ridicule reduces its capacity for winning the unquestioning compliance which is at the heart of civil authority. The Senate should not cease to seek ways to curb excesses, of its committees or individual members, which tarnish the corporate dignity of the body.

Perhaps this has relevance for those two oft-denounced institutions of the Senate, the filibuster and the seniority system. There is weight to the argument that the filibuster has never killed a measure a determined majority really wanted and that the time consumed in its debate of a civil rights measure in 1964 was not disproportionate to that required by the Executive and the courts in their efforts to advance civil rights. Nevertheless epithets like "obscene spectacle" were applied to it without challenge, and it would have been hard to find a defense of the filibuster outside the South. What is almost universally regarded as wrong can be maintained by government only at great cost. Perhaps time will prove that a filibuster like that in 1964 was exactly what was needed to make a more effective limitation possible.

Some modification of the seniority rule seems under a like burden of public disapprobation. Most Americans are required by law or private usage to retire by age seventy at the latest; social security and many private pensions are available earlier than that. Common experience suggests to most people that this is about right. They have observed the diminution of powers which ordinarily occurs at that age. Perhaps congressmen are different; certainly exceptional individuals are. But who is to say who is exceptional? That is why a rule is required. At the minimum, a committee might be permitted to decide for itself in the case of its chairman.

These changes and many others will be suggested, and some will be made. No human institution is above criticism or beyond reform. Nevertheless the history of the republic and the prestige of the modern Senate attest to its basic vitality and to its deep-rooted representativeness, and by inference to the judicious use of power by the men who run it.

SIX
CONGRESS, THE DURABLE PARTNER

T is ironic that the representative assembly, whose great historic achievement was the taming of the executive, is now almost every-where submissive once more to him and his establishment. The notable exception among national legislatures is the Congress of the United States. Congress cannot match the drama of the presidency but any day it sits it can remind the executive that it must be taken into account. Its leaders are men of political substance and its members can, even in their individual capacities, influence public policy. My purposes are to state briefly some reasons why Congress has maintained its place in the constitutional partnership, to consider some of the factors which affect that partnership, and to suggest some lines of inquiry which would keep a generation of legislative scholars busy and out of trouble.

I. NEVER THE TWAIN SHALL MEET

Even in a country where a fairly high percentage of a sample of the populace manages to miss almost any political question, it is a fair bet that most people know that our government is based on a separation of powers, modified somewhat by so-called checks and balances. Perhaps some of that group also know that this

Ralph K. Huitt, "Congress, The Durable Partner," in *Lawmakers in a Changing World*, edited by Elke Frank, © 1966. Reprinted by permission of Prentice-Hall, Inc., Englewood Cliffs, New Jersey.

formula is supposed to protect the people from tyranny, and that our forefathers were confident it would. Their confidence was shared by most of the liberal philosophers of their time. But the Founding Fathers were, above all else, practical men; they were not so much interested in a scientific separation of powers as they were in drawing on the lessons of experience to make a workable structure for the future. What they did do in deference to that shibboleth of separation which has had such an enormous influence on American political history was to provide in their Constitution that a man who holds office in one branch cannot simultaneously serve in another. At the same time, they softened the separation with checks and balances, drawing again upon experience, and by the admirable terseness of the document which they drew, they left their equally pragmatic descendents largely free to distribute and share powers as current exigencies seemed to require. The result is an untidy but, on the whole, eminently successful system. Nevertheless, there have been and are tensions in the system produced by contrary pulls of separation and commingling. Let us look first at some of the effects of separation and later at the numerous accommodations between legislature and executive which have worked to dampen those effects.

Separate systems of power

The process by which the English Parliament developed responsible party government is too well known to need repeating. Why should not the American system go the same way—to the extent the Constitution permits? A President elected by a majority of the people, working through a majority of his own party in Congress, should be able to enact a fair share of the program he has promised. Only some structural changes—policy committees made up of committee chairmen to adopt appropriate bills, party caucuses to pledge support to them—reinforced by a measure of public understanding of the value of responsible parties, are needed, according to earnest critics. Why have not such steps been taken? Why, in houses where most partisans vote with a majority of their party most of the time, do the blandishments of the President go unheeded, often at the most critical times?

The fragmentation of party power followed naturally from the need of Congress to establish some source of information separate from the executive and some mechanism for independent consideration of the merits of bills. In a parliamentary system the members can, at least in good logic, listen to the bureaucracy, because their own leaders are said to control the bureaucracy. But in the congressional system the bureaucrats are "they"; the men who more or less control them belong to the President. A committee was the answer: first an *ad hoc* committee, then a standing committee, then a standing committee with specialized jurisdiction. Such a committee perforce becomes a locus of power. So in time do its own subcommittees which, often over the strenuous exertions of the committee chairman, also carve out jurisdictions that they are quick to defend.

Even the dispersal of power in a committee system might not be irreparable if a party leadership could select the chairmen. But this is an exhausting procedure, often holding up appointments until most of the business is settled. The answer, as everyone knows, has been chairmanship selection by seniority, which often brings good and experienced men to power but which also, by definition, elevates those least answerable to a central party leadership. The President is not unlike a king forced to deal with feudal barons. He has certain advantages of identity with the national interest and superior visibility, as the king did, but he too must respect the rules of the game, which limit severely what he can command.

When these factors are reinforced by all the forces of localism inherent in federalism, accentuated by a long history on a vast continent with poor communication, the basic underpinnings of responsible party government are lacking.

Separate institutional influences on behavior

The separation of personnel in the American system means a separation of *institutions,* and that separation has, in behavioral terms, profound influence on the day-to-day operations of American government. The Constitution, to repeat, says simply that the same man cannot hold office in both branches at the same time. A parliamentary system may actually separate powers very neatly; the minister may distinguish nicely between his executive and his legislative role. But he *can* have both roles at the same time, and so mediate between the legislature as an institution and the executive as an institution. Not so here; the institutions are clearly divided and so are the roles that go with each. What this means in behavioral terms is worth some exploration.

No dissertation on the term "institution" need be attempted. We mean simply a pattern of behavior of great stability and predictability, including the expectations people have that the pattern will be maintained. People know what behavior to expect in a church, a court of law, a college classroom. It is convenient but not essential to have an appropriate building and symbolic trappings; men have made and accepted a church in the hold of a ship at sea. What is necessary is that the participants behave according to expectations. Confusion comes when behavior appropriate to one institution is employed in another. This was the case in the televised controversy between Senator McCarthy and the Army, in which some judicial forms were bootlegged into a legislative hearing. On the other hand, appropriate behavior validates the collective actions people take.

If men brought up in our tradition were cast upon a desert island, they would know (without a political scientist among them) that policy should be adopted by a majority, that a project should have a leader, and that an accused man should be tried by his peers, however ignorant or biased they might be. It is accepted procedure, appropriate behavior, that legitimizes social action. The social function of a court, say, is not so much the administration of justice (who can say when it deals justly?) as it is the deciding of quarrels and the imposing of sanctions, even to the taking of life, in a way society accepts as legitimate.

Needless to say, men who are inducted into any social system in which they hope to be accepted try to learn the appropriate behavior. The literature on this process of socialization is extensive and need not be reviewed here. What is worth emphasis is that men who spend much or most of their adult lives in a social system as highly institutionalized as Congress and the bureaucracy, where careers are long and status and influence depend so much on tenure, are profoundly shaped in their attitudes by the institution itself. The institution is not the only or necessarily even the most important influence, of course, but its effect can be seen in some of the ineradicable suspicions and adversions which legislators and administrators develop toward each other, which persist even when they work productively and cooperatively together. The principal purpose of this essay will be to suggest some of the differences in the institutional fabric of legislature and executive, and the influence these differences have on the people who are associated with them.[1]

It should go without saying that the Court is a distinct institution, encrusted with the habits of centuries.[2] Like the Presidency and Congress, it is a political (as well as a legal) institution, sharing their power to make choices as to who shall get what. The Court—and especially the Supreme Court of the United States—legislates boldly and with remarkable political acumen, pushing to the testing point what Congress and the country will take. We leave it out of our discussion only because it is not part of the problem we have chosen to consider.

It is not quite accurate to say that we will contrast legislature and executive; what we really mean in the latter case is the bureaucracy. The political officers of the executive branch are a different breed than the bureaucrats. They form a kind of quasi-institution. They are not self-selected, as congressmen generally are, nor do they enjoy the tenure of either the bureaucracy or most members of Congress. They are creatures of the President, existing officially on sufferance. Their institutional life and influence on the system have largely escaped analysis and that is a pity.[3] The bureaucracy, on the other

---

[1] A good picture of the life of a member of the House of Representatives may be found in Charles Clapp, *The Congressman: His Work as He Sees It* (Washington, D.C.: The Brookings Institution, 1963) and Clem Miller (ed. John W. Baker), *Member of the House: Letters of a Congressman* (New York: Charles Scribner's Sons, 1962). The life of the Senate is depicted in William S. White, *Citadel* (New York: Harper and Row, Publishers, Inc., 1956) and Donald R. Matthews, *U.S. Senators and Their World* (Chapel Hill: University of North Carolina Press, 1960). A pioneering investigation of the role perceptions of members of four state legislatures is that of John C. Wahlke, Heinz Eulau, William Buchanan, and LeRoy Ferguson, *The Legislative System: Explorations in Legislative Behavior* (New York: John Wiley and Sons, Inc., 1962). If my hypothesis that the legislature *as an institution* affects the behavior of its members is correct, the significance of the latter work for students of Congress is obvious.

[2] The influence of the Court on its members has frustrated Presidents throughout our history. For an interesting contemporary example of a dramatic conversion, see the account of the transformation of Mississippi's Supreme Court Justice Tom P. Brady from a race-baiting white supremacist to a champion of the U.S. Constitution in *Time*, October 22, 1965, pp. 94–96.

[3] Richard E. Neustadt, in David B. Truman, ed., *The Congress and America's Future* (Englewood Cliffs, N.J.: Prentice-Hall, Inc., 1965), pp. 116–20, makes an interesting case for the common stakes of elective politicians. His viewpoint is primarily that of an acute observer of the executive branch. See also Dean E. Mann (with Jameson W. Doig), *The Assistant Secretaries: Problems and Processes of Appointment* (Washington, D.C.: The Brookings Institution, 1965).

hand, is as old as human organization, and its habits, cries, and protective coloration have been subjected to intensive analysis. Moreover, it should be a safe wager that bureaucratic influence far outweighs that of the political executive officers, excepting possibly the President himself.

A good place to begin a study of any institution in which people make a living is with the conditions of employment. How are jobs got and kept? What influences salaries and promotions? These considerations probably influence the performance of professors, to take a ready example, more than the standard protestations of university presidents about the relative importance of good teaching.

The differences in the vocational aspects of the two branches of the national government are striking. The congressman is a politician whose first rule of life is to take care of himself. Characteristically, he is self-selected and self-promoted. It is he who decides that the public needs him in the first place and it is he who must persuade the public this is so at each election. Generally speaking, the national party cannot help him or hurt him very much. If the local party organization is strong, this simply means that the self-selection process must employ other channels. His tenure likewise depends mostly upon his own efforts; he can be a statesman only so long as the people in his constituency are willing to let him be one.

The bureaucracy is another matter. The bureaucracy is peopled overwhelmingly by men and women who came into the service through a merit system examination, who rise in grade through largely non-competitive promotions, and who can look forward to retirement on a rather generous retirement plan. Everything in their professional lives underscores the slow but sure. They come to have faith in rules and procedures. The elements of risk and combat, of rewards and punishments that often are disproportionate and unfair—elements with which politicians live daily—are minimized.

It would seem reasonable to assume that self-selection assures generally that different kinds of men go into the separate branches. Certainly it is doubtful that either the politician or the bureaucrat could breathe easily in the environment of the other. Be that as it may, the distinct demands of each branch enforce differences.

A congressman may come from any vocation and he is required by his job to be a generalist. It is true that he specializes somewhat on his committee, and indeed may develop considerable expertise. Nevertheless, he is required to vote on a staggering variety of complicated bills, about most of which he will try to have at least a minimum understanding. The bureaucrat, on the other hand, is virtually required to be a specialist of some sort. Even if he is one of that handful of college graduates who come in as some kind of management intern, he soon finds his niche and concentrates on it if he is to move up the ladder. He is accustomed to operations in which a wide variety of experts can be brought to bear on a problem. As a matter of course he refers problems to the specialists whose skills are most appropriate to them.

The institutional fabrics into which these different kinds of men fit themselves are likewise distinctive. In Congress all members technically are peers, and at the time of the vote they are absolutely equal. The same weight of numbers which took the congressman to his house ultimately determines every issue on its floor. In the bureaucracy nothing is decided that way. The hierarchy of influence and responsibility is clearly understood; the distinctions between staff and line are appreciated; and status is reflected even in the kinds of furniture permissible to an office and the order of names on a route slip.

Furthermore, even the kinds of evidence which are acceptable in these different kinds of institutions are sharply differentiated. A congressional committee makes no attempt to get all the facts and may joyfully accept what it knows not to be facts. It is interested in hearsay, in opinion, in the shibboleths, however nonrational, around which men rally and fight. This is not to discount the careful amassing of expert testimony which many committees do; the point is simply that Congress is a representative assembly, a popularly elected body, and what may be studiously ignored in a courtroom may be exactly what a congressional committee most needs to hear. The bureaucracy, on the other hand, is a matchless machine for assembling all kinds of facts, for taking into account all kinds of expert advice. Congress itself is ultimately utterly dependent on the bureaucracy for most of the information upon which it acts.

The process by which each branch makes policy is likewise its own. Congress makes policy deliberately. The laying down of rules of general applicability for the future is its avowed business. Generality indeed is forced upon it by the complexity of modern life. Legislatures learned more than a century ago that they cannot legislate in detail for very much of the varied life they seek to regulate. The bureaucracy is capable of making policy determinations of breathtaking scope, but theoretically at least its task is to "fill in the details" of general policy, and its characteristic mode is day-by-day administration, employing standards, rules, and similar bureaucratic tools to fashion a general design.

What has been said here is familiar; any student could elaborate it from his classroom notes. The recitation nevertheless has a point: in this national government of separated institutions different kinds of men, operating in different kinds of institutional fabrics, proceed in different ways to perform much the same functions for the political system. This has operational significance: the leaders of pressure groups do not hesitate to seek from one branch what they fail to get from another but, unless they are incredibly naive, they will adapt themselves carefully to the behavior appropriate to each. It also has significance for understanding the tensions and suspicions between branches which are endemic in the system. Perhaps most important, it suggests the crucial influence of the institution itself, with all its historic antecedents, on the behavior of the people who make their lives in it.

II. BUT OF COURSE THEY DO MEET

Despite what has been said so far, the element of collaboration between Congress and executive is far more decisive in the operation of the American system than the fact of physical separation; law and the imperatives of politics require it to be. The modifications of separation affected by the checks and balances, incorporated in the Constitution more as accommodations to experience than as an exercise in theory, are in law quite substantial. There is no need to itemize the familiar constitutional assignments of power to make the point. In practice, the separation breaks down even more. It is trite to mention the familiar designation of the President as "chief legislator." He has accepted the role happily, sending a steady stream of messages and bills to Congress in the opening months of each session. Congress, on the other hand, appears to take seriously its obligation to supervise the administration of legislation. In the Legislative Reorganization Act of 1946, Congress assigned oversight responsibility along with legislative jurisdiction to its standing committees. Congress also has invented a score of devices for "overseeing administration" (or for "meddling," depending upon the point of view).

Some of the most recent—and annoying to administrators—are the use of formal legal devices to give congressional committees the last word over certain kinds of administrative actions. Probably much more important in the long run is the growing practice of the House of Representatives of passing one-year authorizations, requiring agencies to pass bills over again next year. Needless to say, if legislative advice has not been heeded in that first year unhappy accountings must be made in the second year. It may be, however, that the real significance of the one-year authorization is that the legislative committees in the House are jealous of the Appropriations Committee and do not wish to see it exercise the only check on the administration of programs during the several years of their authorized life.

The exercise of commingled powers is carried out by the two branches with a degree of pragmatism which reduces complaints of violations and overreachings to the level of political rhetoric. As Roland Young pointed out in his fine study of congressional politics in World War II, neither Congress nor the President has much to say about encroachments when the result achieved is good.[4] It is when a particular venture goes badly that the other side is open to the charge of constitutional poaching.

Even when all this is admitted, as it would readily be by sophisticated observers, there is not much in the literature which describes the extent to which the executive and legislature share the policy process at almost every turn. It is not easy to generalize from the rich and varied studies of particular aspects of the relationship which do exist. Subject to the test of systematic analysis, I suggest that Congress plays rather a more important part in legislation than its critics usually suggest, and that it would be easy to overstate what Congress does to supervise administration.

Congress as legislature

Some critics have assigned Congress largely a passive role in legislation. It has been suggested that the President now initiates, Congress reacts.[5] This is superficially true. Even when the impetus comes from Congress, as it did in the legislative response to Sputnik, congressional

[4] Roland Young, *Congressional Politics in the Second World War* (New York: Harper and Row, Publishers, Inc., 1956).

[5] Samuel P. Huntington, "Congressional Responses to the Twentieth Century," in David B. Truman, ed., *op. cit.*, pp. 22–25.

leaders like to wait for the Administration bill to have something to work on. But what is easy to miss is the origin of many bills which in time pick up enough support to become "Administration bills." One or more members of Congress may have originated the idea and done all the spade work necessary to make it viable. One thinks of the lonely voice of George Norris in the 1920s calling for a Federal river project which became, in a different political climate, the Tennessee Valley Authority.[6] Other crusades have taken less time to succeed. Area redevelopment and water pollution control are projects which began in Congress. Examples are offered in the absence of systematic analysis. It is worth mention that the individual member may engineer a public policy. I remember watching a Canadian audience, including many members of its Parliament, listen enthralled to the account of Congressman Thomas Curtis, a minority member from Missouri, of his successful effort to enact a law suggested by a woman constituent.

Needless to say, the committees of Congress maintain a large measure of control over what goes into a bill and what happens to it, regardless of its origin. A striking case occurred in the early days of the second session of the 89th Congress. The Administration had proposed the conversion of loans to college students of money directly supplied (90 per cent of it) by the government to private bank loans guaranteed by the government. There was much opposition to the proposal, based largely on the fear that the new program could not be put in operation soon enough to meet the needs of students that year. The subcommittee of the House Education and Labor Committee which handles higher education, chaired by Congresswoman Edith Green of Oregon, met in executive session and voted unanimously to keep the National Defense Education Act loan program as it was (i.e., a direct loan program). The reason given by Mrs. Green was that the colleges needed to know what they could count on for the next school year. What is significant is the absolute confidence of the subcommittee, challenged by no one, that the change could not be made without their approval. If that confidence were not justified, the colleges obviously could not base their plans on the subcommittee action.

[6] Henry C. Hart, "Legislative Abdication in Regional Development," The Journal of Politics, XIII (1951), 393–417.

It may be remarked that this was a negative action. Critics of Congress, particularly those of the liberal persuasion, have emphasized that Congress is obstructive, that it cannot act affirmatively.[7] As Presidents have encountered obstacles to liberal programs, these critics have urged overhaul of structure and procedure to make Congress more responsible (i.e., more responsive to the President and the constituency that nominates and elects him). But in the first session of the 89th Congress, with a topheavy Democratic majority that included some seventy generally liberal freshmen, President Johnson got approval of a massive domestic legislative program that might normally have taken twenty years. The critics were not mollified. It was the work of a transient political genius, they said; soon Congress would go back to its normal nay-saying role. But such was not the case. In the second year of that Congress the President decided, under the pressure of war and threatened inflation, to hold the line on spending. The committees in both houses, legislative and appropriations alike, would have none of it; they set about expanding the programs of the year before and inventing new ones. This bit of legislative history may require a simple explanation: that elections do count and representation does work.

Emphasizing the congressional role in legislation is not an exercise in redundancy; it is given pertinence by the volume of literature arguing that Congress is impotent. It would be misleading, nevertheless, not to put Congress in the context of a system and suggest the roles of other participants. The notion of a legislative system that includes executive, courts, interest groups, press, local constituencies, and perhaps others, is useful but not precise enough. It might be more helpful to conceive of a set of "policy systems," in which all parties involved in a particular category of issues share regularly in the making, alteration, and execution of policy. This would recognize the specialization necessary to effective political action. A particular policy is made by the people in the agencies, public and private, who are interested in and know about that policy area. There is an almost continuous interchange among committee members, their staffs, the executive (that is, agency personnel, White House staff, and private persons appointed to "task forces," and the like), and representatives

---

[7] For a selection of the writings critical of Congress, see Ralph K. Huitt, "Democratic Party Leadership in the Senate," [pp. 136–158 of the present book—Eds.].

of private associations at almost every stage of the process, from the first glimmer of an idea to compromises in conference and to administration of the act.[8] Careful research would be necessary to establish the extent to which these generalizations are true and where the breakdowns occur, but it is a fair guess that members of the appropriate committees are seldom if ever taken by surprise by executive initiative in legislation. Indeed, much initiation is simply the reasonable next step in the view of those within a given policy system and it is so recognized on all sides, even though there is opposition to it.

Congress as overseer

The relationship of Congress to the administrative performance of the bureaucracy is equally important and invites careful study.[9] Students of representative assemblies at least since the time of John Stuart Mill have said that control of the government—the oversight function—is probably the most important task the legislature performs. It is easy to get the impression that the bureaucracy lives under the heavy frown of congressional supervision all the time. Certainly it is not pleasant to be interrogated by a congressional committee, nor to find oneself in the headlines which are congenial to the politician but not to the civil servant. But for the most part it is the politicians in the agencies, the expendable men, who face the committees in open hearings. Congressmen complain that they reach understandings with the political people which are not kept by the agency's operating personnel, who are largely beyond the reach of Congress. Without careful comparative studies designed to explore the range of patterns of relations which exist, it is hazardous to suggest generalizations. But perhaps it is not out of order to make some tentative comments based on observation.

The first would be the prediction that appropriate studies will show that not much "oversight" of administration, in a systematic and continuous enough manner to make it mean very much, is practiced. The appropriations committees probably do more than the legislative committees (which, not surprisingly, are more interested in legislation),

[8] For an example of this, see Stephen K. Bailey's classic case study, *Congress Makes a Law* (New York: Columbia University Press, 1950). Ernest S. Griffith refers to this coalescence of interests as a "whirlpool" in his *Congress: Its Contemporary Role*, 3rd ed. (New York: New York University Press, 1961).

[9] For a careful analysis of the process, see Joseph P. Harris, *Congressional Control of Administration* (Washington, D.C.: The Brookings Institution, 1964).

and the House Appropriations Committee does more than the Senate committee (because it is bigger, hears the agencies first, and permits its members no other committee assignments). Most legislative oversight occurs when hearings on new bills or authorizations occur. Closer scrutiny is likely to result from the personal interest of a chairman or ranking member, the sudden interest of the public in a program or a member's hunch that interest can be aroused, or the relationship (amounting virtually to institutional incest in a separation-of-powers system) which arises when a chairman fills the agency's top jobs with his own former staff members. The individual member's interest in administration is likely to be spurred by a constituent's protest, which subsides when the matter is taken care of.

III. WHAT SHOULD BE DONE

If the argument in the beginning of this essay—that there are similarities among particular political institutions in roughly comparable systems and that these institutional influences significantly affect behavior—has merit, then research on the legislature might profitably attempt to be comparative.

Comparative studies of legislative-administrative relations in the English parliamentary and the American presidential-congressional systems as an example, might be worth doing. The legislature and bureaucracy in both countries stem from the same root, the feudal Great Council which advised the king. Some of its members were barons who belonged to the Curia Regis, a part of his permanent court which developed into the professional bureaucracy. The other members of the Great Council were barons invited, usually three times a year, to consult with the king and consent to taxes. They were joined in time by representatives of the communities. From these occasional meetings the bicameral legislature evolved, while the professional bureaucracy is an outgrowth of the Curia Regis itself. Thus it is that our practices and procedures (and this is true of our courts as well) bear everywhere the marks of English experience. These are worth tracing and explaining.

But our histories have diverged and there are differences. Leaving aside the tendency of some Americans to idealize the British system, what price have we paid in friction and inefficiency for an arrangement which forces the legislature and bureaucracy to negotiate without the legislator-minister as intermediary? Is that lack so decisive as some other factors that accompany it? Say, that the Member of Parliament generally is powerless to do much and the Member of Congress is not? Or that the Member of Parliament may hope for genuine power only in the executive (and so shapes his efforts that way) while a ranking Member of Congress almost surely would sacrifice power if he were to join the executive? To what extent, on the other hand, has institutional separation been bridged in the American system by the shared interest and expertise of committee and agency people, and by their mutual dependence? These questions lead not to statements of abstractly ideal systems but to an attempt to weigh the costs and gains of alternative arrangements.

What is most difficult, obviously, is to sort and assess the relative weights of influences that bear on a man in public life. The argument of this essay is that the institutional influence is a powerful one, that it shapes attitudes and values and produces a shared way of life— so much so that a seasoned member of almost any legislature in the Western world almost surely would be more at home on the floor of either house of the American Congress than most American bureaucrats would be. If this is so, it suggests that the influence of an institution in all its historic dimensions may be stronger than those which are products of a peculiar national experience. The hypothesis should be worth exploring.

The idea of studying the legislature—or any other political institution—in a comparative way is attractive. If political systems may profitably be compared, why not political institutions? It may be that legislatures appear in a system at a certain stage of development, that they perform similar political functions whatever the system, that they affect the behavior of their members in ways that are enough alike to be significant.

Needless to say, there is much of crucial importance to be done on Congress without regard to other systems or to other institutions within the American system.[10] Research on Congress with a behavioral bent has come a long way, it seems to me, in the last ten or twelve

[10] Most of the remaining material is taken from a working paper prepared by the author for a conference of congressional scholars who met at Airlie House, Warrenton, Virginia, on May 20, 1964, to launch the American Political Science Association's Study of Congress. The Study of Congress is financed by the Carnegie Corporation and directed by the author and Robert L. Peabody. Most of the topics upon which scholars of the Study of Congress are working were taken generally from these suggestions.

years. Our discipline has produced a generation of scholars sensitive to the influence on the behavior of Congressmen of the various roles they assume in the related subsystems of Congress, and to the influence on Congress of the external system with which it interacts. We have sliced into our problem enough ways to give us a notion of what is there and some confidence that we know how to proceed. What we still lack, even with the extensive descriptive and prescriptive work of several generations of predecessors, is any very clear idea, to put it simply, of how Congress works—how its principal parts do their jobs and how they are related to each other.

Empirical research can and should provide us with analytical descriptions of Congress, its subsystems, and its relations with its environment; these should (1) fill in the research gaps, suggesting models and relevant variables for future research; and (2) provide some basis for stating the functions Congress performs for the political system, evaluating the performance, and pointing out alternative structural arrangements and modes of action which seem realistically to be open to Congress. Until we have reasonably adequate models, can identify significant variables, and can know what a deceptively simple action like a recorded vote probably means, the machines stand ready to give us more help than we can use. Until we have some idea about what needs of the system are served by Congress and how it serves them, the laundry-ticket lists of congressional reforms are no more than statements of personal preferences.

Research on Congress might be categorized many ways. The categories which will be suggested here are no better than some others that might be chosen, but they should help to organize discussion. Two categories that are obvious enough are the internal system, with its norms and roles, and the relations of this system with the external system, its environment. A third category might be that of policy, or process; the budget or economic policy or foreign policy or defense, might be considered, with the approach not separating internal and external systems, but combining them as the legislative system for that kind of policy. A fourth category might deal with purely facilitative concerns. What kinds of changes would help Congress get on with its job, whatever that job is conceived to be? Improvements in personnel recruitment, pay for Congressmen, vacations, scheduling, and other items affecting the Congressman's life might readily fall into a single category, perhaps even into a single study.

The internal system

The study of the power structure of each house—and they probably should be studied separately—might begin with the elected leaders.[11] We should not be satisfied with a description of the way the present incumbents operate; this would be little more than good journalism, at best. What is the range of behaviors open to the incumbent of a leadership position? What rewards and punishments were available to Mr. Rayburn in the time of his maximum prestige? What does an intangible like "prestige" mean and how can it be translated into power? What happened in the years of Mr. Rayburn's waning personal powers? How does the House work when the Speaker is ineffective? A close study of the division of labor among the elected leadership on both sides of the aisle, preferably with some attention to history to gain some sense of alternative possibilities, might require the collaboration of several people.

The Senate clearly is a separate study. The floor leadership seems to vary even more widely with incumbent and circumstance than the Speakership; it has fewer institutional props to support it. One crucial variable certainly is the leader's own perception of his role. Another is the occupant of the White House, whether he is of the same party as the Senate majority, and if so, what he expects of the leader and what their relations are. How can the formal party organs, such as the policy committees and the conferences, be used? Recent history suggests a cynical answer, but less recent history does not; Wilson's leader relied heavily on the conference in one of the most productive legislative periods in our history and there are senators now who argue the conference need not be useless.

In each house, the relations of the elected leaders with the committee chairmen should be explored. How does a "strong" elected leader approach his chairmen? Does he attempt to establish priorities among bills? Influence their content? Or does he just take the committee product and try to move it on the floor? These questions are doubly complicated in the House by the power of the Rules Committee. Recent history suggests at least superficially that the Speaker's

11 See David B. Truman, The Congressional Party (New York: John Wiley and Sons, Inc., 1959); Ralph K. Huitt, "Democratic Party Leadership in the Senate" [pp. 136–158 of the present book]; Charles O. Jones, Party and Policy-making (New Brunswick, N.J.: Rutgers University Press, 1964).

principal tool is a showdown or threat of it, a weapon as likely to blow up as it is to shoot. But what about periods when Speaker and committee chairmen worked in close accord? What then was their relation with strong committee chairmen?

Perhaps no study could be more rewarding than a systematic comparative analysis of committees. Some useful and suggestive work already has been done. How do the norms of other committees differ from those found by Professor Richard Fenno to prevail in the House Appropriations Committee?[12] Are the norm systems different and more permissive in less prestigious committees? How are members recruited to committees? What does the freshman member know about this fateful decision about his career? What kind of socialization does he go through?

The chairmen should be the targets of close analysis. This means, among other things, scrutiny of the operation of seniority. It is easy to attack or defend seniority; what does not commend itself to scholarship apparently is the empirical question of its effects. How many committee majorities actually are frustrated by the tyranny of their seniority chairmen? How is this putative authoritarianism accomplished? Can committee majorities break out? What rules do they need—or are the rules already on the books? What happens when a new chairman faces 180 degrees away from his predecessor (say, Langer succeeds McCarran, Eastland follows Kilgore, on Senate Judiciary)? How does a committee deal with a senile chairman? Are there institutional devices for going around him and how well do they work? Answers to questions like these can take a lot of the fun out of the debate over seniority.

Relations among committees also are important. We think especially of the experience of legislative committees which see their floor successes at the authorization stage put in hazard by the appropriations committees. And the relations of the spending with the taxing committees. What problems come from the inescapable overlapping of committee jurisdictions? How do like committees in the two houses get along? Why do the two spending committees often fight when the taxing committees collaborate easily and well? Who wins in conference? Does it vary from committee to committee? Does the

---

[12] "The House Appropriations Committee as a Political System: The Problem of Integration," *American Political Science Review,* LVI (June 1962), 310–324.

seniority system at the conference stage really deliver control of the ultimate product to the oligarchies of the houses?

The norm system in the Senate has been studied to some effect, but the same cannot be said for the House.[13] Both chambers are worth more attention. What is the range of permissible behavior in each? Systematic analyses of the "outsider," who helps to define the norms by pressing at their boundaries, might be useful. What are the sanctions in these institutionalized groups which have almost no control over the selection of their members? Who is the "outsider"? Is he a personality type? Are there significant correlations with state or district, with socio-psychological origins? In what ways may he be said to be "effective"? In what ways may he be functional, in what ways dysfunctional, for the system?

The chamber floor as terrain for legislative combat might also be a focus of study. What is the relationship between the formal and the informal rules? What advantages, if any, does the skilled parliamentarian enjoy? What difference would a change in rules make? What are the strategies which might be employed by the men who lead floor fights? The literature recounts occasional coups by which advantage has been gained through knowledge and use of the rules. What is not clear is whether legislators divide labor as lawyers do, with a counterpart on the floor of the skilled advocate who takes the prepared case to the courtroom, or whether there is enough to parliamentary advocacy to justify specialization.

Another actor who occupies an ambiguous place in the power structure is the professional staff man,[14] an ambiguous figure because his influence has been both underrated and overrated. Surely he is more than a facilitator, more than extra hands to relieve the legislator of errand-running, more than a trained research mind to end legislative dependence on bureaucrat and lobbyist. Surely he is less than the real power behind the throne, as the frustrated lobbyist, and even the staff man himself, sometimes thinks he is. What is he like, this bright and ambitious man who submerges his own career aspirations in those of another? What does he want, what does he think he can get? How

---

[13] Matthews, op. cit., Ch. 5; Huitt, "The Morse Committee Assignment Controversy: A Study in Senate Norms," *American Political Science Review*, LI (June 1957), 313–329 [pp. 113–135 of the present book], and "The Outsider in the Senate," *ibid.*, LV (September 1961), 566–575 [pp. 159–178 of the present book].

[14] See Kenneth Kofmehl, *Professional Staffs of Congress* (West Lafayette, Indiana: Purdue University Press, 1962).

does *he* perceive his role, its satisfactions and limitations? Some remarkable men have served members of Congress; some have gone on to serve two Presidents who have come out of the legislature. There is a great study to be made of the professional staff man and his relations with his principal by the legislative scholar who can enter upon it with his preconceptions firmly under control.

Relations with the external system

The importance of the web of relationships existing between Congress and the President, bureaucracy, parties, interest groups, press, and constituencies is so patent that almost any well-designed study of any of these relationships could have significance. Let me suggest only two or three.

One need which must be met before the computers really can serve us is the construction of more sophisticated models of systems of outside influence which press upon a member of Congress. The party is an example.[15] Many roll-call studies have made use of "party votes," so designated because a stated majority of one party opposed a similar majority of the other. Indices of cohesion and other measures are built from them and statements are made about the influence of party on members or on this or that bloc. The curious thing is that our model of the party in the basic texts is much more sophisticated than that. A reasonably competent student in the freshman course can write that the major party "is a federation of state and local parties." Why is not this model carried over into research on Congress? Suppose that two members bearing the same party designation split their votes on a roll call. Might it not be that one is voting with the national committee party, the other casting an opposing vote *with* a state or local party which bears the same name—in a word, *both* are casting party votes?

A similarly simplistic view of *the* constituency often is employed.[16] A conception of the constituency as all the people of voting age

[15] An excellent bibliography on the subject has been compiled by Charles O. Jones and Randall B. Ripley, *The Role of Political Parties in Congress* (Tucson, Arizona: University of Arizona Press, 1966).

[16] For sophisticated analyses of congressional relations with constituencies employing survey research techniques and systematic interviews, see Warren E. Miller and Donald E. Stokes, "Constituency Influence in Congress," *American Political Science Review*, LVII (March 1963), 45–56; and Charles C. Cnudde and Donald J. McCrone, "The Linkage Between Constituency Attitudes and Congressional Voting Behavior: A Causal Model," *ibid.*, LX (March 1966), 66–72.

living in the district or state is bound to lead to remarkable results. Everyone knows that the constituency so conceived will have opinions on very few issues indeed. Nevertheless, the member talks about his constituency; he says he follows its wishes sometimes or all the time, and it is not safe to assume without proof that this is double-talk or that he is a dunce. On the contrary; his perhaps tacit concept of constituency is more complicated: he responds to *different* constituencies on different issues. He may try to paint an image of himself in the broadest strokes as an "economiser," say, for the vast number of voters who will try to remember *something* about him when they go to the polls, while at the same time he works to amend one line of a bill to please a half-dozen labor leaders who can make or break him by the kind of voter-registration effort they put on. These are "constituencies"—the people of varying degrees of influence, knowledge, and intensity of feeling who are aware of and respond to particular issues. The students of public opinion long ago learned that if they defined "public" as all the people living in a society there usually would be no public opinion. Because this was a nonsense result they defined the term in a variety of ways that would support analysis. That is what we must do with the concept "constituency."

Inasmuch as "party" and "constituency" in this sense are systems of influence, why not go for help with our models to the persons presumably influenced, the members of Congress themselves? How do *they* perceive party and constituency? The same kinds of questions might be asked about interest groups, bureaucracy, or any other putative system of influence.

One further need may be suggested. In the systematic comparative study of committees close attention should be paid to the patterns of relations between committees and the bureaucratic agencies they supervise. An unassailable truism of legislative literature makes "legislative oversight" a basic congressional task. But what goes on under the label "oversight"? Consider some of the conventional tools. Appropriations: do the subcommittees really get to the heart of the matter? Investigation: is anything really changed after the dust settles? Confirmation: what difference does it really make in agency operations *who* the top man is? Detailed legislation: but isn't it the lesson of the last century that Congress must delegate to administrators the burden of legislating in detail? Studies of the oversight exercised by particular committees make clear that some of them exercise no supervision over the agencies assigned them and have no desire to do it; others have a variety of relationships, some of which would be hard to call oversight. What determines the character of the committee's concern about administrative performance? Some of the hypothetical variables are the personality of the chairman and his perception of his role, the character of the agency and its program, the degree of constituency involvement in the program, the character and quality of the committee's professional staff. Careful and realistic additions to the literature on oversight will find an eager audience among the bureaucrats themselves.

Policy-making process

It is not easy for a feudal system to make national policy. Whatever the advantages of dispersed centers of power (and I believe they are many), the capacity to make and carry out a plan is not among them. It is common for Congress to have inflationary and deflationary programs underway at the same time, to take away with one hand what it gives with the other. Some of our studies might profitably abandon the single house as a subsystem and look at the way one kind of policy is made across the board.[17] What is the budget process? This might be broken into spending and taxing (as Congress does it). How is foreign policy, or defense policy, fashioned? If Congress wanted to make a real effort to effect coordination in the making of some kind of national policy, what devices might be employed that have been proved by congressional experience to be useful for that purpose? If stronger party leadership generally were desired, what organizational arrangements might be strengthened, what inhibited? What would be gained and what would be the price?

These last questions, we might say finally, should be part of every study. Congress changes, as all living things must change; it changes slowly, adaptively, as institutions change. But structural arrangements are not neutral; they will be used by those who can get control of them for whatever purposes the controllers have in mind. Changes, therefore, may have unforeseen consequences. What changes seem possible of accomplishment, given Congress's history and present structure? Who seems likely to benefit, who will pay? These are questions our discipline has taught us to ask.

[17] For representative studies, see Holbert N. Carroll, *The House of Representatives and Foreign Affairs* (Pittsburgh: University of Pittsburgh Press, 1958); Aaron Wildavsky, *The Politics of the Budgetary Process* (Boston: Little, Brown and Co., 1964).

SELECTIVE
BIBLIOGRAPHY

Alexander, De Alva S. *History and Procedure of the House of Representatives.* Boston: Houghton Mifflin, 1916.

American Political Science Association. *The Reorganization of Congress.* Washington, D.C.: Public Affairs Press, 1945.

American Political Science Association. "Toward a More Responsible Two-Party System," *American Political Science Review,* XLIV (1950), Supplement.

Anderson, Lee F., Meredith W. Watts, Jr., and Allen R. Wilcox. *Legislative Roll-call Analysis.* Evanston, Ill.: Northwestern University Press, 1966.

Bailey, Stephen K. *Congress Makes a Law.* New York: Columbia University Press, 1950.

Bailey, Stephen K., and Howard D. Samuel. *Congress at Work.* New York: Holt, Rinehart and Winston, 1952.

Bauer, Raymond A., Ithiel de Sola Pool, and Lewis Anthony Dexter. *American Business and Public Policy: The Politics of Foreign Trade.* New York: Atherton, 1963.

Belknap, George M. "A Method for Analyzing Legislative Behavior," *Midwest Journal of Political Science,* II (1958). Pp. 377–402.

Bentley, Arthur F. *The Process of Government.* Chicago: The University of Chicago Press, 1908.

Berdahl, Clarence A. "Some Notes on Party Membership in Congress," *American Political Science Review,* XLIII (1949). Pp. 309–321, 492–508, 721–734.

Beyle, Herman C. *Identification and Analysis of Attribute-Cluster-Blocs.* Chicago: University of Chicago Press, 1931.

Bibby, John F. "Committee Characteristics and Legislative Oversight of Administration," *Midwest Journal of Political Science,* X (1966). Pp. 78–98.

Bibby, John F., and Roger Davidson. *On Capitol Hill: Studies in the Legislative Process.* New York: Holt, Rinehart and Winston, 1967.

Bolling, Richard. *House Out of Order.* New York: Dutton, 1965.

Bone, Hugh A. *Party Committees and National Politics.* Seattle, Wash.: University of Washington Press, 1958.

Brimhall, Dean R., and Arthur S. Otis. "Consistency of Voting by Our Congressmen," *Journal of Applied Psychology, 32* (1948). Pp. 1–14.

Brown, George R. *The Leadership of Congress.* Indianapolis: Bobbs-Merrill, 1922.

Burns, James MacGregor. *Congress on Trial.* New York: Harper & Row, 1949.

Burns, James MacGregor. *The Deadlock of Democracy: Four Party Politics in America.* Englewood Cliffs, N.J.: Prentice-Hall, 1963.

Carroll, Holbert N. *The House of Representatives and Foreign Affairs.* Pittsburgh: University of Pittsburgh Press, 1958. Rev. ed., Boston: Little, Brown, 1966.

Clapp, Charles L. *The Congressman: His Work as He Sees It.* Washington, D.C.: Brookings Institution, 1963.

Clark, Joseph S. *Congress: The Sapless Branch.* New York: Harper & Row, 1964.

Congressional Quarterly Service. *Congress and the Nation, 1945–1964.* Washinton, D.C.: Congressional Quarterly Service, 1965.

Cooper, Joseph. "Congress and Its Committees," unpublished Ph.D. dissertation, Harvard University, 1960.

Cooper, Joseph. *Reorganization and Reform in the U. S. House of Representatives.* Washington, D.C.: Brookings Institution (forthcoming).

Cummings, Milton C., Jr. *Congressmen and the Electorate.* New York: Free Press, 1966.

Cummings, Milton C., Jr., and Robert L. Peabody. "The Decision to Enlarge the Committee on Rules: An Analysis of the 1961 Vote," in Robert L. Peabody and Nelson W. Polsby, eds., *New Perspectives on the House of Representatives.* Chicago: Rand McNally, 1963. Pp. 167–194.

Dahl, Robert A. "The Concept of Power," *Behavioral Science, 2* (1957). Pp. 201–215.

Dahl, Robert A. *Congress and Foreign Policy.* New York: Harcourt, Brace & World, 1950.

Davidson, Roger H., David M. Kovenock, and Michael K. O'Leary. *Congress in Crisis: Politics and Congressional Reform.* Belmont, Calif.: Wadsworth Publishing Co., 1966.

De Grazia, Alfred, coord. *Congress: The First Branch of Government.* Washington, D.C.: American Enterprise Institute for Public Policy Research, 1965.

Dennison, Eleanor E. *The Senate Foreign Relations Committee.* Stanford, Calif.: Stanford University Press, 1942.

Dexter, Lewis A. "Congressmen and the Making of Military Policy," in Robert L. Peabody and Nelson W. Polsby, eds., *New Perspectives on the House of Representatives.* Chicago: Rand McNally, 1963. Pp. 305–324.

Dexter, Lewis A. "Marginal Attention, Pressure Politics, Political Campaigning, and Political Realities," *International Review of History and Political Science* I (1964). Pp. 115–123.

Dexter, Lewis A. "The Representative and His District." *Human Organization, 16* (1957). Pp. 2–13. Reprinted in Robert L. Peabody and Nelson W. Polsby, eds., *New Perspectives on the House of Representatives.* Chicago: Rand McNally, 1963. Pp. 3–29.

Dexter, Lewis A. "What Do Congressmen Hear: The Mail," *Public Opinion Quarterly, 20* (1956–57). Pp. 16–27.

Eulau, Heinz, and Katherine Hinckley. "Legislative Institutions and Processes," in James A. Robinson, ed., *Political Science Annual.* Indianapolis: Bobbs-Merrill, 1966, I. Pp. 85–189.

Eulau, Heinz, John C. Wahlke, William Buchanan, and Leroy C. Ferguson. "The Role of the Representative: Some Empirical Observations on the Theory of Edmund Burke," *American Political Science Review,* LIII (1959). Pp. 742–756.

Evans, Rowland, and Robert Novak. *Lyndon B. Johnson: The Exercise of Power.* New York: New American Library, 1966.

Ewing, Cortez A. M. *Congressional Elections, 1896–1944: The Sectional Basis of Political Democracy in the House of Representatives.* Norman, Okla.: University of Oklahoma Press, 1947.

Farnsworth, David N. *The Senate Committee on Foreign Relations: A Study of the Decision-Making Process.* Urbana, Ill.: University of Illinois Press, 1961.

Farris, Charles D. "A Method of Determining Ideological Groupings in the Congress," *Journal of Politics, 20* (1958). Pp. 308–338.

Fenno, Richard F., Jr. "The House Appropriations Committee as a Political System: The Problem of Integration," *American Political Science Review,* LVI (1962). Pp. 310–324.

Fenno, Richard F., Jr. "The House of Representatives and Federal Aid to Education," in Robert L. Peabody and Nelson W. Polsby, eds., *New Perspectives on the House of Representatives.* Chicago: Rand McNally, 1963. Pp. 195–235.

Fenno, Richard F., Jr. "The Internal Distribution of Influence: The House," in David B. Truman, ed., *The Congress and America's Future.* Englewood Cliffs, N.J.: Prentice-Hall, 1965. Pp. 52–76.

Fenno, Richard F., Jr. *The Power of the Purse: Appropriations Politics in Congress.* Boston: Little, Brown, 1966.

Ferber, Mark. "The Democratic Study Group: A Case Study," unpublished Ph.D. dissertation, University of California, Los Angeles, 1964.

Fiellin, Alan. "The Functions of Informal Groups in Legislative Institutions: A Case Study," *Journal of Politics, 24* (1962). Pp. 72–91.

Froman, Lewis A., Jr. *The Congressional Process: Strategies, Rules and Procedures.* Boston: Little, Brown, 1967.

Froman, Lewis A., Jr. *Congressmen and Their Constituencies.* Chicago: Rand McNally, 1963.

Froman, Lewis A., Jr., and Randall B. Ripley. "Conditions for Party Leadership: The Case of the House Democrats," *American Political Science Review,* LIX (1965). Pp. 52–63.

Galloway, George B. *Congress at the Crossroads.* New York: Crowell, 1946.

Galloway, George B. *History of the House of Representatives.* New York: Crowell, 1962.

Galloway, George B. *The Legislative Process in Congress.* New York: Crowell, 1953.

Goodwin, George, Jr. "The Seniority System in Congress," *American Political Science Review,* LIII (1959). Pp. 412–436.

Goodwin, George, Jr. "Subcommittees: The Miniature Legislatures of Congress," *American Political Science Review,* LVI (1962). Pp. 596–604.

Gray, Charles H. "A Scale Analysis of the Voting Records of Senators Kennedy, Johnson and Goldwater, 1957–1960," *American Political Science Review* LIX (1965). Pp. 615–621.

Green, Harold, and Alan Rosenthal. *Government of the Atom: The Integration of Powers.* New York: Atherton, 1963.

Gross, Bertram M. *The Legislative Struggle: A Study in Social Combat.* New York: McGraw-Hill, 1953.

Harris, Joseph P. *Congressional Control of Administration.* Washington, D.C.: Brookings Institution, 1964.

Hasbrouck, Paul D. *Party Government in the House of Representatives.* New York: Macmillan, 1927.

Hilsman, Roger. "Congressional-Executive Relations and the Foreign Policy Consensus," *American Political Science Review* LII (1958). Pp. 725–744.

Hinckley, Barbara. "Interpreting House Midterm Elections: Toward a Measurement of the In-party's 'Expected' Loss of Seats," *American Political Science Review* LXI (1967). Pp. 694–700.

Holcombe, Arthur N. *The Political Parties of To-day: A Study in Republican and Democratic Politics.* New York: Harper & Row, 1924.

Huitt, Ralph K. "The Congressional Committee: A Case Study," *American Political Science Review,* XLVIII (1954). Pp. 340–365.

Huitt, Ralph K. "Congressional Organization and Operations in the Field of Money and Credit," in William Fellner, *et al.,* eds., *Fiscal and Debt Management Policies.* Englewood Cliffs, N.J.: Prentice-Hall, 1963. Pp. 399–495.

Huitt, Ralph K. "Democratic Party Leadership in the Senate," *American Political Science Review,* LV (1961a). Pp. 333–344.

Huitt, Ralph K. "The Internal Distribution of Influence: The Senate," in David B. Truman., ed., *The Congress and America's Future.* Englewood Cliffs, N.J.: Prentice-Hall, 1965. Pp. 77–101.

Huitt, Ralph K. "The Morse Committee Assignment Controversy: A Study in Senate Norms," *American Political Science Review,* LI (1957). Pp. 313–329.

Huitt, Ralph K. "The Outsider in the Senate: An Alternative Role," *American Political Science Review,* LV (1961b). Pp. 566–575.

Huitt, Ralph K. Book Review of Donald R. Matthews, *U.S. Senators and Their World,* in *American Political Science Review,* LV (1961c). Pp. 401–402.

Jewell, Malcolm E. "Evaluating the Decline of Southern Internationalism Through Senatorial Roll Call Votes," *Journal of Politics, 21* (1959). Pp. 624–646.

Jewell, Malcolm E. *Senatorial Politics and Foreign Policy.* Lexington, Ky.: University of Kentucky Press, 1962.

Jewell, Malcolm E., and Samuel C. Patterson. *The Legislative Process in the United States.* New York: Random House, 1966.

Jones, Charles O. "Inter-Party Competition for Congressional Seats," *Western Political Quarterly,* XVII (1964). Pp. 461–476.

Jones, Charles O. *Minority Party Leadership in Congress.* Boston: Little, Brown (forthcoming).

Jones, Charles O. "The Minority Party and Policy-making in the House of Representatives," *American Political Science Review,* LXII (1968). Pp. 481–493.

Jones, Charles O. *Party and Policy-making: The House Republican Policy Committee.* New Brunswick, N.J.: Rutgers University Press, 1964.

Jones, Charles O. "Representation in Congress: The Case of the House Agriculture Committee," *American Political Science Review,* LV (1961). Pp. 358–367.

Jones, Charles O. "The Role of the Congressional Subcommittee," *Midwest Journal of Political Science,* VI (1962). Pp. 327–344.

Jones, Charles O., and Randall B. Ripley. *The Role of Political Parties in Congress: A Bibliography and Research Guide.* Tucson, Ariz.: University of Arizona Press, 1966.

Keefe, William J., and Morris S. Ogul. *The American Legislative Process: Congress and the States.* Englewood Cliffs, N.J.: Prentice-Hall, 1965; rev. ed., 1968.

Kessel, John H. "The Washington Congressional Delegation," *Midwest Journal of Political Science,* VIII (1964). Pp. 1–21.

Key, V. O., Jr. *Southern Politics in State and Nation.* New York: Knopf, 1949.

Kofmehl, Kenneth. "The Institutionalization of a Voting Bloc," *Western Political Quarterly,* XVII (1964). Pp. 256–272.

Kofmehl, Kenneth. *Professional Staffs of Congress.* West Lafayette, Ind.: Purdue University Press, 1962.

Kovenock, David M. "Communications and Influence in Congressional Decision-making," paper delivered at the American Political Science Association Meeting, Chicago, 1964.

Kovenock, David M. "Influence in the U.S. House of Representatives: Some Preliminary Statistical 'Snapshots,'" paper delivered at the American Political Science Association Meeting, Chicago, 1967.

Lowell, A. Lawrence. "The Influence of Party Upon Legislation in England and America," *Annual Report of the American Historical Association,* I (1901). Pp. 321–542.

Luce, R. Duncan, and Arnold A. Rogow. "A Game Theoretic Analysis of Congressional Power Distributions for a Stable Two-party System," *Behavioral Science, 1* (1956). Pp. 83–95.

McInnis, Mary, ed. *We Propose: A Modern Congress.* New York: McGraw-Hill, 1966.

Macmahon, Arthur W. "Congressional Oversight of Administration: The Power of the Purse," *Political Science Quarterly,* LVIII (1943). Pp. 161–190, 380–414.

MacNeil, Neil. *Forge of Democracy: The House of Representatives.* New York: McKay, 1963.

McPhee, William N., and William A. Glaser, eds., *Public Opinion and Congressional Elections.* New York: Free Press, 1962.

MacRae, Duncan, Jr. *Dimensions of Congressional Voting: A Statistical Study of the House of Representatives in the Eighty-first Congress.* Berkeley: University of California Press, 1958.

MacRae, Duncan, Jr. "A Method for Identifying Issues and Factions from Legislative Votes," *American Political Science Review,* LIX (1965). Pp. 909–926.

MacRae, Duncan, Jr., and Hugh D. Price. "Scale Positions and 'Power' in the Senate," *Behavioral Science, 4* (1959). Pp. 212–218.

Manley, John F. "The House Committee on Ways and Means: Conflict Management in a Congressional Committee," *American Political Science Review,* LIX (1965). Pp. 927–939.

Marwell, Gerald. "Party, Region and the Dimensions of Conflict in the House of Representatives, 1949–1954," *American Political Science Review,* LXI (1967). Pp. 380–399.

Masters, Nicholas A. "Committee Assignments in the House of Representatives," *American Political Science Review,* LV (1961). Pp. 345–357.

Matthews, Donald R. *U.S. Senators and Their World.* Chapel Hill, N.C.: University of North Carolina Press, 1960.

Mayhew, David R. *Party Loyalty Among Congressmen: The Difference Between Democrats and Republicans, 1947–1962.* Cambridge, Mass.: Harvard University Press, 1966.

Meller, Norman. "Legislative Behavior Research," *Western Political Quarterly,* XIII (1960). Pp. 131–153.

Meller, Norman. "Legislative Behavior Research Revisited: A Review of Five Years' Publications," *Western Political Quarterly,* XVIII (1965). Pp. 776–793.

Miller, Clem. *Member of the House: Letters of a Congressman,* ed. John W. Baker. New York: Scribner, 1962.

Miller, Warren E., and Donald E. Stokes. "Constituency Influence in Congress," *American Political Science Review,* LVII (1963). Pp. 45–56.

Munger, Frank J., and Richard F. Fenno, Jr. *National Politics and Federal Aid to Education.* Syracuse, N.Y.: Syracuse University Press, 1962.

Neustadt, Richard E. "Presidency and Legislation: The Growth of Central Clearance," *American Political Science Review,* XLVIII (1954). Pp. 641–671.

Neustadt, Richard E. "Presidency and Legislation: Planning the President's Program," *American Political Science Review,* XLIX (1955). Pp. 980–1021.

Patterson, Samuel C. "Legislative Leadership and Political Ideology," *Public Opinion Quarterly,* XXVII (1963). Pp. 399–410.

Peabody, Robert L. "The Enlarged Rules Committee," in Robert L. Peabody and Nelson W. Polsby, eds., *New Perspectives on the House of Representatives.* Chicago: Rand McNally, 1963. Pp. 129–164.

Peabody, Robert L. *The Ford-Halleck Minority Leadership Contest, 1965.* New York: McGraw-Hill, 1966. Eagleton Institute Case No. 40.

Peabody, Robert L. "The House Republican Leadership: Change and Consolidation in a Minority Party," in Allan P. Sindler, ed., *Case Studies in American Government and Politics.* Boston: Little, Brown, 1969.

Peabody, Robert L. "Party Leadership Change in the House of Representatives," *American Political Science Review,* LXI (1967). Pp. 675–693.

Peabody, Robert L., and Nelson W. Polsby, eds. *New Perspectives on the House of Representatives.* Chicago: Rand McNally, 1963.

Polsby, Nelson W. *Congress and the Presidency.* Englewood Cliffs, N.J.: Prentice-Hall, 1964.

Polsby, Nelson W. "The Institutionalization of the U.S. House of Representatives," *American Political Science Review,* LXII (1968). Pp. 144–168.

Polsby, Nelson W. "Two Strategies of Influence: Choosing a Majority Leader, 1962," in Robert L. Peabody and Nelson W. Polsby, eds., *New Perspectives on the House of Representatives.* Chicago: Rand McNally, 1963. Pp. 237–270.

Pressman, Jeffrey L. *House vs. Senate: Conflict in the Appropriations Process.* New Haven, Conn.: Yale University Press, 1966.

Price, H. Douglas. "Are Southern Democrats Different? An Application of Scale Analysis to Senate Voting Patterns," in Nelson W. Polsby, Robert A. Dentler, and Paul A. Smith, eds., *Politics and Social Life: An Introduction to Political Behavior.* Boston: Houghton Mifflin, 1963. Pp. 740–756.

Rice, Stuart A. "The Behavior of Legislative Groups: A Method of Measurement," *Political Science Quarterly,* XL (1925). Pp. 60–72.

Rice, Stuart A. *Quantitative Methods in Politics.* New York: Knopf, 1928.

Riddick, Floyd M. *The United States Congress: Organization and Procedure.* Manassas, Va.: National Capitol Publishers, 1949.

Rieselbach, Leroy N. "The Demography of the Congressional Vote on Foreign Aid, 1939–1958," *American Political Science Review,* LVIII (1964). Pp. 577–588.

Rieselbach, Leroy N. *The Roots of Isolationism: Congressional Voting and Presidential Leadership in Foreign Policy.* Indianapolis: Bobbs-Merrill, 1966.

Riker, William H. "A Method for Determining the Significance of Roll Calls in Voting Bodies," in John C. Wahlke and Heinz Eulau, eds., *Legislative Behavior: A Reader in Theory and Research.* New York: Free Press, 1959 Pp. 377–384.

Riker, William H. "The Paradox of Voting and Congressional Rules for Voting on Amendments," *American Political Science Review,* LII (1958). Pp. 349–366.

Riker, William H., and Donald Niemi. "Stability of Coalitions on Roll Calls in the House of Representatives," *American Political Science Review,* LVI (1962). Pp. 58–65.

Ripley, Randall B. *Majority Party Leadership in Congress.* Boston: Little, Brown, 1969.

Ripley, Randall B. *Party Leaders in the House of Representatives.* Washington, D.C.: Brookings Institution, 1967.

Ripley, Randall B. "The Party Whip Organizations in the United States House of Representatives," *American Political Science Review,* LVIII (1964). Pp. 561–576.

Robinson, James A. *Congress and Foreign Policy-making.* Homewood, Ill.: Dorsey Press, 1962; rev. ed., 1967.

Robinson, James A. *The House Rules Committee.* Indianapolis: Bobbs-Merrill, 1963.

Rothman, David J. *Politics and Power: The United States Senate, 1869–1901.* Cambridge, Mass.: Harvard University Press, 1966.

Saloma, John S. *The Responsible Use of Power, a Critical Analysis of the Congressional Budget Process.* Washington, D.C.: American Enterprise Institute for Public Policy Research, 1964.

Scher, Seymour. "Conditions for Legislative Control," *Journal of Politics,* 25 (1963). Pp. 526–551.

Scher, Seymour. "Congressional Committee Members as Independent Agency Overseers: A Case Study," *American Political Science Review,* LIV (1960). Pp. 911–920.

Shapley, L. D., and Martin Shubik. "A Method for Evaluating the Distribution of Power in a Committee System," *American Political Science Review,* XLVIII (1954). Pp. 787–792.

Sharkansky, Ira. "An Appropriations Subcommittee and Its Client Agencies: A Comparative Study of Supervision and Control," *American Political Science Review,* LIX (1965). Pp. 622–628.

Smith, Frank. *Congressman from Mississippi.* New York: Pantheon, 1964.

Smith, Robert A. *The Tiger in the Senate: The Biography of Wayne Morse.* Garden City, N.Y.: Doubleday, 1962.

Snowiss, Leo M. "Congressional Recruitment and Representation," *American Political Science Review,* LX (1966). Pp. 627–639.

Tacheron, Donald G., and Morris K. Udall. *The Job of a Congressman.* Indianapolis: Bobbs-Merrill, 1966.

Truman, David B., ed. *The Congress and America's Future.* Englewood Cliffs, N.J.: Prentice-Hall, 1965.

Truman, David B. *The Congressional Party: A Case Study.* New York: Wiley, 1959.

Truman, David B. *The Governmental Process.* New York: Knopf, 1951.

Turner, Julius. *Party and Constituency: Pressures on Congress.* Baltimore: Johns Hopkins Press, 1951.

Turner, Julius. "Primary Elections as the Alternative to Party Competition in 'Safe' Districts," *Journal of Politics, 15* (1953). Pp. 197–210.

Wahlke, John C. "Behavioral Analyses of Representative Bodies," in Austin Ranney, ed., *Essays on the Behavioral Study of Politics.* Urbana, Ill.: University of Illinois Press, 1962. Pp. 173–190.

Wahlke, John C., and Heinz Eulau, eds. *Legislative Behavior: A Reader in Theory and Research.* New York: Free Press, 1959.

Wahlke, John C., Heinz Eulau, William Buchanan, and LeRoy C. Ferguson. *The Legislative System: Explorations in Legislative Behavior.* New York: Wiley, 1962.

Westphal, Albert C. F. *The House Committee on Foreign Affairs.* New York: Columbia University Press, 1942.

White, William S. *Citadel: The Story of the U. S. Senate.* New York: Harper & Row, 1956.

White, William S. *The Taft Story.* New York: Harper & Row, 1954.

Wildavsky, Aaron. *The Politics of the Budgetary Process.* Boston: Little, Brown, 1964.

Willoughby, W. F. *Principles of Legislative Organization and Administration.* Washington, D.C.: Brookings Institution, 1934.

Wilson, Woodrow. *Congressional Government.* Boston: Houghton Mifflin, 1885; New York: Meridian Books, 1956.

Wolfinger, Raymond E., and Joan Heifetz, "Safe Seats, Seniority, and Power in Congress," *American Political Science Review,* LIX (1965), Pp. 337–349.

Young, James S. *The Washington Community, 1800–1828.* New York: Columbia University Press, 1966.

Young, Roland. *The American Congress.* New York: Harper & Row, 1958.